THE ORGANISATION IN ITS ENVIRONMENT

£4

THE ORGANISATION IN ITS ENVIRONMENT

Business in the Mixed Economy

J. Harvey

M

First edition 1980
Reprinted 1982, 1983

Published by
THE MACMILLAN PRESS LTD
London and Basingstoke
Companies and representatives
throughout the world

Filmset in Great Britain by
Vantage Photosetting Co. Ltd.
Southampton and London

Printed in Hong Kong

British Library Cataloguing in Publication Data

Harvey, J, *b.* 1917
    The organisation in its environment.
    1. Economics
    2. Civics, British
    I. Title
    330'.02'4658   HB171.5

    ISBN 0–333–27196–3
    ISBN 0–333–27197–1   Pbk

Contents

PART IV   THE PUBLIC SECTOR

PART V   GOVERNMENT STABILISATION POLICY

Preface

The primary aim of this book is to provide a basic text covering 'The Organisation in its Environment', the common core modules 3 and 4 of the Business Education Council (BEC) National Awards. It could also be used as an introduction to Higher National Awards courses.

Because the syllabus draws on a number of disciplines – in particular economics, government and politics, and law – a textbook can adopt alternative approaches. First, it could take the learning objectives of the BEC syllabus, dealing with each in turn. The weakness of this is that it might simply describe topics in a rather unrelated way. Second, it can give a bird's-eye view of how the UK is organised to provide the goods and services required by the community, explaining principles, suggesting reasons and provoking thought, but at the same time seeking to integrate the syllabus topics within the broad structure. The latter is the method adopted by this book. But, to reassure teachers and students that the learning objectives are covered, the relevant chapters are indicated on page x.

The 'organisation' is interpreted widely, covering firms in the private sector and government departments, the nationalised industries, local authorities and other quasi-government bodies in the public sector. While such organisations may differ in structure and objectives, all are engaged in some form of production and the book shows how they are interrelated through this.

Nevertheless, their particular operations are so complex that rarely can their policies be explained by reference to a single section of the text. Thus the real task of analysing real-life situations and of integrating modules and the general and learning objectives is reserved for the exercises and projects provided in the accompanying workbook. In short, the textbook should be regarded primarily as the basic tool-kit which can be used to unravel the actual problems facing all organisations.

At all times, the needs of beginners have been kept uppermost. As far as possible, the formal disciplines of economics, government, law, etc., have been avoided. Nevertheless, especially when a topic falls mainly within the field of economics, some elementary theory to show how analysis can proceed has been introduced. This has two main advantages: first, there is nothing so practical as sound theory; second, should the student wish to proceed later to a more formal study of economics, his thinking will already have been directed along the right lines.

In conclusion I would like to thank my two editors, Nick Brealey and John Winckler, for their enthusiasm, encouragement and hard work, without which this book could not have been possible.

Coverage of learning objectives

Learning objective		Relevant chapters	Learning objective		Relevant chapters
A	1	1	F	1	7, 8
	2	1, 14		2	7, 10
	3	1		3	8
	4	1		4	8
	5	1		5	8
B	1	1, 8	G	1	8
	2	1, 8, 14		2	14
	3	3, 5, 9		3	7
C	1	1, 4		4	7
	2	1, 11		5	8
	3	2, 3	H	1	20
D	1	2		2	20
	2	2		3	20
	3	2		4	20
	4	2	J	1	6
	5	2		2	6
E	1	3		3	6
	2	3		4	6
	3	9		5	4, 5, 6
	4	9		6	4, 6
	5	9	K	1	4, 5, 14
	6	10		2	6, 14
	7	12		3	18
	8	11		4	20
	9	12, 13	L	1	3, 15, 16, 17, 18, 19, 20, 21
	10	13		2	18
	11	13		3	15
	12	12		4	1, 17
	13	12	M	1	4, 5, 11, 16
	14	12		2	4, 16
	15	13	N	1	4, 5, 6
	16	12		2	5, 6
	17	11		3	5, 6
	18	11	P	1	5, 16, 17
	19	11	Q	1	4, 21
	20	12, 13			
	21	11, 12, 13			

Part I

The Organisation in its Environment: A Profile

1 Business Organisations and the Environment

I Production for wants

Why organisations are formed

The essential activity of man is living. But this has many aspects – providing for material needs, deriving satisfaction from work, appreciating art, music and nature, satisfying spiritual longings, living in harmony with his fellows and enjoying freedom from enslavement by others. The promotion of such objectives is usually helped by organisations – firms, trade unions, clubs and societies, museums, churches, charities and governments.

The purpose of these organisations is to bring together people having common interests and, through their *combined* efforts, promote the extent to which those interests can be secured or enjoyed. They may do this simply by bringing people with like interests together on the principle that the whole is greater than the sum of the parts. Thus, through the state, citizens can combine their defence efforts. Similarly, football supporters' clubs organise individual fans into groups to stimulate their team by cheering and singing together. Usually, however, organisations go further, actively promoting objectives. Thus the state employs trained Armed Forces, while supporters' clubs raise funds to be spent in ways which will help the team win matches.

Characteristics of all organisations

Whatever the form and purpose of the organisation, there are common features:

(1) They have *rules*, either written or tacitly accepted. Written rules usually state the objectives of the organisation, the structure of the governing body, the appointment of officials and the powers which they can exercise. Thus, as we shall see, a state has a 'constitution' and companies have 'Articles of Association'. In contrast, relationships within the family, e.g. in running a farm, are often governed by custom.

(2) There is a decision-making body with a recognised

hierarchy of authority, usually provided for in the rules. Thus, in the organisation of the government of the UK, Parliament has the ultimate supremacy, while with companies, shareholders have, at least in theory, the final say.

(3) Officials are chosen (and often paid) to perform specific tasks. Thus we have the monarchy, the Prime Minister, departmental ministers, the managing director of a company and the Chairman of a football club.

(4) Records are usually kept of decisions in order to avoid future dispute or misunderstanding, and information may be stored for the guidance of members. Thus companies keep minutes of the proceedings of Boards of Directors, and summaries of the accounts are distributed to those providing capital.

(5) Provision is usually made for co-ordinating the work of the different institutions and departments within the organisation. This is especially important in government and large business organisations.

Providing for material wants

This book concentrates on the main aspect of man's well-being – his material standard of life. Generally speaking, the more goods and services he possesses, the richer his life, or (as it is often put), the higher is his welfare. However, while it is usually true, this conclusion may have to be modified: the production of more goods may be at the cost of longer working hours, more accidents at work, pollution of the environment, higher juvenile delinquency (as mothers work outside the home), social divisions and political unrest. As we shall see, such considerations will have to be taken into account when looking at man's economic progress.

The justification for limiting the scope of this book is that man's main concern is the improvement of his material standard of life. In poor countries this is obvious; but even in the more advanced countries, such as the UK, earning a living and spending income still dominate man's life. Indeed, it is often asserted that people are too 'materialistically minded'.

The business organisation

Furthermore, this book looks at production basically from the viewpoint of the business organisation – what form it takes, its objectives, the efficiency it achieves, the difficulties it encounters and the environmental background within which it has to work. These topics will be discussed in broad terms with respect to business organisations generally. The details of how individual firms use their accountants, personnel officers, etc., to deal with their own particular problems will be only briefly touched upon since they form the subject-matter of other modules.

The fundamental function of the business organisation is to assemble and direct the resources of the community to produce those goods and services which the community wants (see Figure 1.1). It has to ascertain what goods and services to produce, obtain funds to purchase the appropriate resources, organise production by those resources as effectively as possible and decide who shall benefit from what is produced.

Fig. 1.1
The role of the firm

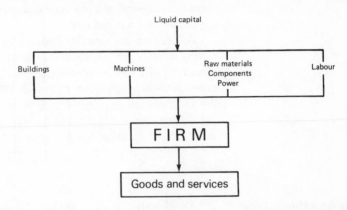

Objectives of the
business organisation

Since production covers all activities directed to satisfying wants (see below), the business organisation can take different forms, including government departments and local authorities (see Figure 1.2). For the sake of brevity, we shall refer in future to all these different business organisations as 'firms'. Omitted, however, are voluntary bodies, such as Housing Associations, Shelter and Christian Aid; while they organise production to satisfy needs, moral and religious motives overshadow economic considerations and we shall therefore not examine them.

It will be observed that Figure 1.2 divides firms into the private sector and the public sector. In the former, firms are owned and controlled by private persons, usually the capital having been subscribed by them. While the government may influence the policy of such firms indirectly, it cannot exert direct ownership control. In contrast, it does have ultimate control over public-sector 'firms', either continuously, as with government departments, or as the final arbiter, as with nationalised industries and local authorities. Indeed, public-sector capital comes mainly from government sources. Such direct control is vital to the government in furthering its economic and social objectives.

The two sectors also differ in their overriding objectives. Unlike private firms which are profit-motivated and therefore have to produce goods and services for which there is a market demand, public-sector firms are supported by government funds to provide for community-defined needs. This is true particularly of government departments and local authorities, but at times nationalised industries may be required to put wider community

Fig. 1.2
Forms of business
organisation

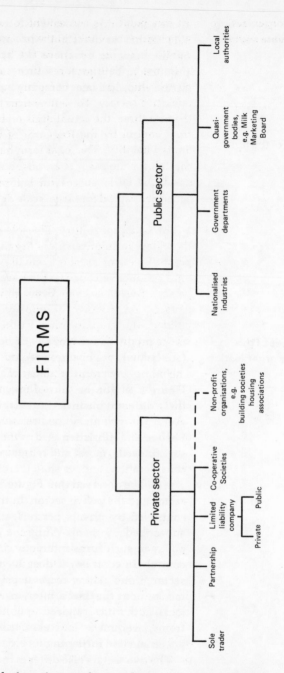

aims before financial considerations, with subsequent losses
being covered by the government. Thus British Rail has maintained unprofitable local branch lines for social reasons, while the
Central Electricity Generating Board has been required to invest
in coal-fired plants to relieve unemployment and provide more
time for assessing the environmental risks of nuclear energy.

Types of organisation in the private sector

At this point it is convenient to examine briefly the legal forms which firms may take in the private sector, postponing a study of public-sector organisations to Chapter 14.

In the private sector a firm can trade as a sole proprietor, partnership, private company, public company or as a co-operative society. For a new firm the choice really rests between the first three, the actual decision being largely based on freedom from control by the Registrar of Companies as opposed to unlimited liability. The legal form hardly affects its ability to raise capital, for, unless it is an offshoot of a large parent company, it has to be fairly successful before outsiders can be induced to subscribe capital for large-scale development.

1 The sole proprietor The sole proprietor or 'one-man' firm is the oldest form of business organisation. Even today, from the point of view of numbers, small firms predominate, but in their total productive capacity they are far less important than companies. Such one-man firms range from the window-cleaner working on his own account to the farmer, shopkeeper and builder who employ other workers and may even own many separate units. Nevertheless these businesses all have the same characteristic of being owned and controlled by a single person. This person decides the policy of the firm, and it is he alone who takes the profits or bears the losses. This makes for energy, efficiency and a careful attention to detail. In addition the only accounts he has to submit are to the Board of Inland Revenue for income-tax assessment and to the Customs and Excise Department if registered for VAT. He does not have to pay corporation tax.

As a form of business organisation, however, the sole proprietor suffers from five main disadvantages.

First, such a firm can only develop slowly because sources of capital are limited. The success of the venture, especially in its early stages, depends mainly on the person in charge, and nobody is likely to provide capital unless he has that confidence in the proprietor which comes from personal contact. Hence the main source of capital is the owner's savings, plus any money he can borrow from relatives or close friends. In time development may be financed by 'ploughing back' profits, but this will probably be a slow process and sole traders generally remain comparatively small.

Second, in the event of failure, not only the assets of the business but also the private assets and property of the proprietor can be claimed against by creditors. In short there is no limited liability.

Third, if profits are high, income tax paid on annual profits may be larger than would have been paid through corporation tax. This is because income may be taxed at a high marginal rate of tax, whereas corporation tax is 42 per cent if a company's profits are less than £60,000 and with marginal relief up to £100,000 when tax is 52 per cent. This would leave more funds for ploughing back into the business.

Fourth, it is more difficult to transfer part of a business than to transfer shares of a company.

Fifth, there is lack of continuity; on the retirement or death of the owner a one-man firm may cease to function.

Because of these disadvantages the sole proprietor is mainly confined either to businesses which are just setting up, or to certain industries, such as agriculture and retailing, where requirements of management make the small technical unit desirable.

2 The partnership   More capital is available when persons join together in a 'partnership', though not more than twenty (with the exception of certain professions, such as solicitor and accountant) may do so. Each partner provides a part of the capital and shares the profits on an agreed basis. Yet the amount of capital which can be raised in this way is still inadequate for modern large-scale business. Thus partnerships remain relatively small, predominating in retailing, insurance broking and underwriting, and the professions (doctors, surveyors, consulting engineers and lawyers), where the capital provided is not so much in the form of money as in experience and professional skill, each partner often specialising in a particular branch.

Nor is the partnership without its snags. The risk inherent in unlimited liability is increased because all partners are liable for the firm's debts irrespective of the amount of capital which each has individually invested. Only if a partner takes no share in the management of the firm, and there is at least one ordinary partner, can he enjoy limited liability. Second, since any action taken by one partner is legally binding on the others, not only must each partner have complete confidence in them but the risk inherent in unlimited liability increases with the number of partners. Finally, at any time one partner may give notice to end the partnership, while it is automatically dissolved upon the death or bankruptcy of a partner. To preserve the business, surviving partners may be put to great expense and trouble in buying the partner's share or finding a purchaser acceptable to everyone.

3 The joint-stock company   The joint-stock company dates from Tudor times when England's foreign trade began to expand. Instead of a trading ship being owned by one person, it was financed by a number of people who bought 'shares' in a company formed for the purpose. However, since they enjoyed no limited liability, people were reluctant to join such companies: by purchasing only one share a person risked not only the money invested but all his private assets should the company be forced into liquidation. Moreover, this made it impossible to adopt the technique of spreading risks by investing in a number of companies.

The Industrial Revolution, with the introduction of machines and factory organisation, made it essential that more capital should be available to industry. So in order to induce small savers to invest, Parliament granted limited liability in 1855.

Today the joint-stock company is the most important form of business organisation. The advantages it enjoys over the partnership are limited liability, continuity, the availability of capital (since investors can spread their risks and sell their shares easily) and, should the need arise, ease of expansion. Indeed, some kinds of businesses (e.g. computers) could not be operated on a small scale. Here firms have to start as joint-stock companies, either being sponsored by important interests, or else developed as subsidiaries of existing large firms.

Against these advantages, however, the small company in particular has to consider certain snags. Additional cost is incurred in submitting the annual accounts etc., to the Registrar of Companies, while the company's corporation tax could exceed the income tax which would have been paid had the business been carried on as a sole trader or partnership. Furthermore, any assets of the company which have been built up over the years will increase the value of the original shares (usually owned by the family), so that when the time comes to wind up the company, e.g. owing to retirement, this increase will be subject to capital-gains tax. Finally, if the company is expanded by the issue of more shares, the original owners may lose control or even be subject to a takeover bid.

Forming a company is a simple process; indeed certain firms specialise in selling 'ready-made' companies over the counter. The *Memorandum of Association* governs the relationship of the company with the outside world, and states the name of the company, the address of its registered office, its objects, the limited liability of its members and particulars of the authorised share capital. The *Articles of Association* govern the company's internal management, for example regarding the powers of directors and the transfer of shares. On receipt of the above two documents and the appropriate fee, the Registrar of Companies issues a Certificate of Incorporation and, once the directors have taken up their shares, a Certificate of Trading.

Joint-stock companies are of two main kinds, private and public.

a The private company

A private company, while conferring the advantage of limited liability, allows a business to be privately owned and managed. The formalities involved in its formation are few, but the Companies Act, 1948, imposes conditions restricting its size and the sale of shares to the public.

Thus the private company is particularly suitable for either a medium-sized commercial or industrial organisation not requiring finance from the public, or for a speculative venture where a small group of people wishes to try out an idea and is prepared to back it financially to a definite limit before floating a public company. While private companies are considerably more numerous than public companies, their average capital is much smaller.

b The public company

To obtain a large amount of capital it is necessary to form a public company (having a minimum of seven shareholders) and then apply for a Stock Exchange quotation. The affairs of the company have to be advertised in at least two leading London newspapers, while, if no new issue is being made, a supply of shares has to be made available sufficient to make dealing and the price fixed realistic.

Once the introduction has been completed, the capital can be raised by offer to the public, as described in Chapter 13.

It should be noted that a new Companies Bill is currently proceeding through Parliament to implement the EEC second directive on company law. It covers a new definition of public company, the share capital of companies and the distribution of profits to shareholders.

4 Multi-national firms   Many firms, e.g. Unilever, Shell, Renault and Metal Box, operate internationally by producing goods and components in different countries. While the host country benefits from their productive investment, problems can arise. First, the multinational firm may take advantage of the different rates at which profits are taxed by different countries by pricing components so as to ensure that the bulk of its profits occur in the country having the lowest rate of tax. Second, payments between countries may be accelerated to a country whose currency is likely to appreciate and held back from a country whose currency is likely to depreciate. Such 'leads' and 'lags' help to bring about the currency movement anticipated.

5 Co-operative societies   Although there were many co-operative socieities in operation before the Rochdale Pioneers, 1844, it was these twenty-eight workers who started the modern co-operative movement. By subscribing a few pence per week they accumulated an initial capital of £28, with which they rented a store and started trading with small stocks of flour, oatmeal, sugar, butter and candles. Profits were distributed to members in proportion to their purchases. Today the number of retail co-operatives societies in Great Britain and Northern Ireland is 227 and the trade accounts in value for 7 per cent of Britain's retail trade. In addition these retail societies largely provide the capital and control the operations of the Co-operative Wholesale Society.

The minimum shareholding in a retail co-operative society is usually £1. Only if a full share is held does a member enjoy voting rights, but each member has only one vote irrespective of the number of shares held. Until fairly recently societies distributed profits as a dividend in proportion to the value of the member's purchases over the period. Today, however, most societies make use of the National Dividend Stamp scheme run by the Co-operative Wholesale Society. Stamps are given to customers in proportion to their purchases, and a book of stamps can be redeemed for 40p cash, 50p in goods or a 50p deposit in a share account, in which case a bonus of an extra 10p is usually added. Not only has this system allowed the co-operative shops to compete in price with the supermarkets but it is much cheaper to operate than the old 'divi' method. Nor does the member have to wait at least six months before receiving the dividend, while the national stamp can be given by other traders, e.g. petrol stations.

The co-operative societies described above are organised directly by consumers and are therefore called 'consumers' co-operative societies'. Producers have also formed 'producers' co-operative societies' to market their members' produce. They are chiefly important in agriculture, particularly where production is carried on by many small farmers, as in Denmark, New Zealand and Spain. Nevertheless they have been slow to develop in the UK. Instead marketing difficulties have been dealt with by the government setting up Marketing Boards.

Co-operatives have also been established in manufacturing, e.g. the Meriden Motor Cycle workers' co-operative, which was established with government aid when threatened with closure. A highly successful retail co-operative is the John Lewis Partnership, while building societies can be regarded as 'co-operative' ventures.

II The material standard of living

Table 1.1 shows the contribution made by each broad industrial group to the total output of the UK in 1977. While an account of how these figures are compiled is postponed until Chapter 15, an initial inspection raises two fundamental questions: (1) What is meant by 'production'; and (2) Why is production limited?

The meaning of 'production'

It will be observed that Table 1.1 includes the value of services rendered, e.g. in public health and education, as well as the output of farmers, miners and manufacturers. How is this justified?

The very early economists considered that only work in the extractive industries (agriculture, mining and fishing) was productive. In his *Wealth of Nations*, 1776, Adam Smith added manufacturing, but he was specific in excluding persons who merely rendered services.

This was illogical. People work, and production takes place, in order to satisfy wants. Consequently people who render services must be regarded as being productive. The soldier, actor and footballer are all satisfying wants. Similarly, in a factory the clerk

Table 1.1 *Output by industry of the UK, 1978 (current prices)*

	(£ million)
Agriculture, forestry and fishing	3,715
Mining and quarrying	4,467
Manufacturing	40,690
Construction	8,610
Gas, electricity, and water	4,772
Transport	7,677
Communication	4,011
Distributive trades	14,687
Insurance, banking, and finance and business services	5,170
Public administration and defence	10,197
Public health and educational services	9,674
Other services	18,680
Ownership of dwellings	8,578
Total domestic output	140,928
Residual error	1,071
Net property income from abroad	836
GROSS NATIONAL PRODUCT AT FACTOR COST	142,835
less capital consumption	−18,310
NATIONAL INCOME	124,525

Source: *National Income and Expenditure* (Blue Book) London, HMSO, 1979.

who calculates the wages is just as productive as the man who makes the nuts and bolts. All are helping to produce the final product, a good satisfying wants.

Wants can take different forms. Most people like a newspaper to read at the breakfast table; thus the boy who takes it from the shop to the customer's letter-box is productive. Most people, too, prefer to buy their potatoes weekly; thus the farmer or merchant who stores them through the winter is satisfying the wants of consumers, and are similarly productive. Utility is created not only by changing the *form* of our scarce resources but also their *place* and *time*.

For certain purposes it may still be useful to classify industries broadly. *Primary industries* cover the first steps in the productive process – agriculture, fishing, mining and oil-prospecting. *Secondary industries* use the raw materials of the extractive industries to manufacture into their own products – flour, clothing, tinned salmon, steel girders, petrol, and so on. *Tertiary industries* are concerned with the provision of services – transport, communications, distribution, commerce, government and professional and other services. What we find is that as over time national output grows, an increasing proportion is provided by the tertiary industries (see also p. 31).

Factors determining a country's material standard of living

Table 1.1 also shows that in 1978 total net production of the UK was limited to £124,525 million. Since people can only enjoy what they produce, this limits their material standard of living, which we can take as being roughly equal to average national income per head. The factors which set this limit can be classified as internal and external, the latter resulting from economic relationships with the rest of the world.

The most important *internal* factors are:

1 Original natural resources   Obviously, 'natural resources' cover such things as mineral deposits, sources of fuel and power, climate, fertility of the soil and fisheries around the coast, but also included are geographical advantages, such as navigable rivers or lakes, which help communications.

While national income increases as new techniques or transport developments allow natural resources to be exploited, the exhaustion of mineral resources works in the opposite direction. Moreover, where a country's economy is predominantly agricultural, variations in weather may cause its national income to fluctuate from year to year.

2 The nature of the people, particularly of the labour force   Other things being equal, the standard of living will be

higher, the greater the proportion of workers to the total popula
tion and the longer their working hours.

But the quality of the labour force is also important. This wil
depend upon the basic characteristics of the people – their health
energy, adaptability, inventiveness, judgement and ability to
organise themselves and to co-operate in production – togethe
with the skills they have acquired through education and
training.

3 Capital equipment   The effectiveness of natural resource
and of labour depends almost entirely upon capital equipment
Thus machinery is necessary to extract oil and minerals, a turbine
generator to harness a waterfall, and hotels to exploit Spanish su
and beaches. Similarly, the output of workers varies almost in
direct proportion to the capital equipment and power at thei
disposal. Indeed the most important single cause of materia
progress is investment, the addition to capital.

If this is so, the question has to be asked as to why we do no
have more investment? The answer is simply that we can ac
cumulate capital only by postponing current consumption. In
everyday language more jam tomorrow means less jam today. A
simple example will make this clear.

Suppose a peasant farmer has been tilling the ground with a
primitive spade. By working twelve hours a day he can cultivate
two acres. Obviously, if he had a plough which could be drawn by
his oxen, it would help him considerably. How can he obtain it?
Three ways are open to him:

(a) He could reduce the land he cultivates to $1\frac{1}{2}$ acres, using the
three hours saved on tilling to make the plough.

(b) He could reduce his leisure and sleeping time from twelve to
eight hours, using the extra four hours for making the plough.

(c) He could decide not to consume some of the produce already
harvested, exchanging it instead for the plough.

Whichever method is chosen entails some present sacrifice.
With (a) and (c) the farmer has less to eat, lowering his standard
of living. With (b) he has to forgo some leisure. In short he has to
draw in his belt or work harder. But the reward comes when he
has the plough: with twelve hours' work a day he can now
cultivate four acres, thereby doubling his standard of living.

One other point emerges from this illustration: the more fertile
his land, the easier it is for the farmer to increase his income. If,
because of the poverty of the soil, sixteen hours were required to
dig his two acres, our farmer would have found it more difficult to
obtain his plough. He could not reduce his consumption below the
subsistence level; nor could he go without essential sleep. Similarly, countries on extremely low living standards are in a vicious
circle which can only be broken by economic aid from richer

countries or by enforced five-year plans which ruthlessly cut current consumption, as in the USSR, China and Cuba.

Naturally our farmer will have to devote time to repairing the plough. So long as it is capable of cultivating four acres, we can say that capital is being 'maintained intact'. Where capital is not maintained, it is being 'run down' or 'depreciated'.

We can now see why governments encourage investment: it has important consequences for future living standards.

4 The organisation of resources   To achieve the maximum output from scarce factors of production, they must be organised efficiently. Have we the correct proportion of machinery to each worker? Is the production of the particular good being carried on in the best possible locality? Could the factors be better deployed within the factory? Such questions have to be answered by persons organising production.

5 Knowledge of techniques   Technical knowledge is the result of research and invention. Further capital expenditure is required to develop discoveries. Thus before we can utilise our present knowledge of nuclear energy, much capital expenditure is required. Nevertheless the rapid increase of the standard of living of the UK over the last hundred years has largely been due to the development and application of new inventions such as the steam-engine, the internal combustion engine, electrical power and electronics.

6 Political organisation   A stable government promotes confidence and thereby encourages saving and investment in long-term capital projects.

To the above we have to add what can be termed *external* factors:

7 Foreign loans and investments   A net income from foreign investments means that a country obtains goods or services from other countries without having to give goods and services in return, and vice versa. Generally speaking, welfare from this source is only likely to fluctuate over a long period.

8 The terms of trade   In the short run fluctuations in the terms of trade are likely to be far more important in changing material welfare, especially if the country, as with the UK, has a high level of imports and exports.

By the *terms of trade* we mean the quantity of another country's products which a nation gets in exchange for a given quantity of its own products. Thus, if the terms of trade move in a nation's favour, it means that it gets a larger quantity of imports for a given quantity of its own exports (see p. 27). This happens because the prices of goods imported have fallen relatively to those exported. Thus the 1973 increase in the price of oil reduced the standard of living of the importing countries and raised that of the oil producers.

9 Gifts from abroad   Gifts made to countries for purposes of economic development and defence improve the standard of living of the receiving countries.

III The firm and its environment

The response of firms to their environment

Whatever form the firm takes it has to be responsive to its environment, seeking to be as efficient as possible within the constraints imposed. The environment embraces a number of influences. Some, such as changes in the price of the product, are specific, affecting the firm directly; others, such as government measures to combat inflation, are general, providing the background for the operations of all firms. (See Figure 1.3 at the end of the chapter for a diagrammatic representation.)

Environmental influences differ in importance according to the type of organisation. Thus private-sector firms are mainly concerned with the immediate factors which influence the markets for their products, particularly demand – what people are able and willing to pay (see p. 96). In contrast, government organisations, such as the Department of Education and Science, the National Health Service and local authority housing committees, respond to what are considered to be the 'needs' of people for education, health services and housing rather than their ability to pay. Since the decision as to what constitutes such 'merit goods' is largely subjective, politics is a further environmental influence.

Moreover, firms vary in their responsiveness to changes in their environment. Thus if an industry is highly competitive, a firm will have to adapt quickly to a change in demand or it will lose out to rival firms. A monopoly, on the other hand, would be under less pressure.

Many environmental factors will be discussed under topic headings. At this stage, however, it is useful to draw them together in outline, classifying them into (1) specific, immediate influences, and (2) general, background influences.

1 Specific influences   *(a) Market factors: price relative to costs.* In the private sector the overriding influence on the firm will be the price at which the product sells relative to the cost of production. A profit will encourage the firm to expand; a persistent loss will eventually force the firm out of business.

(b) *Availability of capital and labour.* As we shall see, expansion of the organisation may be restricted by lack of funds. Private firms come up against the imperfections of the capital market (see p. 137); public-sector organisations may be restricted in the services they can provide by the government's reluctance to increase taxation or charges, or its inability to borrow additional funds. Similarly, a firm may have to curtail its activities through a shortage of skilled labour.

(c) *Physical factors.* These often decide the location of firms, e.g. shipbuilding, or what they produce, e.g. agriculture. They may even limit a firm's expansion on its existing premises.

(d) *Government measures.* Government action, both legal and administrative, may affect a firm directly. Thus the law may impose price control or insist on safety precautions within the factory, while Ministers may forbid a merger or refuse planning permission. Similarly, in the public sector some projects may be encouraged by government action, e.g. providing financial support for British Leyland, raising the TV licence fee for the BBC, increasing grants to local authorities.

(e) *Trade-union policy.* Demands for higher wages, threats of strikes and actual stoppages affect firms both in the private and public sectors.

(f) *Social and psychological attitudes.* Firms have to assess the likely reactions of consumers to price rises, standardisation of the product, delays on delivery time, inefficient after-sales service, etc. But it is in dealing with labour that psychological and social considerations are paramount, for productivity depends not only on the wage offered but also on job satisfaction, the avoidance of boredom, loyalty to the firm and future prospects.

(g) *Events abroad.* Where a firm is highly dependent upon export markets, it may be affected by events outside its control, e.g. import duties on its goods, a United Nations' sanctions decision, joining the EEC, the cancellation of export orders through a change of government in the importing country.

2 General influences (a) *Government direction of the economy.* The government is responsible for securing full employment, a stable price level and growth of national output. The policies it adopts, and the success it achieves, provide the background for firms' operations. Thus a booming economy encourages firms to invest; the possibility of a recession makes them consider retrenchment. Likewise, in the public sector a healthy economy allows expenditure on services to expand more easily since the tax base also expands.

(b) *The rate of growth of income.* The current level of national income will determine partly firms' production plans. In addition income can be expected to grow over time, and firms must respond accordingly by changes in their products (see p. 117), especially where production plans have to be made well ahead, e.g. new car and aeroplane models.

(c) *Demographic changes.* Changes in the population – its size, composition, level of education and geographical distribution – occur over the long period (see Chapter 2). Nevertheless firms, and the government in particular, must provide for foreseeable changes, e.g. for housing, education and recreational facilities.

(d) *Political climate.* While private firms are influenced by the attitude of the government in power to the private-enterprise system and respond favourably to political stability, it is the public sector which is directly affected by swings in the political pendulum. In general Labour governments are more favourable to the expansion of the public sector than are Conservative governments.

(e) *Social and psychological attitudes.* Over time people's way of looking at life changes, especially as they become better off. Thus in recent years more emphasis has been placed on the quality of life, e.g. preventing pollution, and securing future living standards, e.g. nature conservation, preserving buildings of special architectural or historic interest. Today, too, there is a movement away from higher wages towards a thirty-five hour working week, longer holidays, etc. Firms have to respond to such aspirations in their policy decisions.

(f) *International events.* In Chapter 20 we study the importance of international trade to the UK. This dependence means that firms can be affected by a variety of world events, e.g. a change in the exchange rate of the £ sterling, political unrest in Africa or the Middle East, additional defence commitments in response to Soviet rearmament. Probably the major single event in recent years was the 1973 steep rise in oil prices following the Arab–Israeli war, for this was largely responsible for the subsequent world recession.

The approach of this book

In the limited space available it would be impossible to consider all the above influences in detail. Attention will be drawn to them when dealing with particular topics, e.g. monopoly and government policy, labour and trade unions and employment protection, taxation and the redistribution of income. But of these influences, two are of overriding and immediate importance: (1) price, especially for firms in the private sector; and (2) government policy, as it deals with particular problems in the private sector, directly organises the government's own production or takes measures to stabilise the economy generally.

This book concentrates, therefore, on these two major influences. The first requires an examination of the operation of the market economy, the second a basic knowledge of how the government functions in the context of British democracy. Before considering these, however, we must look at the population of the UK – the consumers of goods and services and the owners of the labour, capital and land which produce those goods.

**Fig. 1.3
The firm and its
environment**

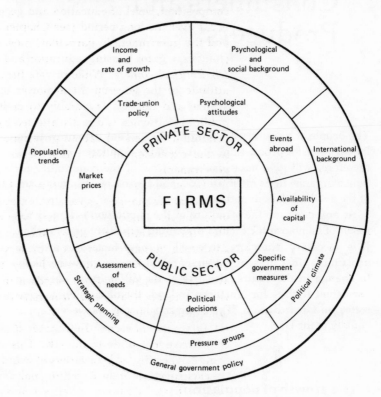

2 The Population as Consumers and Producers

The people of a country are its consumers. They also provide the labour force for production. A study of the population of the UK, therefore, will give us a bird's-eye view of the community for which organisations must provide, and also of the size and nature of the available labour source.

At any one time the structure of the population is largely the result of demographic factors prevailing some fifty years earlier. It is necessary, therefore, to consider these factors in order to explain the UK's present pattern of population and how it is likely to change in the future. Because of the difficulty of obtaining consistent figures for Northern Ireland, the discussion concentrates on Great Britain. The basic conclusions, however, apply equally to the UK.

I The growth of population

Table 2.1 *Population (in 000's) 1801–1971*

Date	Great Britain (England, Wales and Scotland)	Northern Ireland
1801	10,501	—
1851	20,816	1,443
1901	37,000	1,237
1951	48,854	1,371
1961	51,250	1,425
1971	53,979	1,536

Source: *Annual Abstract of Statistics*, London, HMSO.

Table 2.1 and Figure 2.1 reveal that while the UK's population increased quite rapidly during the nineteenth century, there was a marked falling off in the rate of increase in the twentieth century. This poses three main questions: (a) Why was there such a rapid growth of population during the nineteenth century? (b) Why has the rate of growth fallen so markedly during the twentieth century? (c) What is likely to happen during the rest of the twentieth century?

Fig. 2.1
Growth of the population, 1801–1971

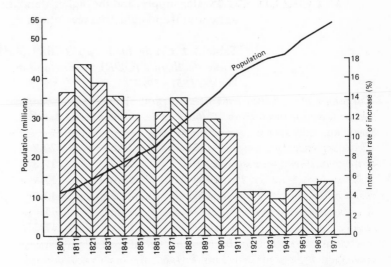

Causes of changes in the rate of growth

The factors affecting population changes are shown in Figure 2.2. On the one hand we have the natural increase – the excess of births over deaths; and on the other hand we have migration – the balance between immigration (inwards) and emigration (outwards). In fact, apart from the years 1931–41 and 1951–61, Great Britain has lost by migration about half a million people each decade. Changes in the rate of growth, therefore, have resulted chiefly from changes in the natural increase.

Fig. 2.2
Factors affecting population

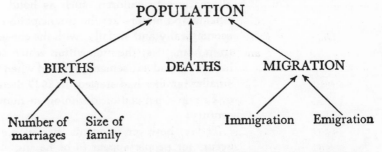

For our purposes crude rates are adequate for examining changes in the rate of births and deaths. The *crude birth rate* (CBR) is the number of births per year per thousand of the population. For example, if the total population is 50 million and the number of births in the year is 1 million, the CBR equals 20. Similarly, the *crude death rate* (CDR) is the number of deaths per year per thousand of the population.

Table 2.2 indicates the reason for the high rate of increase during the nineteenth century – while the birth rate remained high, there was a considerable fall in the death rate. The latter was the result of improved medical knowledge, better sanitation and water supply, and the higher standard of living following the agricultural and industrial revolutions.

Table 2.2 *Crude birth rate (CBR) and crude death rate (CDR) for England and Wales, 1851–1977*

Date	CBR	CDR
1851	35.5	22.7
1900–2	28.7	17.3
1950–2	16.0	11.9
1961	17.9	12.0
1971	16.2	11.6
1977	11.8	11.7

But the situation changed in the twentieth century. The death rate did not fall so rapidly. More important, the birth rate fell considerably. The reason was a fall in the average size of family – from between five and six children to just over two. A variety of factors contributed to this: improved methods and social acceptance of birth control; the increased economic burden of parenthood, due, for instance, to the gradual raising of the school-leaving age; the higher standards which parents generally set themselves for their children's welfare; the growth of competing alternatives to children, such as holidays, foreign travel, the cinema and motor-car; the emancipation of women, politically, economically and socially, with the consequent desire to be free from home ties; the momentum which social example, smaller houses and advertisement provided when the movement towards smaller families had started. In 1949 there was a real possibility of Britain's population declining in number by the end of the century!

Today, however, it seems that such a decline is unlikely to occur, for people appear to be having slightly larger families. Various reasons can be suggested for this: younger marriages, greater economic prosperity, increased government help to the family man and more facilities for young mothers to resume work. Even so, over the past thirty years population projections have been continually revised downwards, for, after the 'baby booms' immediately after 1945 and in the early 1960s, the birth rate has fallen, and continues to do so. The size of the family appears to be settling only slightly above the 1930 level. While couples are marrying younger, they postpone having children so that wives can continue working full time, while smaller families enable them to resume work sooner. In this they are aided by improved methods of contraception.

While any projections of population are dependent upon the reliability of assumptions, especially as regards births and migration, it now seems likely that the population of the UK will be about 57 million at the end of the century. Whether such an increase is desirable or not will now be examined.

II The implications of changes in the size of the population

The Malthusian theory of overpopulation

Until the middle of the eighteenth century the population of Britain grew slowly. But from then on it became more rapid, and in 1798 the Reverend Thomas Malthus's first essay on *The Principle of Population as it affects the Future Improvement of Society* made it a major subject of discussion.

Malthus began from two postulates: (a) that the passion between the sexes is necessary and will remain nearly in its present state; and (b) that food is necessary to the existence of man. Given these two postulates, his arguments forced him to conclude that: (a) the population will, if unchecked, double itself every twenty-five years; and (b) the means of subsistence can, at a maximum, increase by only the same amount every twenty-five years. In other words, while population multiplies in a geometric progression, food supplies increase in an arithmetic progression.

The first conclusion was based on information collected by Malthus on the populations of various countries. But the second was supported by no evidence whatsoever. In order to substantiate it, Malthus appealed to the 'known properties of land'. Here he was virtually relying on the *law of diminishing returns* (see p. 145), though this was not precisely stated until some fifty years later.

From these two conclusions the important result followed that the power of population to increase was 'infinitely greater than the power of the earth to produce subsistence for man'. In short there would always be a tendency for the population to outrun the means of subsistence.

If man cannot live without food, what, Malthus asked, kept population within its means of subsistence? The answer he found in certain 'checks'. First, there were 'positive checks', involving misery – famine, war, disease, epidemics. Second, there were 'preventive checks' which, with one exception, all involved 'vice', including contraception. The exception was 'moral restraint', by which was meant that people deliberately refrained from marrying at an early age. Since this was a remote possibility, the outlook for civilisation was gloomy: in the long run there could only be a subsistence level of existence for people. Moreover, social policies to alleviate poverty would be self-defeating.

Malthus's 'blind spots'   Although at the beginning of the nineteenth century Malthus's views were widely accepted, the final tragedy of starvation, the logical outcome of his two conclusions, has not occurred. Where, therefore, did Malthus go wrong?

First, we must note that to some extent his argument was illogical, for he did not answer the fact, well known at the time, that in spite of the rapid increase in the population over the previous fifty years, people on the average were no worse off. This showed that the means of subsistence must at least have increased in proportion. Had Malthus possessed a precisely formulated law of diminishing returns, he could have based his argument on a fixed total supply of land which would sooner or later make itself felt as the population increased. Second, Malthus was preoccupied with people as consumers. He failed to see that, by and large, a consumer is also a producer, for 'with every mouth God sends a pair of hands'. Here again a fixed supply of land with consequent diminishing returns could have overcome this objection. Third, Malthus failed to foresee change. On the one hand the geometric increase in Britain's population did *not* occur, because of emigration and, above all, through the reduction in the size of family. On the other hand improved agricultural techniques and the vast increase in imports meant that Britain's food supplies were not limited to increasing in an arithmetic progression.

Thus Malthus's arguments have validity only when there are fixed resources, such as land or energy reserves. It is, for instance, the limited supply of land which brings about a Malthusian situation in the Far East today and, as we shall see, increases Britain's difficulties as she tries to produce a larger proportion of her foodstuffs at home.

The concept of an   To Malthus, increasing numbers were a bad thing, as they
'optimum population'   pressed on the means of subsistence and lowered the standard of living. But his views lost ground towards the middle of the nineteenth century, for as the capital investment of the Industrial

Revolution began to yield benefits, the standard of living was seen to be keeping pace with the increase in population.

Indeed, at the turn of the century, Professor Edwin Cannan showed that population could be too small to take full advantage of available knowledge. For example, a larger population might justify large-scale production with more use being made of division of labour, specialised machines and technical discoveries. In short a doubling of the population could lead to more than doubling production.

Since, therefore, population could either be too large or too small, there must be an intermediate point where it is just right. The optimum population is that population at which, given existing technical knowledge, capital equipment, and exchange possibilities with other countries, average output per head is at a maximum. Thus if we refer to Table 9.2 on p. 145, the optimum population for the example given would be four labourers. It follows that any country is over- or under-populated if its population is respectively more or less than the optimum.

But the concept of an optimum population is not without difficulties. In the first place it is unjustifiable to apply the conditions of 'given existing technical knowledge, capital equipment, and exchange possibilities' and then to speculate as to what production would be if the population were larger or smaller. Had the population increased differently, these variables themselves would have been different. The same mistake is apparent in J. S. Mill's argument in the middle of the nineteenth century that the world would have been better off if, with the improvements that had taken place, population had been more restrained. The truth is that such improvements would not have taken place, for a large and rapidly growing population accumulates knowledge and equipment differently from a smaller or slowly growing one. Even more important is that, from the practical point of view, the concept is of little help. Any optimum population at which a country was aiming would only remain the optimum so long as technical knowledge, etc., did not change. Thus, before an optimum was achieved, some new figure would have taken its place. All that can be done, therefore, is to consider the present composition of the population, forecast the population which will result from it, and then relate this population to likely changes in capital accumulation and technical discoveries.

We now apply this procedure to a study of Britain's population.

The advantages to Great Britain of an increasing population

An increasing population has certain advantages which stimulate growth:

(1) *It increases the size of the home market.* The additional output needed for a larger population should benefit industries working under conditions of decreasing costs, e.g. aircraft,

computers, nuclear reactors. It should be noted, however, that this applies only if the extra output is provided by existing firms and not by additional firms entering the industry. Moreover, it is possible to obtain large-scale economies by specialising on a narrow range of goods and exporting, e.g. Switzerland.

(2) *It facilitates labour mobility.* With an increasing population unemployment resulting from the immobility of labour is a less intractable problem. This is because the decline of the old industries is slower and can be covered by natural wastage with fewer redundancies, while expanding industries can obtain most of their additional workers from new entrants to the labour force.

(3) *It encourages investment.* An increasing population makes it easier to maintain the level of replacement investment. More than that, the extra consumer demand necessitates additional investment in machinery, factories, schools, houses, transport, etc. Consequently it stimulates improved techniques, thereby accelerating the replacement of existing equipment.

(4) *It promotes vitality.* By weighting the age distribution in favour of youth, an increasing population provides more workers for a given number of retired persons and makes for energy, mobility, inventiveness and the willingness to accept new ideas.

It should be noted that the disadvantages of a decreasing population could be stated as the opposite of these.

The disadvantages of an increasing population

Against the advantages given above, it is necessary to set certain disadvantages which may make it difficult for an increasing population to raise present living standards. Resources have to be used in adding to capital equipment instead of producing consumer goods or improving existing buildings. The growing population in Britain since the war, for example, has delayed slum-clearance and rehousing schemes, for new houses for the extra people have had to be built.

Above all, an increasing population adds to the pressure on the fixed supply of land available in Britain. The saying that 'with every mouth God sends a pair of hands' ignores two important facts. The first is that not every person is a producer – for a time the additional mouths have to be provided with food, education, etc., by the working group. The second is more important – the increase in the number of labourers on a fixed amount of land may well bring the law of diminishing returns into operation, with a consequent fall in living standards.

It is the law of diminishing returns which pinpoints the problem of increasing numbers. With the Far Eastern countries there is simply a lower output per head, as extra people have to obtain their subsistence from a fixed amount of land. But for Britain the problem is presented in a slightly different form. Some of her additional food supplies can be produced at home by improving techniques. But in the main, Britain produces her food in her workshops by exporting machinery, cars, electrical equipment, etc., for the meat, cereals, fruit, etc., that she requires. What Britain has to ask, therefore, is: can exports be increased sufficiently to pay for the extra imports required by the larger population? In short can she maintain a healthy balance-of-payments position so that she suffers no reduction in her standard of living if population grows?

Throughout the nineteenth century Britain proved that this was possible. Indeed, a balance-of-payments surplus allowed her to invest heavily abroad. But since then the problem of finding and holding foreign markets has become more acute, reflected in her frequent balance-of-payments difficulties.

Moreover, it must be remembered that a given increase in the population necessitates a much larger proportional increase in exports if the standard of living is to be maintained. Any expansion of present food production in Britain could encounter rapidly diminishing returns. Most of the extra foodstuffs, therefore, would have to come from abroad (not just 50 per cent, which is the present proportion). In addition the extra population would require imported goods, such as cameras and cars. Finally, to increase exports much of the raw materials from which they are made would have to be imported.

Nor does this take into consideration any possible deterioration in Britain's terms of trade. Will there be as much raw materials and foodstuffs available from the underdeveloped countries as they industrialise and improve their own incomes? Or will the latter lead to a vastly increased demand for British exports? At present the rising price of North Sea oil is moving the terms of trade in Britain's favour.

Finally, with population growth environmental problems intensify. As city congestion increases and more open space is required for housing, roads and industry, arguments for conservation and control of pollution gain momentum.

Conclusion

At present Britain is managing to support increasing numbers while improving living standards. But the over-all level of the future population must be watched by the government and, if necessary, influenced by the level of child benefits and immigration policy. Social as well as economic considerations have to be taken into account.

In the Far East a Malthusian situation exists. While the death rate is falling through better medical services, the birth rate remains high. By the end of the century an almost doubled population could be seeking to live with little increase in land. Possible solutions are birth control, improved agricultural techniques, the development of export industries and economic aid from developed countries.

III The age distribution of the population

Any change in birth or death rates will affect the age distribution over time. Thus the boom in births after 1945 and in the early 1960s produced a bulge in new young workers some sixteen years later.

The present over-all pattern is of an ageing population brought about by the fall in the rate of increase during the twentieth century (see Figure 2.3). Until the end of the century the working age group should form a slightly higher proportion (65 per cent) of the total population, but those under 15 years will fall to 20 per cent and those over 65 rise to 15 per cent.

**Fig. 2.3
Changes in the age distribution of the population of Great Britain, 1851–1971**

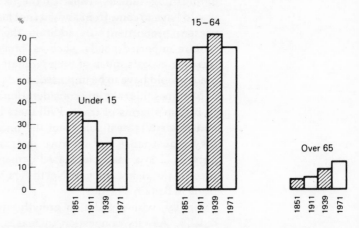

The effects of an ageing population

It should be noted that in part this trend is due to a normal development, the fall in mortality. This means that we have to adjust to the change: trying to prevent it by raising the birth rate will also increase the size of the population, which, as we have seen, presents problems.

It is essential, therefore, to anticipate the possible economic, social and political difficulties resulting from changes in the age structure so that the necessary adjustments can be planned in advance.

1 Economic   First, there is an increased dependence of retired persons on the working population. Current wants can only be provided for by current production. An ageing population means that the proportion of workers to consumers is falling. Whereas in

1851 there were over twelve people of working age to every person over 65 years of age, in 1978 there were only 4½. One particular result will be the increased burden of retirement pensions, more pensioners having to be supported by proportionately fewer contributors.

Second, a changing pattern of consumption will result. An ageing population means, to take extreme examples, that bath-chairs will be wanted in place of prams, walking-sticks in place of hockey sticks, tea in place of milk. For many of these new 'wants' consideration has to be given well in advance. We must, for instance, make more provision for aged couples when planning a housing programme. On the other hand, the bulges of the late 1940s and early 1960s have to be provided with housing and jobs or further education respectively.

Third, an older labour force is less mobile. In the past expanding industries have obtained labour from young persons just starting their working lives, while the decaying industries have declined fairly smoothly by not replacing workers as they leave or retire. However, where the working population is static in size, expanding industries have to draw older workers from the declining industries. 'Teaching old dogs new tricks' and moving them to new areas is not always easy (see pp. 182–3). A high level of unemployment increases the difficulties, for it is the older workers in the declining industries who are likely to remain out of a job the longest. Thus both the government and firms must provide training schemes and relocation incentives.

Fourth, an older population tends to be less progressive. While older people are more patient and experienced than younger people, the latter excel in energy, enterprise, enthusiasm and the ability to adapt themselves and to learn new skills.

2 Social   Where old people are more numerous and live longer, their children find greater difficulty in caring for them. Thus there is an increasing need for the state to provide home-care services (such as meals-on-wheels and home-helps), old people's homes and geriatric wards in hospitals.

Similarly, there is a greater demand for advice from citizen's advice bureaux since older people need more help in sorting out difficulties relating to housing, gas and electricity bills and social-security benefits.

3 Political   Political decisions have to be made as a result of the disadvantages of an ageing population. To what extent should younger generations be augmented by a liberal immigration policy, bearing in mind the social stresses which could arise? Can adequate defence be provided by the use of more sophisticated weapons, or will the falling proportion of young people necessi-

tate conscription? Should TV and radio programmes give greater weight to the type of entertainment preferred by old people? And, since older people own the larger share of the nation's capital but are adverse to taking risks, should the state assume responsibility for providing funds for the riskier types of enterprise, such as North Sea oil prospecting and development, the building of nuclear power stations, and the exploration of outer space?

Indeed, the ageing population may even influence the type of government elected, older people tending to be more conservative.

IV The industrial distribution of the working population

The working population

The population of GB in 1977 was estimated to be 54,315,000 persons. Of these 25,717,000 persons are described by the Department of Employment as 'the working population'.

The working population is defined as persons, over school-leaving age, 'who work for pay or gain or register themselves as available for such work'. It therefore includes all persons who are: (a) in civil employment, even if they are over retirement age or are working only part time; (b) in the Armed Forces; (c) registered as unemployed. Excluded by the definition are: (a) children under 16 years of age and students above 16 years of age who are receiving full-time education; (b) persons, such as housewives, who do not work for pay or gain; (c) persons who, having private means, do not need to work; (d) retired persons.

The size of the working population depends upon:

(1) The numbers within the 16–65 age group.

(2) The activity rates within this group, especially as regards young persons and female workers. The tendency over the last twenty years has been for a higher proportion of young persons to remain in further education, thus reducing their activity rate. On the other hand, a higher proportion of women are now entering the working population. The expansion of the service and light manufacturing industries has provided increased job opportunities for women, while the changed attitude to women workers is reflected in the Equal Pay Act, 1970, and the Sex Discrimination Act, 1975. Above all, the smaller family, the availability of crèches and school dinners, and new labour-saving domestic appliances have allowed married women to work.

(3) The extent to which people over retiring age continue to work, something which is largely influenced by the level of pensions.

(4) The employment opportunities available, the tendency

being for the working population to contract in a depression (mainly through the withdrawal of married women).

Changes in the industrial distribution of the working population

Table 2.3 shows that the chief changes in the distribution of the working population between 1901 and 1975 were as follows:

(1) A large decrease in the percentage of the population employed in the primary (extractive) industries – agriculture and mining.

(2) A relatively small decrease in the percentage employed in secondary – manufacturing and construction – industries.

(3) A relatively large increase in the tertiary industries – distributive trades, public administration and services – with the notable exception of domestic servants.

The basic explanation of these broad changes can be found in the increase in real income (which more than doubled) over the period. In this respect, the changes are merely a continuation of the trend of the previous century. As income increases, people

Table 2.3   *Industrial distribution of the working population, 1901–1977*

	Distribution (%) Great Britain		Numbers (000's) GB
	(1) 1901	(2) 1977	(3) 1977
Agriculture, forestry and fishing	9·0	1·5	381
Mining and quarrying	5·8	1·3	347
Manufacture (including gas, electricity and water supply)	32·6	29·3	7,544
Construction	8·1	4·8	1,228
Transport and communication	9·3	5·6	1,428
Distributive trades		10·4	2,682
Financial, professional and scientific services	15·4	18·1	4,662
Public administration	1·4	6·2	1,583
Catering and domestic services	15·3	3·4	873
Miscellaneous services	2·0	5·6	1,445
Armed Forces	1·1	1·3	327
Registered unemployed	—	5·4	1,390
Employers and self-employed	—	7·1	1,825
TOTALS	100·0	100·0	25,714

Sources: Col. (1) compiled from Colin Clark, *Conditions of Economic Progress* (quoting Booth, *Journal of Royal Statistic Society,* 1856). Cols (2) and (3) compiled from *Annual Abstract of Statistics.*

tend to spend a smaller proportion of it on food, and more on comforts and luxuries. In 1901, for example, the average labourer spent 60 per cent of his income on food; by 1977 it had fallen to 23 per cent. Now the distribution of labour between industries is largely a reflection of the way in which people spend their incomes. Thus, as agriculture declined in relative importance, workers moved into the new luxury industries, particularly those providing services.

But there have been other influences at work, especially important in explaining changes within these broad groups. Briefly these influences are:

(1) changes in exports (e.g. mining), or in imports (e.g. agriculture);

(2) improved techniques and increased use of machines (e.g. agriculture, construction, transport, mining);

(3) the increase in exchange (e.g. insurance, banking and other services);

(4) the increase in state activities (public administration);

(5) the acceptance of women workers in industry and commerce, where high wages attracted them from domestic service.

V The geographical distribution of the population

Geographically, the population of the UK is dominated by two features: it is concentrated, and it is urban. Both are the result of moving from an agricultural to an industrial economy.

The concentrated nature of the population

As a result of the Industrial Revolution industry migrated to the coalfields which were located in the Midlands and north of England. And today, even though electricity frees industry from being located on the coalfields and the basic industries of these areas have declined, they still remain important centres of industry and population (see Figure 2.4). There are two main reasons for this. First, many industries remain on account of acquired advantages, particularly the availability of labour (see p. 198). Second, new industries have been attracted by the government's Development Area policy (see p. 292).

Nevertheless, since the Second World War the main areas of natural expansion have been the Midlands and South-east England (particularly London and the Home Counties). In comparison the coalfield and rural areas have declined. This is what one might expect with the expansion in the demand for light engineering and electrical products, aircraft, motor-vehicles, consumer durable goods, luxury goods and services of various kinds, and

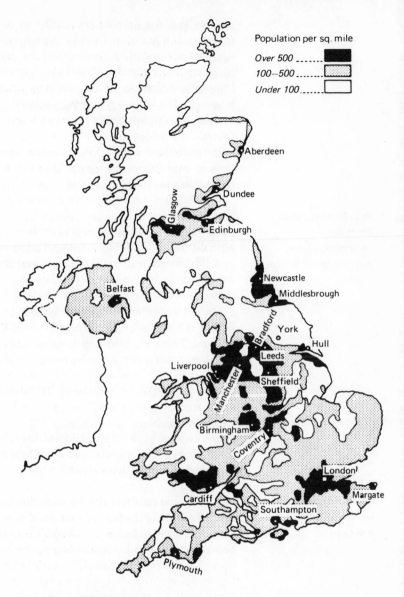

Fig. 2.4
Distribution of the UK
population

Population per sq. mile

Over 500
100–500
Under 100

the relative decrease in demand for the products of agriculture
and heavy industry. The result is that at present 55 per cent of the
population live in a coffin-shaped area, with south Lancashire
and west Yorkshire at the northern end, the Midland region
forming the broader centre and the London area at the southern
end.

**The urban nature of
the population**

This concentration of population is in towns (unlike the concentration in the Nile and Ganges deltas which consists mainly of
rural communities). Eighty per cent of the population of England

and Wales is urban. More than this, 30 per cent of Great Britain's population lives in the seven conurbations (where there is a continuous built-up area) of Greater London, south-east Lancashire (Manchester), the west Midlands (Birmingham), central Clydeside (Glasgow), west Yorkshire (Leeds and Bradford), Merseyside (Liverpool) and Tyneside (Newcastle).

Changes in population take place, however, within the main centres. As towns become too crowded, or as the standard of living improves, or as offices take over residential areas, so people tend to move from the centre to the suburbs, or even further, commuting to work by car and public transport.

Problems resulting from the concentration of population in urban areas

The concentration of population in large urban areas has certain advantages. Such areas can offer better and more specialised schools, shops, entertainment and other services. Fast road, rail and air communications facilitate travel between cities. They can usually provide a variety of employment opportunities, enabling firms to recruit the different types of labour they require. But conurbations often involve travelling long distances to work within the urban area, putting a heavy stress on the transport system. There are also problems of inner-city decay, with poor housing, inadequate schools, pollution and lack of open spaces. Moreover, with fewer social ties, the lower community spirit results in vandalism and petty crime. Above all, where these areas are faced with the decline of major local industries, there is a 'regional' problem (see Chapter 17). Not only do government organisations have to respond to these conditions, but the development of urban areas may itself lead to the reorganisation of local and regional government.

We must now return to the problem discussed in Chapter 1 of the limited nature of the UK's income and therefore of the standard of living of her population. We look at it first in its wider setting – how man responds by economising.

3 The Background to Business Activity: The Problem of Scarcity

I The economic problem

Man's standard of living has always been limited by the resources at his disposal. Thus, as a hunter, how well he lived was mainly determined by the abundance of game and the effectiveness of his weapons. Today we face the same problem of scarce resources. Just think of the extra things we could buy if our incomes were larger – new clothes, up-to-date kitchen furniture, a better car, a hi-fi tape recorder, a cine-camera. Indeed the list has no end, for, even as these wants were satisfied, new wants would arise. You just cannot get a quart out of a pint pot. This is the *economic problem* – unlimited wants, very limited means.

While we can never completely overcome the difficulty, we can,

Fig. 3.1 The economic problem

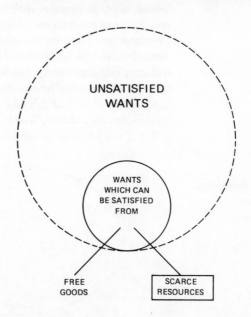

UNSATISFIED
WANTS

WANTS
WHICH CAN
BE SATISFIED
FROM

FREE
GOODS

SCARCE
RESOURCES

by 'economising', make the most of what we have. Thus the housewife buys that assortment of goods which will give maximum satisfaction from her limited housekeeping allowance. Similarly, the student strives to make his grant go as far as possible. And the businessman takes decisions which will achieve the maximum return on capital. The government, too, has to economise in order to make the most of the nation's resources as it plans its spending.

Usually economising does not mean a complete rejection of one good in favour of another, but rather deciding to have a little bit more of one and a little less of the other. In short, as we shall see, it involves choices at *the margin*.

It is against this backcloth of limited resources that all decisions of consumers and firms have to be made (see Figure 3.1).

II Economic systems

The role of the economic system

In primitive economies the individual uses his resources directly to provide what he wants. Thus Robinson Crusoe had to decide how much time to spend hunting, fishing, growing corn and relaxing in the sun according to the strength of his preferences for meat, fish, bread and leisure. Similarly, in a subsistence economy, the farmer's output is mainly for his own family's needs.

Today, however, decisions as to what shall be produced are linked only indirectly with the actual consumer. Man now specialises in production, obtaining the variety of goods he wants by exchange. Thus on the one hand we have what we will term 'households', the units which both consume goods and services and supply the resources, mainly labour, to produce them. On the other hand, we have 'firms', the organisations which decide what goods and services to produce and use the resources supplied by households accordingly (see Figure 3.2).

But if the greatest possible satisfaction is to be obtained from

Fig. 3.2
The flow of goods and services in an economic system

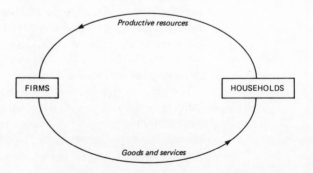

limited resources, there must be a link between households and firms. Put briefly, the following questions have to be answered:

(1) *What* goods and services shall firms produce?
(2) *How much* of each good and service shall be produced?
(3) *How* shall the goods and services be produced?
(4) How shall products be *divided* between households?

To solve these problems we need some form of economic system; in short the economic system provides the link between households and firms.

Different forms of economic system

Man's first exchanges were quite simple: there was a direct swap of one good for another. Eventually a 'go-between' – money – was developed allowing goods to be 'priced' and sold in markets. The subsistence economy had now evolved into the *market economy* where answers to the above questions flow from people's decisions in the market.

In contrast to the market economy there is the *command* or *centrally directed* economy (closely resembling Communism). Here the state decides what to produce and directs the factors of production accordingly. Furthermore what is produced is distributed according to the decisions of the central body, the emphasis being 'to each according to his need' rather than on financial ability to pay.

Our task now is to examine in turn the respective strengths and weaknesses of these two systems.

III The market economy

Outline of the market mechanism

With the market economy emphasis is laid on the freedom of the individual, both as a consumer and as the owner of resources.

As a consumer he expresses his choice of goods through the price he is willing to pay for them. As the owner of a factor of production he seeks to obtain as large a reward as possible. If consumers want more of the good than is being supplied at the current price, this is indicated by their 'bidding up' the price. This increases the profits of firms and the earnings of factors producing that good. As a result, resources are attracted into the industry, and supply expands. On the other hand if consumers do not want a particular good, its price falls, producers make a loss, and resources leave the industry.

The price system therefore indicates the wishes of consumers (subject to the existing distribution of income) and allocates the community's productive resources accordingly (see Figure 3.3). There is no direction of labour; people are free to work wherever they choose. Efficiency is achieved through the profit motive;

Fig. 3.3
The allocation of
products and
resources through the
market economy

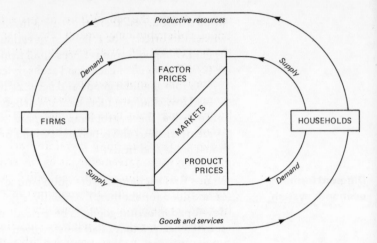

owners of factors of production sell them at the highest possible
price, while firms keep production costs as low as they can in
order to obtain the highest profit margin.

Who receives the goods produced depends upon factor earnings. If firms produce a better good or improve efficiency, or if
workers make a greater effort, they receive a higher reward,
giving them more spending power to obtain goods in the market.

In this way the price system acts, as it were, like a marvellous
computer, registering people's preferences for different goods,
transmitting these preferences to firms, moving factors to produce the goods, and deciding who shall obtain the final products.
Thus, motivated by private enterprise, the four problems inherent
in economising are solved automatically.

**Defects of the market
economy**

Unfortunately, in practice the market economy does not work
quite so smoothly as this. Nor are its results entirely satisfactory.

First, some vital *community goods*, such as defence, police,
justice and national parks, cannot be adequately provided
through the market. This is mainly because it would be impossible to charge a price since 'free-riders' cannot be excluded.
Indeed, in most advanced countries, the state usually goes further. Thus it may take responsibility for *public goods* where there is
no reduction in the quantity available for others when one person
has more, e.g. TV programmes, parks, roads and bridges, the
cost being covered by taxation. Moreover, it usually provides a
safety net when people are unemployed, sick or old, and gives
assistance towards *merit goods*, such as education, housing,
museums and libraries, where people might underspend either
through ignorance or miscalculation of future benefits.

Second, it is those consumers with the most money who have
the greatest pull in the market. As a result resources may be
devoted to producing luxuries for the rich to the exclusion of

necessities for the poor. While this is really brought about by the unequal distribution of wealth rather than by the market system, the fact is that the latter tends to produce, and even to increase, such inequality.

Third, the competition upon which the efficiency of the market economy depends may break down. An employer may be the *only* buyer of a certain type of labour in a locality. If so, he is in a strong position when negotiating rates of pay with individual workers. The state may therefore have to intervene, e.g. with minimum wage agreements, as in the 'sweated' industries. Similarly, on the selling side, one seller may be able to exclude competitors. This puts the consumer in a weak position because he cannot take his custom elsewhere.

Fourth, competition itself may sometimes lead to inefficiency. Small units may be incompatible with achieving the economies of large-scale production. Duplication of research and competitive advertising may waste resources. Uncertainty as to rivals' plans may hold back investment.

Fifth, consumers' sovereignty may be distorted by large firms which use extensive advertising simply to convince consumers that the goods they have produced are just what people want.

Sixth, in practice the price mechanisms may function sluggishly through imperfect knowledge or immobility of factors of production (see Chapters 11 and 17). As a result supply is slow to respond to changes in demand.

Seventh, the private profit motive does not always ensure that *public* wealth (as distinct from the sum total of *private* wealth) will be maximised. There may be *social benefits* (often referred to as 'spillovers' or 'externalities'). Thus, in providing a car park, a supermarket attracts customers; but there is an additional social benefit in that it reduces congestion for all road users. On the other hand there can be a *social cost*. A manufacturer does not consider the soot which falls from his factory chimney on the nearby washing-lines. Although not a cost to him, it is to the community around.

Last, and most important, in a market economy where individuals decide what to produce, resources may remain unemployed because firms as a whole consider that profit prospects are poor.

IV The command economy

Central decision-making

With the command economy the decisions regarding 'What, how much, how, and for whom?' are taken by an all-powerful planning authority. It estimates the assortment of goods which it considers people want and directs resources into producing them. It also decides how the goods produced shall be distributed among the community. Thus economic efficiency largely depends upon how accurately wants are estimated and resources allocated (see Figure 3.4).

Fig. 3.4
The allocation of resources and products through a command economy

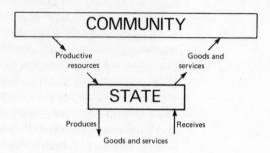

Merits of the command economy

The merits of the command economy correspond closely to the defects of the market economy. The central planning authority can: (1) allow for the uneven distribution of wealth when planning what to produce and in rewarding the producers; (2) ensure that adequate resources are devoted to 'community', 'public' and 'merit' goods; (3) eliminate the inefficiencies resulting from competition; (4) use its monopoly powers in the interests of the community, e.g. by securing the advantages of large-scale production, rather than to make maximum profits by restricting output; (5) use advertising to inform rather than simply to persuade or 'brainwash'; (6) allow for external costs and benefits when deciding what and how much to produce; and (7) employ workers in order to keep them occupied although to do so may be unprofitable in the narrow sense.

Defects of the command economy

Nevertheless the command economy has inherent defects which lay it open to criticism on both economic and political grounds.

First, estimating the satisfaction derived by individuals from consuming different goods is impossible. But some help can be obtained by introducing markets, changes in prices signalling possible changes in wants.

Second, many officials are required to estimate wants and to direct factors of production. Inasmuch as such officials are not needed in a market economy they represent wasted factors of production. Moreover, the use of officials may lead to bureaucracy – excessive form-filling, 'red tape', slowness in coming to decisions and an impersonal approach to consumers. At times, too, officialdom has been accompanied by corruption.

Third, even when wants have been decided upon, difficulties of co-ordination arise. On the one hand wants have to be dovetailed and awarded priorities. On the other hand, factors have to be combined in the best proportions. Usually plans are co-ordinated through numerous committees, directed at the top by a central planning committee. Yet members of this committee would be primarily politicians with little experience of administration, especially in coping with the difficulties of managing a large organisation (see p. 138).

Fourth, it is argued that state ownership of resources, by reducing incentives, diminishes effort and initiative. Direction of labour may mean that persons are dissatisfied with their jobs; officials may play for safety in their policies (see p. 237). Thus production may be less than under private enterprise.

Fifth, and probably the most important, is the political danger. Once individuals have given power to the state to decide what is good for them, to own all factors of production and to direct labour, it may eventually seize absolute political power. Individuals would then exist for the state, and not the state for the individual. Thus the ultimate decision between a market economy and a command economy (in their extreme forms) really hinges on whether people prefer to run the risk of dictatorship or to accept the defects of the market economy, providing they can choose their own jobs.

V Britain's mixed economy

The 'middle way'

Fortunately a community does not have to make a complete choice between the two. Instead it can compromise, using the state, not as a dictator, but rather as a wise father who allows his children much personal freedom but plans ahead to avoid many of the pitfalls into which they might stumble.

Thus, in an attempt to get the best of both worlds, the UK has a 'mixed economy' in which four-fifths of production is carried out by the private sector through the market (but subject to varying degrees of government control), while for the other fifth the government is directly responsible through the public sector. Moreover, chiefly by income redistribution and subsidies, the government influences the allocation of the goods and services produced.

Summary of the objectives of government economic policy

The objectives of government economic policy in the UK fall into three broad categories: allocation of resources, stabilisation of the economy, and redistribution of income.

The government may influence the allocation of resources by itself producing goods and services. This occurs when they would not be provided adequately by the private sector, as with public goods, or when they can be produced more efficiently by the state, as with the nationalised industries and certain activities of local authorities, e.g. roads and libraries. We consider the organisations concerned with these functions later in this book.

But other defects of the market mechanism are often dealt with by influencing the functioning of the price system in order to: (a) protect individuals from the operations of powerful interests, such as monopolies; (b) overcome frictions, e.g. in the movement of labour; (c) mitigate shortages when these would entail hardship, as with housing; (d) allow for the external costs and benefits of a firm's own plans, e.g. as in planning controls.

In general the government modifies the operation of the price system either by physical controls or market intervention. The most rigid form of physical control is by legislation. For example, 'hard' drugs and pornographic literature must not be sold freely, and certain forms of cigarette advertising are forbidden. Controls can be flexible, however, when they are administered by the authorities under general powers conferred by Act of Parliament. Thus under the Town and Country Planning Acts, local authorities exercise planning functions which take into consideration the external costs and benefits from the particular uses of land or of the buildings erected. As we shall see, other direct controls operate over certain prices, proposed mergers of firms and foreign trade.

Alternatively the government can avoid the rigidity of physical controls by its own intervention in the market. Thus it can adjust its own demand and supply to affect price, as with government bonds (see p. 310) and foreign-exchange rates (see p. 339). Or it may influence demand, supply and price by indirect taxes and subsidies.

While such intervention is best discussed under the specific topics, other government policy is more widespread in its effects and is therefore considered separately. Thus Chapters 16–20 cover full employment, price stability, regional development, economic growth, the redistribution of income through government expenditure and taxation, and international trading relationships.

Political decisions   It will be appreciated that many economic decisions involve subjective judgements; that is, they cannot be made solely by an objective appraisal of the facts but depend to some extent on personal views in interpreting facts. Thus the relative size of the public sector and the extent to which the government interferes with the operations of firms in the private sector are determined largely by the political philosophy of the elected government.

In theory government decisions should reflect the views of the community. Whether they do or not depends upon a country's political organisation. Our next task, therefore, is to examine briefly the major difficulties of democratic government and to describe the main lines upon which British government is carried on and the major institutions involved, particular attention being given to the management of the economy.

Part II

The Government of the UK

4 The Problem of Government

I Introduction

Man's major objectives

From earliest times man's main activities have been concerned with providing for his needs and defending himself from attack. The two objectives are related: since resources are limited, the temptation exists for others to seize them.

On the other hand man has learned that both objectives can be achieved more effectively through co-operation. Thus total output is increased if persons do that job at which they are relatively best (see p. 13). Similarly with defence there is safety in numbers. So men came together in communities: settlements were sited at the intersection of trade routes and in easily defended positions.

The need for government

But when people live in communities (indeed, even as a family) rules are necessary to regulate the relationships of individuals within the community or to promote the wider interests of the community as a whole. Thus communities formulated rules: there is now some form of government. Such rules not only covered personal behaviour, as with many of the Ten Commandments, but decided how defence should be organised and paid for. At first, however, economic activities were fairly free from state supervision: provided private-property rights were respected and contracts enforceable, transactions through the market proceeded smoothly and efficiently.

In time, however, any form of government changes, as regards both its structure and powers. For instance, in England it was soon realised that trade could be made to contribute to the costs of government. Thus in the fourteenth century England was taxing the export of wool. Two centuries later, government interference in the economy was extended by the Mercantilist policy, where the taxation of imports and the encouragement of exports had the wider objective of strengthening the national economy. To do this the government had to assume considerable powers of control.

This illustrates the basic problem of organising government; while sufficient powers must be given to the government so that it can carry out the wishes of the people effectively, there must be some check on those powers developing into unbridled authority. The fact is that people who govern like exercising power. Or, as Lord Acton put it: 'Power tends to corrupt and absolute power corrupts absolutely.' Hence the government, like any other club or society, has to be run according to recognised principles and rules which lay down the institutions which may be set up and the powers that they can exercise. Moreover, if this 'constitution' is to work satisfactorily, it must prove flexible to changing needs, be understood and accepted by the people, and respect the opinion of minority groups.

The branches of government

It is usual to divide government into three branches, corresponding to the three main functions of government:

(1) Rules, i.e. laws, have to be laid down to regulate people's actions in the wider interests of the community. Thus all road users proceed faster when everybody keeps to the left and overtakes on the right. These laws are passed by the legislative branch of government – Parliament.

(2) Laws have to be administered, finance raised and the state run efficiently. These tasks fall to the executive branch of government – the Prime Minister, Cabinet and government departments.

(3) The laws have to be interpreted and enforced. This is the function of the courts – the Judiciary.

In Britain all three are connected by the Crown (see Figure 4.1). Later we study each in more detail.

**Fig. 4.1
The three branches of government**

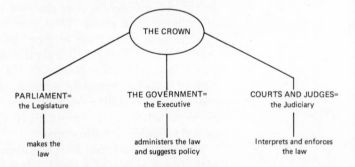

PARLIAMENT=	THE GOVERNMENT=	COURTS AND JUDGES=
the Legislature	the Executive	the Judiciary
makes the law	administers the law and suggests policy	Interprets and enforces the law

Solving the problem of government

A constitution then has two broad aims: (1) allowing people to choose a government having effective powers to carry out their wishes; and (2) ensuring that ultimate control is retained by the people. Before examining the organisations of government it is helpful to consider these broad aims, for they eventually determine the lines upon which institutions work.

1 A government with effective powers   At least once in five years Britain has a general election. Voters put a cross against the name of the candidate they want as Member of Parliament for the constituency in which they live.

But, like the iceberg, more lies below the surface than appears above. This is because the candidates belong to a party. In Britain there are two major parties, and the government is formed from that party which wins most seats. Thus when a person votes he is not merely selecting an MP; he is choosing which party he would like to govern.

In this way people choose the government; and, because each party has put forward a programme of its basic proposals, the people also exercise some control over the policies to be followed. But in order to understand how this makes for *effective* government we have to digress a little in order to discuss the *sovereignty of Parliament.*

The first thing we have to ask regarding the three branches of government is: 'Does the constitution allow one to exercise power over the others?' If so, we say that branch is 'sovereign'. In Britain Parliament is sovereign because it can limit the powers of all other institutions by its exclusive, unlimited and supreme authority to make law. No other body, e.g. local authorities, enjoys legal powers unless so authorised by Parliament; Parliament can pass any law, even one affecting the rules of government, and there is no body which can overrule Parliament by declaring a law illegal. On the other hand, it is only a *legal* sovereignty. Because Parliament has to submit to periodic elections, it is the people who hold *political* sovereignty.

But how does the sovereignty of Parliament secure effective powers for the government? The answer is through the party system (see p. 52). The government is formed from the party which can command a majority in the House of Commons. But since one of the two major parties usually holds an over-all majority, it means that the government can control Parliament so long as it maintains party discipline. Thus the party system puts the legal sovereignty of Parliament at the disposal of the government, whose majority enables it to implement its policies. Occasionally the government may meet obstacles, e.g. through the opposition of the House of Lords, lack of time, or a revolt by its own MPs, but by and large it can rely on its majority to overcome obstruction so that Parliament virtually rubber-stamps bills laid before it. The main check on the government is its awareness that it will be judged at the next general election.

2 A government under the ultimate control of the people
This aim depends upon the *rule of law* being obeyed. In essence the rule of law says that any interference with the freedom of the individual must be 'lawful' i.e. covered by law. So if the government wants new powers to control the individual's way of life, it

has first to obtain an Act of Parliament. The law, therefore, has two functions. First, it sanctions action in the interests of the people as a whole; and second, it is a protection against arbitrary government. Thus not only is the sovereignty of Parliament the means of securing powers but it is a link in the ultimate chain of control (see Figure 4.2).

**Fig. 4.2
The flow of power in
British government**

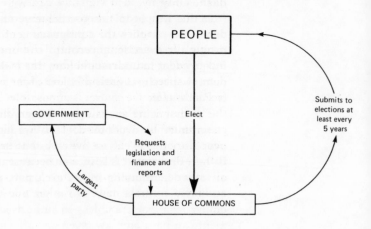

In itself, however, the rule of law is no safeguard against an unscrupulous government. So long as it controls Parliament any government can secure vast powers quite lawfully. Or it could arrange for the police and Armed Forces to be manned by its own puppets, and so extend its power by force. Nor have the British people any constitutional requirement to prevent this happening. Instead there are simply certain devices which form an 'early-warning sytem': a non-partisan Speaker to ensure that minority views are heard in the House of Commons, an Opposition with the duty of criticising the government, a free press to publicise such criticism, judges who are independent of the government, and so on. Any government seeking despotic powers would first have to suppress such institutions in order to stifle the criticism which is allowed, indeed provided for, in the normal working of the constitution. Thus censorship of the press, imprisonment without trial, etc., are the danger signals alerting the people to the government's ultimate aim.

In the final analysis, therefore, the government can only do what the people will stand for – and this will depend upon their basic philosophy. The British hold dear the freedom of the individual to plan and live his own life, and this freedom finds expression in ways they accept as commonplace: the right to leave the country, Speaker's Corner, Hyde Park, or a march to Trafalgar Square to protest against government policy.

Preserving liberty

But noble sentiments are not enough; freedom can be easily lost. No government with despotic intentions would try to eliminate all critics in one fell swoop. Instead it would brainwash the people with propaganda, and then deal with the warning signals one by one, and as unobtrusively as possible.

The ultimate guarantee of liberty, therefore, is watchfulness, so that action can be taken when the warning signals first begin to flash. Only by such vigilance can we ensure that power flows from the people to the government, and not vice versa. Thus democracy implies the continuous control over the government through free elections, constant and organised criticism and an independent judiciary upholding the law. It shows itself in freedom of speech, of assembly and of the person, for without such freedoms effective control is impossible. Nor in this context must the economic relationships between the government and the community be overlooked. Thus we have to consider whether people are free to choose their jobs and to spend their incomes. Or is there direction of labour, restriction on the movement of capital or state determination of spending patterns? Indeed, in practice, economic controls may be the prelude to loss of political freedoms.

II Parliament

Strictly speaking Parliament consists of the House of Lords, the House of Commons and the Queen in Parliament. In practice, however, the powers of the House of Lords have been truncated to limited revising and delaying functions. It is the House of Commons which is the dominant part of the legislature, and we shall concentrate on this.

Elections to the House of Commons

Since the UK has a population of 55 million, government has to be organised through elected representatives. *General elections* have to be held at least every five years. But Parliament rarely runs its full term, the Prime Minister preferring to call an election when his party's prospects appear favourable rather than wait until the last minute. By-elections are held on the death, retirement or disqualification of a member. There are 635 constituencies in the UK, each of which, as far as possible, has about 60,000 electors who elect one MP. In practice there is little chance of a candidate being elected unless he is backed by a major party, in particular the Conservative Party or the Labour party.

In order to vote a person must be over 18 years of age and have his name on the register of electors and not be disqualified, e.g. by being an alien. The register is drawn up yearly, and to be included a person must be resident in the constituency on the qualifying date, 10 October.

The candidate obtaining the most votes at an election becomes the MP for that constituency irrespective of the number of votes obtained by his rivals. The main advantage claimed for this 'first past the post' system is that, when there are only two parties, it gives stable and effective government since one is bound to have a majority. Whether it leads to consistency of policy where swings of the political pendulum occur is, however, debatable. Some people argue that if some form of proportional representation were used in elections, other parties, particularly the Liberal party, would be more fairly represented, providing a moderating influence on the more extreme measures of successive Labour and Conservative governments.

Political parties

The main way in which people exert influence over government is through political parties. These parties organise opinion on national issues, formulating policies which they feel will meet the wishes of as many people as possible. Consequently national affairs obtain priority over narrow sectional interests.

But certain organisations, such as trade unions and the Confederation of British Industry, are of national significance, and often, therefore, influence the policies adopted. Indeed, to exert pressure they may, like the trade unions, be a constituent part of a major party. Other pressure groups and interests, e.g. co-operative societies, the National Union of Teachers, the Police Federation and the National Farmers' Union, sponsor MPs to promote their objectives in Parliament or, like companies, provide funds to help the party most sympathetic to their aims. Even comparatively minor interests, e.g. the Lord's Day Observance Society, the Child Poverty Action Group, the National Association of the Self-employed and the Property-owners Federation, can exert pressure. At elections all their members have votes and they want to know where a party stands on issues of vital concern to them. Hence, in order to win their support, parties make concessions to such views whenever possible.

Nor are interests' activities limited to influencing parties during elections. Continual pressure is put on the government throughout its term of office to make concessions to their views through press and TV propaganda, speeches by sponsored MPs both inside and outside Parliament, parliamentary lobbying, rallies, marches and demonstrations.

In formulating alternative policies upon which the electorate can decide parties clarify and explain political issues. As regards elections they select candidates, stimulate interest and work to see that likely supporters take the trouble to vote.

Above all, parties provide the link between the electorate and the government. If MPs were independent of any party connection, there would be no guarantee that the policies they advocated would be supported by other MPs. The electorate, therefore, would have no effective control over policy since this would be formulated by bargaining between different groups of MPs in Parliament. In such horse-trading sectional rather than national interests could be paramount.

With the party system, however, the MP is a member of a national party committed to specific policies if returned to power. Thus in choosing between candidates at an election voters are really deciding which party should form the government and which policy should be pursued.

More than that, because the government is formed from the majority party, it can rely on its policies being backed by the House of Commons. Through parties, therefore, effective government is possible. On the other hand, while democracy must ensure that a government has effective powers, it must also see that those powers are exercised by consent. Hence it is essential that a continuous searchlight is directed on every aspect of the government's conduct of affairs. The main responsibility for this rests with *Her Majesty's Opposition*, formed from the second largest party in the House of Commons. The Opposition watches, questions and criticises the government, trying to prove

Fig. 4.3
The path of choice through parties

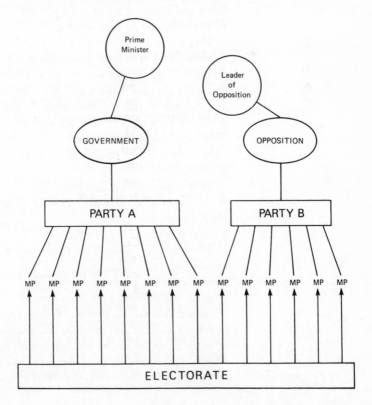

to the electorate that, given the chance, it could do better. Its criticism must therefore be constructive, containing credible alternative policies. If, at a general election, the electorate votes for a change of policy, the Opposition is available and organised through its 'shadow Cabinet' to take over with the minimum of upset (see Figure 4.3).

Functions of the House of Commons

1 Legislation   While a Bill has to be passed by the House of Commons and the House of Lords and assented to by the Queen before it can become law, it is the House of Commons which usually takes the initiative.

Legislation falls into two main categories: public bills and private bills. Both types have to follow a formal procedure in order to secure publicity for and full discussion of its provisions and to ensure that its wording secures its objectives. At all stages interests can seek to make the bill more acceptable to their views.

Public bills are concerned with the general law which applies to the community as a whole. Most are government bills, but a few are introduced by private members. We shall concentrate on the former.

Most government bills have their origin in the policies submitted to the electorate. In addition the departments themselves may initiate legislation. This may result from administrative experience, the report of a Royal Commission or Committee of Inquiry, or the influence of a pressure group.

Preparing a bill for submission to Parliament may take many months, and it may be preceded by other government publications. A Green Paper sets out various alternatives for discussion. Pressure groups make their views known. Government departments concerned are also consulted. The government then issues a White Paper containing its definite proposals for legislation. Even so, discussion continues, and the government may make concessions in the final draft to ease the Bill's passage through Parliament.

Important and controversial government Bills and all money Bills are introduced in the House of Commons. Others may start their life in the House of Lords. The *first reading* is merely a formal reading of the short title.

The *second reading* is the really important stage. Not only is it concerned with basic principles but, since the arguments are fresh, it excites the most interest. The minister in charge puts the case for the Bill and a leading Opposition spokesman, usually the 'Shadow Minister', replies. Other speakers, including backbenchers, follow, and the debate may continue for two days or so. It is then wound up by an Opposition speaker making the final points, and a leading government spokesman replies. Usually a three-line whip ensures that the Bill is given its second reading.

The details of the Bill are examined in *committee*, and it is then *reported* back to the House, given a *third reading* and sent to the House of Lords. Since the Lords is mainly concerned with improving the details of the Bill, most of its work takes place at the committee stage, usually a Committee of the Whole House. The House of Lords can reject or radically amend a Bill (except a money Bill) but in practice it rarely does so. Under the Parliament Act, 1949, it can delay a Bill for twelve months. Once it has passed both Houses the Bill receives the *Royal Assent.* It then becomes an Act of Parliament.

Backbench MPs also have limited opportunities to present their own public Bills. Such *private members' Bills* may reflect their own particular interests, but more usually are presented on behalf of a pressure group, a fellow MP or even the party.

There are numerous obstacles to MPs getting their Bills on the statute book. If the subject infringes government policy or necessitates public expenditure, the Whips will be put on against it. Time has also to be found for debating it. In practice this means success in the ballot for one of the ten Fridays allocated to private members' Bills. Even then only the first twenty Bills are likely to find time during the session.

Private Bills are distinct from the above. Unlike public Bills, which are concerned with the community as a whole, private Bills are promoted to confer special powers or privileges on particular persons or corporations (especially local authorities and the nationalised industries). Consequently they are subject to separate Standing Orders which lay down a strict time-table. While this protects the interests of affected parties, it makes the procedure long and costly. As a result, where there is opposition, efforts are made to reach an agreement. In this way about half the Bills go through unopposed.

Particularly for local authorities, there is now the simpler procedure for obtaining powers by way of *Provisional Orders* and *Special Procedure Orders.* For both of these investigations of the possible infringement of private interests is carried out by a government department. If the findings are satisfactory, the Minister can make, in the first case, a Provisional Order which has to be confirmed by Parliament through a Provisional Order Confirmation Bill, and, in the second case, a Special Procedure Order which is simply laid before Parliament for twenty-one days during which period petitions objecting to it can be lodged. Opposition to an Order is considered by a committee of the House but stands little chance of being successful since a department is unlikely to make an Order to which Parliament will object.

2 The control of finance   In theory the House of Commons still exercises its traditional role of watching the nation's purse.

Indeed the source of its power was its insistence on 'grievances before Supply'. This gave it control of (a) taxation, and (b) spending. The community requires that taxes shall be imposed according to agreed rules and that government expenditure is for specific, rather than general, purposes and that it obtains value for money. In practice the majority of MPs support the government, the task of controlling finance falls on the Opposition.

(a) *Taxation.* To cover its capital expenditure, e.g. on overseas development, loans to local authorities and the nationalised industries, the government will probably raise funds by borrowing. But to finance its current spending it will have to rely largely on taxation. In all matters of finance the lead has to be taken by the government, and only a Minister can introduce proposals to raise or spend money. This is a wise rule. First, it insists that if the government proposes to spend, it shall also suggest how the money should be raised. Second, it prevents MPs from recommending particular expenditure to favour their own constituencies or special interests.

It is still expected that the government's main tax changes should be presented in the Budget at about the beginning of April. The advantages of an annual Budget are: (i) taxation proposals have to be set out as a whole, allowing their full impact to be assessed; (ii) the House of Commons can exert more effective control, for proposals, if submitted piecemeal, might slip through unchallenged; and (iii) a definite time is allocated for Commons' discussion of tax proposals.

The main disadvantage stems from the fact that the Budget today is not solely concerned with raising sufficient revenue to cover proposed expenditure. Taxation is now a weapon for varying consumers' spending power in order to stabilise the economy. When economic conditions are changing quickly, an annual Budget makes this weapon rather inflexible. The Chancellor of the Exchequer can use the 'regulator' at any time to vary the rates of indirect taxes by up to 25 per cent, or even introduce a 'mini-budget'. But frequent changes still tend to reflect unfavourably on his handling of economic policy.

(b) *Spending.* The money raised by taxation (together with other revenue, such as charges for services and income from Crown lands) goes into the Consolidated Fund, the government account at the Bank of England. Only the House of Commons can authorise withdrawals from this Fund.

With some services – the *Consolidated Fund services* – the authority, once given, is not subject to annual renewal. It is felt that it is better for certain payments, such as the Queen's Civil List and the salaries of judges, the Speaker, the Leader of the Opposition and the Comptroller and Auditor General, to be free from recurrent political controversy.

Proposals for spending on *Supply services*, however, have to be submitted by the government to the House of Commons each year, thereby guaranteeing the Commons the opportunity of reviewing government policies periodically. First, the Commons wants to know what the money is to be spent on. Second, it tries to ensure value for money. Third, it earmarks the money for particular uses. In theory, therefore, the House of Commons maintains a fairly tight rein; in practice slack creeps in. An examination of the main stages of control will show the extent of this.

The Commons seeks to ensure that what the government proposes to spend money on is desirable. However, such spending is largely a corollary of policy. In practice, therefore, Supply Debates, allocated twenty-nine days by Standing Orders, are a vehicle for the Opposition to debate subjects of its own choosing at any time in the session.

Having accepted that expenditure is desirable, the Commons wants to be assured that objectives are being attained as cheaply as possible. The *Expenditure Committee* consists of MPs from all parties. It divides into sub-committees, each of which examines the spending intentions of a small group of departments. The Committee is interested in plans for expenditure and in what alternatives were considered by the department. As a parliamentary committee it has power to send for officials and records and to employ experts to assist investigations. While the Committee makes suggestions to avoid waste of money, its real value lies in its impact on departments: all are forced to watch their spending for fear of criticism.

The House of Commons controls the uses to which taxation shall be put: first, by appropriating the money to different items; second, by checking the actual issue of money from the Consolidated Fund; third, by careful audit to see that the money has been spent on the purposes for which it was earmarked.

A department requiring funds first approaches the Treasury. If the Treasury is satisfied that the money has been authorised, it seeks the approval of the *Comptroller and Auditor General*. He is an officer directly responsible to the House of Commons, whose tasks are to: (i) check the issue of money from the Consolidated Fund by seeing that it was authorised by Parliament; (ii) audit each department's accounts; and (iii) advise the Public Accounts Committee.

The *Public Accounts Committee* consists of fifteen MPs representing all parties and is chaired by a member of the Opposition. It receives and considers the report of the Comptroller and Auditor General, follows up any item which it thinks needs further study, and reports to the House of Commons.

3 Protection of the individual Apart from supporting the government or, through the Opposition, challenging it, the

House of Commons throughout its history has been the main champion of the rights of the individual against the government machine. In spite of the dominance of the government this still applies today, for the simple reason that MPs have a duty, above party, to their constituents.

The main opportunity open to MPs for raising individual grievances is *Question Time,* which occupies nearly an hour each day before the Commons proceeds to public business. Questions can be used to draw attention to individual grievances, to seek information, to impress constituents, to publicise a pressure group, or simply to embarrass the government. Where questions are being used by the Opposition for the latter purpose, answers reveal as little as possible. But a Minister has always to be on his guard against supplementary questions which may immediately follow the original question. While replies will, where necessary, cover up the officials concerned, the fact that the Minister is under fire is bound to disturb the civil servants responsible. Thus questions not only serve to protect individual rights but are a safeguard against civil servants becoming slack and inefficient.

If the MP is still not satisfied with the answers to his questions, he can try to raise the matter when the House adjourns for the day. The *10 p.m. adjournment motion* allows a half-hour debate on subjects chosen by private members. These members are selected by ballot on four days of the week and by the Speaker on the other day. In this way members can pursue individual grievances, for the Minister is expected to be present and reply to questions.

A persistent and resourceful MP can harass the government in other ways if he still feels that a constituent is being unjustly treated. Thus he can enlist the support of an appropriate pressure group, write letters to the press, secure publicity on TV, cite the case as an example of bad government policy, refer the matter to the Ombudsman (see p. 69), and so on.

5 The Government and the Administration

I The Cabinet

The Prime Minister and the selection of the Cabinet

The leader of the party which wins a general election becomes the *Prime Minister*, the head of the government. His first task is to choose the Cabinet, which usually consists of the leading members of his party, most of whom head major departments. The Prime Minister also has to make minsterial appointments outside the Cabinet, e.g. the Ministry of Transport is part of the Department of the Environment. Altogether there are some 100 posts to be filled.

Apart from appointing and dismissing Ministers, the Prime Minister takes the chair at Cabinet meetings and exercises a powerful influence over policy especially when a quick decision has to be made, e.g. in foreign affairs. Through his ability to advise the Queen to dissolve Parliament, he exercises a dominating influence over the House of Commons and over his party, the leadership of which he retains.

The functions of the Cabinet

In order that it can work as a team and arrive at decisions more easily and quickly the Cabinet is restricted to about twenty members. However, in practice most of its work is dealt with by Cabinet committees, only the major political issues being decided by the main Cabinet.

The Cabinet formulates a comprehensive policy covering all major issues both at home and abroad, and then fills in the details of proposals when they come to be implemented. Where appropriate some consultation usually takes place between minority interests and pressure groups in order to make the policy as workable as possible (see p. 54).

Apart from implementing the party's policy, the Cabinet has to decide on important day-to-day issues as they arise, e.g. a major strike, a run on the £ sterling, political upheavals abroad. It must also consider future policy, e.g. on Britain's defence commitments and its relationships with the EEC.

II Government departments

The organisation of government work

The policy decided upon by the Cabinet is implemented by the various departments of state. Thus the particular department:

a draws up the necessary legislation and pilots it through Parliament;

b sets up the organisation for implementing that legislation; and

c carries out the day-to-day tasks imposed by previous legislation.

Altogether there are over thirty departments responsible for administering government policy. Some, such as the Department of Employment and the Department of Health and Social Security, are large and well known, with a network of local offices throughout the country. Others, such as the Exchequer and Audit Department, are small and specialised in their work.

Figure 5.1 shows the main government departments grouped according to the particular sphere of government activity in which they function. In the course of their operations, firms, in both the private and public sectors, will come into contact with most of these departments. Indeed, as we shall see, certain departments, such as the Department of Trade and the Department of Employment, may exercise direct controls over firms.

Fig. 5.1
The main departments of state

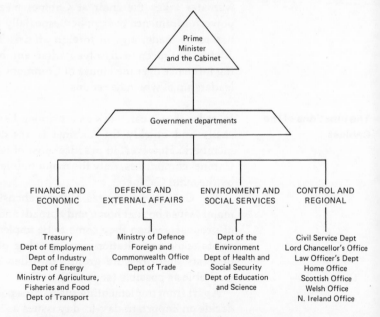

The co-ordination of departments

The division of departments according to function is a convenient form of organisation. The danger, however, is that a department may tend to regard itself as a watertight compartment, whereas

Fig. 5.2
The organisation of a
department

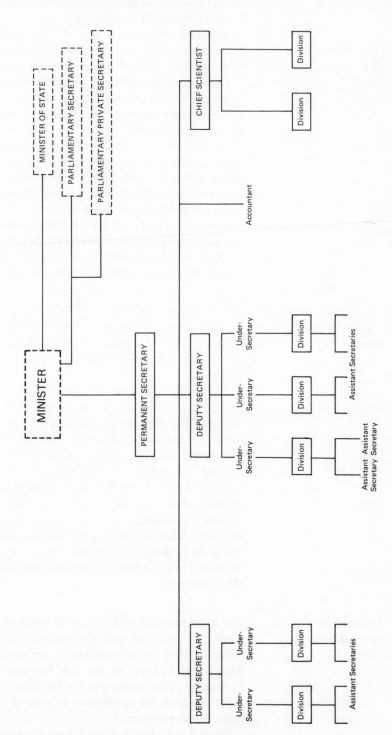

in fact its work overlaps with others. Means must therefore be found of achieving co-ordination.

Much co-ordination is of an informal nature. Those who work in the departments form a unified civil service and follow common methods. More formal means of co-ordination are:

(1) the Cabinet, which co-ordinates policy at the highest level;

(2) the Cabinet Office, which informs Ministries of matters coming before cabinet committees and conveys decisions to the departments affected;

(3) the Treasury, which examines the spending of departments (particularly with regard to securing economies and avoiding waste through overlapping) and often takes the lead in the formation of inter-departmental committees;

(4) inter-departmental committees, consisting mostly of the senior civil servants, which consider the division of responsibility and the possibility of co-operation when the work overlaps; and

(5) the Property Services Agency and the Stationery Office, which arrange for accommodation, office supplies and printing.

The organisation of a government department

Departments differ in size and in the complexity of the work they are called upon to perform. They are therefore left to work out their own internal organisation, and this can vary from one department to another. Nevertheless they have certain features in common.

The basic division of staff is between the political appointments and the permanent officials (see Figure 5.2). As regards the first, most departments are headed by a Minister, usually a Secretary of State in the major departments. Where the work is particularly heavy the present-day practice is to appoint one or two Ministers of State who virtually act on behalf of the Minister.

Under the Minister there are Junior Mininsters, also political appointments. The Minister's immediate deputy is the Parliamentary Secretary (Parliamentary Under-Secretary of State where the Minister in charge is a Secretary of State). Lower down the scale is the Parliamentary Private Secretary. These Junior Ministers help the head of the department in both Parliament and the department.

Ministerial responsibility

The main function of the political heads is to direct the department in accordance with the over-all policy laid down by the Cabinet. They are responsible for the whole of the work of the department and act as the link between the department and Parliament. This means that the Minister must (see Figure 5.3):

(1) interpret the application of over-all cabinet policy to his particular department:

(2) give a clear indication of the policy he wants the department

Fig. 5.3
The Minister and his
department

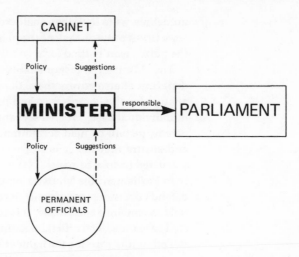

to follow and make sure that the civil servants understand this
policy;

(3) be firm in ensuring that his wishes are carried out;

(4) formulate departmental policy for submission to the
Cabinet; and

(5) represent the department in Parliament.

Parliament is the main political arena, and the Minister, the
political head, is accountable for his department there. He steers
departmental legislation through Parliament and justifies the
Estimates. Above all he is required to explain and defend the
whole of the work of his department to Parliament. This is known
as *ministerial responsibility*.

In essence this means that where it is desired to attack policy
criticism must be directed to the Minister responsible for the
department concerned. Thus, while there is effective government,
responsibility for government (or misgovernment) rests squarely
with the appropriate Minister. In this way the doctrine of ministerial responsibility gives direction to the work of the Opposition
and significance to the probing of MPs at question time. It is the
device by which the government is forced to explain its actions
and to listen to expressions of opinion.

Policy decisions within the department are the ultimate responsibility of the Minister. Having heard the views of his senior civil
servants, he has to exercise two kinds of judgement: (a) whether a
decision can be taken within the department, or should be referred to the Cabinet because political issues are involved; and (b) if
the matter can be dealt with by the department, what action is to
be taken.

It is obvious that the Minister cannot make decisions for every
single case; many have to be left to the Permanent Secretary and
the officials below him. The Minister's duty is to lay down the

guidelines as to how they shall exercise their discretion, or, as it is sometimes put, the task of the politician is to tell the official 'what the public won't stand for'.

The Minister's responsibility for the administration of his department also covers the actions of its civil servants. He has to answer for the competence and judgement exercised by officials in individual cases. If civil servants make mistakes or are incompetent, he will be held accountable; his task is to inspire loyalty and ensure that his senior civil servants can supervise the work entrusted to subordinates.

In Parliament the Minister explains policy, answers questions, defends decisions and shields his civil servants from attack. If he fails to convince the House, it is his job which is at stake, not the civil servant's. The official remains anonymous.

Today it is rare for Parliament to exact the ultimate penalty of requiring the Minister's resignation. If he has been implementing government policy, the Cabinet (and the majority in Parliament) will stand by him. Indeed, even proved incompetence in the department may not lead to the Minister's resignation. The determining factor appears to be the feeling in the party not the volume of criticism in Parliament. If this is running against the Minister, he may decide to resign.

Thus the principle of ministerial responsibility is important in two ways: first, it provides a definite target for the direction of criticism; second, it is a constant reminder to civil servants to watch their step.

The permanent officials

The political head of the department changes if another party comes to power. This has the disadvantage that the new Minister may be an inexperienced layman who has to acquire knowledge as he goes along. Below him, however, and working under his direction, there are permanent officials who remain in office irrespective of any change of government. As civil servants they are politically neutral. Their tasks are:

(1) to advise the Minister on proposed policy, providing information and pointing out possible administrative difficulties, not with the object of being obstructive, but in order to ensure that the policy is workable;

(2) to suggest policy; and

(3) to administer policies decided upon, including the drafting of any necessary rules, orders and regulations.

Where there is any difference of opinion between the Minister and his permanent official, however, the Minister has the final word.

The senior official in a department is the *Permanent Secretary*. He works directly under the Minister, advising on policy and taking responsibility for the permanent officials below him and for the spending of the department. He is assisted by one or more deputy secretaries and usually an accountant, a director of establishments, and perhaps a chief scientist.

The department is usually organised in divisions, each in charge of an Under-Secretary and, below him, assistant secretaries. Each division represents one of the functions of the department, thus allowing civil servants to specialise in particular duties (see Figure 5.2 above).

Not all the permanent officials of a department work in Whitehall. As part of its decentralisation policy the government has encouraged the setting up of offices in the provinces. In any case certain departments, e.g. the Board of Inland Revenue, have a regional organisation, while others in direct contact with the public, such as the Department of Health and Social Security, have local offices.

The Treasury

As the department responsible for the raising and spending of money, the Treasury can be regarded as the lynchpin of the administration. Although its function of managing the civil service passed to the new Civil Service Department in 1968, it still enjoys important supervisory powers:

(1) *It advises on the raising of revenue.* The Treasury is closely concerned with the Budget and, in consultation with the revenue departments, deals with all questions relationg to taxation and the raising of revenue, including forward tax planning.

(2) *It supervises financial transactions.* Many aspects of government policy affect, and are affected by, financial markets and institutions. Thus government borrowing and management of the national debt are not only a major influence on the money and capital markets but have to take account of the current situation in those markets in order to obtain the best possible terms and to preserve an orderly market. The Bank of England carries out monetary policy but the ultimate decisions rest with the Treasury.

Similarly, the Treasury is concerned with the balance of payments, exchange rates and international monetary problems. This means that it has to watch the financial aspects of major policy questions, e.g. the EEC.

On such questions as overseas aid and the government's financial transactions abroad the Treasury is in close touch, not only with the Bank of England, but also with the Ministry of Defence, the Department of Trade and the Foreign and Commonwealth Office.

(3) *It watches the expenditure of departments.* Traditionally the Treasury controls the public purse. No department can ask Parliament for funds without prior Treasury approval; proposed expenditure must be reasonable and secure value for money.

Estimates are submitted to the Treasury annually and these now cover proposed expenditure for the next five years.

(4) *It controls public expenditure to stabilise the economy* (see Chapter 16).

III The Civil Service

The special position of civil servants

As we have seen, the everyday work of departments is carried out by permanent officials, the Civil Service. These civil servants vary in importance from Under-Secretaries and above (the Higher Civil Service), who are responsible for advising Ministers and running their departments, to those at the bottom (ancillary clerical staff, typists and messengers), who carry out the routine work (see Figure 5.4).

Fig. 5.4
The structure of the Civil Service
Notes: (a) total civil servants 500,000 approx; (b) figures in brackets show percentage of total.

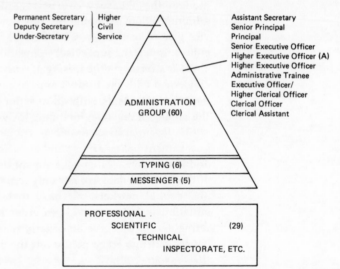

Permanent Secretary
Deputy Secretary
Under-Secretary

Higher
Civil
Service

Assistant Secretary
Senior Principal
Principal
Senior Executive Officer
Higher Executive Officer (A)
Higher Executive Officer
Administrative Trainee
Executive Officer/
Higher Clerical Officer
Clerical Officer
Clerical Assistant

ADMINISTRATION GROUP (60)

TYPING (6)

MESSENGER (5)

PROFESSIONAL
SCIENTIFIC   (29)
TECHNICAL
INSPECTORATE, ETC.

Although, like people in other walks of life, civil servants have a job to do, their employment by the state puts them in a somewhat special position. First, as government employees they traditionally enjoy advantages over other workers as regards permanence of job, sick leave, pension rights, etc. It is essential, therefore, that the right kind of entrant is *recruited*. Second, with no profit yardstick to measure how well government work has been performed, ways have to be found of ensuring that civil servants are *efficient*. Third, although civil servants are closely connected with politics, they must behave with *political neutrality*. Last, as government powers affect the rights of the individual, there must be *safeguards* to ensure that when civil servants make decisions in individual cases they act with humanity and, above all, within the scope of their powers.

These considerations affect the recruitment of civil servants and the methods adopted to ensure their efficiency and accountability, especially as regards the top officials of the Administrative Group, principals and above.

Recruitment

Since 1970 there has been a single Administrative Group, making it possible for an entrant at the bottom to progress smoothly to the top. Recruitment is by open competition, either through interview on the basis of academic qualifications ('O' or 'A' level GCE, a degree, a professional qualification) or by competitive examination. As a rule new entrants are chosen on their general rather than their specialised ability. Thus recruitment for the higher administrative group trainees is by qualifying examination based on most subjects offered in honours degree courses, followed by a two-day series of tests and interviews before selection boards. It is obvious that persons who have to handle secret documents and serve Ministers impartially must have integrity of character. Furthermore, they must be temperamentally suited to the work and, if they are in close contact with the public, have a pleasing personality. The above method of selection can test for character, temperament and personality, qualities which are difficult to assess through an academic examination. Tests have been re-designed so that science candidates are not at a disadvantage compared with arts candidates.

Efficiency

On the whole civil servants do not enjoy a good press. It is often thought that they spend too much time reading newspapers and drinking tea, and passing official papers from one department to another. Or, as one wit put it, 'Like the fountains in Trafalgar Square, they play from 10 to 4.' While this is a grossly distorted view, it does indicate concern as to whether the Civil Service is as efficient as it might be. To assess the position we have to examine its personnel and how they are organised.

As regards the *type of recruit* many critics argue that the methods of selection have tended to place all the emphasis on intellectual ability and integrity. This was satisfactory so long as government activities were confined mainly to traditional functions and watching over the private sector. In recent years, however, the state has moved into fields formerly filled by private enterprise – health insurance, pensions, export credit, loans for investment, and so on. Does a person looking mainly for security have those qualities, such as drive and initiative, essential to the success of the new activities?

The *Civil Service Department* is responsible for matters relating to the pay, conditions of service, training, promotion, allocation to departments and the organisation of the Civil Service. But a separate unit within this department, the Civil Service Commission, recruits civil servants in order to preserve the independence of recruiting.

Since civil servants are chosen on general ability and potential, it is essential that *training* is adequate for the work they will be called upon to do. At one time training consisted of little more than gaining experience on the job. In recent years more systematic training has been provided. Not only are civil servants encouraged to take courses at universities and colleges of commerce but the Civil Service Department also trains at its own staff colleges.

Bureaucracy

One of the major charges levelled against civil servants is that they are addicted to routine, 'red tape', excessive form-filling and arriving at decisions simply by following precedent. While there may be something in this criticism, it is difficult to see how the Civil Service could work differently.

Any large organisation has to work to a system, and this is only possible if employees follow similar methods. In the Civil Service everything is put down on paper. The standard procedure is to prepare a file on each particular query, and this file is then passed from one person to another for comment and action.

Such a procedure has four main attributes. First, it allows an official to deal concurrently with many different queries. Investigation of a case often means contacting many other civil servants, some of whom may not be immediately available. Were he to pursue one query through to the end as soon as it arrived on his desk, therefore, it would be both frustrating and excessively time-consuming. Second, a common system of work not only facilitates the transfer of civil servants between departments but promotes the unity of the service as a whole. Third, the ever-present threat of a parliamentary question on any matter necessitates a detailed record of every case. Fourth, it enables a departmental policy to be built up. The file on a new type of problem may eventually arrive on the desk of the Permanent Secretary or even the Minister. His decision, once made, is recorded and referred to when similar cases arrive later. The code of policy which emerges introduces consistency, impartiality and fairness to the decisions of civil servants, affording some protection to the individual citizen against capricious and arbitrary treatment. However, another aspect of bureaucracy – undue encroachment on the rights of the individual – must be considered.

Control of the Civil Service

In the course of their duties civil servants make decisions which affect firms and members of the community both in general policy and in individual cases. As regards the first, not only do they advise the Minister but they are largely responsible for drafting delegated legislation. With the second, they touch firms and individuals on such vital matters as import controls, bank loans, subsidies, taxation, pension entitlements, health benefits, unemployment insurance payments, and so on.

Usually the traditions of the service ensure that officials do not exceed their powers by making policy (instead of merely advising) or by riding roughshod over the rights of the individual. Even so there must be some safeguards against the arrogant, power-loving, discourteous, or inefficient civil servant. Such safeguards are:

(1) *The Minister.* A Minister is not likely to be appointed to office unless he has ability and strength of character. The odds, therefore, are that he will harness the experience of his senior advisers to the policy decided upon by the government and not be submissive to their views. Civil servants prefer a Minister who gives a firm lead, accepts full responsibility for decisions made, and shields them from attack in Parliament.

(2) *The Scrutiny Committee.* Pressure of work means that much legislation has to be filled in by officials through rules, orders and regulations, usually referred to as 'statutory instruments'. Parliament itself does not have sufficient time to study all the statutory instruments laid before it. That task falls mainly to the Scrutiny Committee, a select committee of the House of Commons which reports on any statutory instruments seeming to warrant the special attention of the House.

(3) *The Member of Parliament.* Individuals aggrieved by the decisions or actions of officials can always approach their MP. He may take up the matter with the department concerned and, if still not satisfied, raise it in Parliament (see p. 58). The difficulty is that officials may put up a 'smoke-screen', and opportunities to probe further are limited by shortage of parliamentary time. In 1966, therefore, a new form of control was introduced in the 'Ombudsman', officially the Parliamentary Commissioner for Administration.

(4) *The Parliamentary Commissioner for Administration.* If MPs receive complaints of injustice or maladministration by a government department, he may refer the matter to the Ombudsman. This officer has power to call for written or oral evidence, and Crown privilege cannot be claimed by officials to avoid disclosing information. Since reference to the Ombudsman can only be through MPs, the MP is still retained as the traditional investigator of complaints. On the other hand, the procedure does suffer from certain weaknesses. First, the Ombudsman can give no remedy; he simply submits reports to the House of Commons Select Committee for the Parliamentary Commissioner. There is no provision for directly publishing these reports. Sec-

ond, only administrative matters for which a Minister is directly responsible can be considered; the Armed Forces, nationalised industries, the police, and personnel problems within departments are excluded. Recently, however, a system of Health Commissioners has been established, and there are now local government Ombudsmen. Different procedures exist for dealing with police and other complaints outside the parliamentary structure. Third, the fact that the citizen cannot approach the Ombudsman directly may lead to some loss of confidence in him as a representative in disputes with officials. (See Figure 5.5 for a diagrammatic representation of the citizen's relationship with the Civil Service.)

Fig. 5.5
The citizen and the
administration

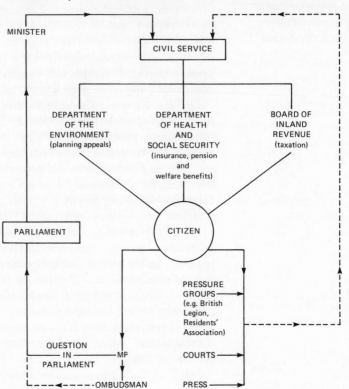

6 The Legal Framework

I The nature and role of law

The relationship of private and public rights and duties

In the British system of government the rights of individuals are paramount. This is enshrined in what is known as the 'rule of law'. First, any infringement of individual rights has to be sanctioned by law. This means that the rights and duties of public bodies can be exercised only in so far as there is a law allowing them to do so. For example, the Board of Inland Revenue can only collect income tax at the rates laid down by the current Finance Act. Second, an individual alleged to have broken the law must be brought to trial speedily and, before he can suffer penalities, his guilt must be established in a court of law according to the proper procedure. Nevertheless, as we shall see, administrative tribunals have modified this requirement.

Laws also regulate relationships between persons. For example, the amount which a landlord may charge a tenant for his dwelling is governed by the Rent Act, 1977, and businesses selling goods to customers have to comply with the Sale of Goods Act, 1893 (see p. 129).

Sources of law

The law recognised by the courts comes from a variety of sources:

(1) *The common law.* Before Parliament passed statutes, the law consisted mainly of accepted customs persisting 'from when the memory of man runneth not to the contrary'. (This idea has been preserved in 'rights of way', e.g. certain footpaths.) In deciding the extent of disputed customary rights the courts established a body of 'common law'.

(2) *Rules of equity.* As the economy of the country developed during the Middle Ages people began to find that for certain cases the common law did not provide remedies. They therefore applied to the Lord Chancellor for justice. The decisions of the Lord Chancellor tended to be followed by his successors, and so a body of law, known as 'equity', was developed to supplement the common law. Thus today the dissolution of partnerships, the foreclosure of mortgages, and bankruptcy jurisdiction are matters dealt with by the Chancery Division of the High Court.

(3) *Statutes.* In the course of time both common law and equity

were either inadequate or inappropriate to deal with changed conditions. Hence new laws had to be passed and old laws amended. This was achieved by Acts of Parliament, which are supreme over all other forms of law, thus upholding the principle of parliamentary sovereignty. Today the bulk of law is in statute form, and its volume has increased as the state has added to its responsibilities in our social and economic life. Indeed, many statutes are only in outline form, the details necessary for their implementation being filled in by rules, orders and regulations (officially termed 'statutory instruments') made by the responsible Minister.

(4) *Case law.* If justice is to be certain, it must be consistent. As far as possible, therefore, judges follow the decisions of higher courts on similar points of law. Thus, in interpreting the law, courts are to some extent making law.

(5) *European Community law.* As a member of the EEC the UK has accepted the Treaty of Rome and other treaties designed to harmonise the policies of the member states. These have the force of law and can override national law, but in order that the Community shall work harmoniously Parliament is expected to respect Community law. Parliamentary sovereignty is preserved by the right to withdraw from membership by repealing the European Communities Act, 1972.

The Council of Ministers and the Commission can make regulations, directives and decisions. *Regulations* are binding on all member states and have the direct and immediate effect of law. *Directives*, on the other hand, need Parliament to pass a law or issue a statutory instrument before they take effect. Thus the Second Directive, 1976, requires a company's name to indicate whether it is private or public, and this is being provided for by a Companies Bill, 1980. *Decisions* apply only to individual organisations, such as a company.

The *European Court of Justice* interprets Community law, and its decisions are applied by British courts. Any member state, Community authority, firm or individual can appeal to the Court if it considers there has been a breach of Community law or if aggrieved by the application of the rules.

(6) *International law.* Firms may occasionally be concerned with international law, e.g. ships must observe the 'rule of the road' at sea. This is usually incorporated in the laws of each country and is thus enforceable through the ordinary courts.

II The need for courts of justice

Criminal and civil cases

Where a citizen offends against society as a whole, he commits a criminal offence and the state prosecutes in a *criminal* court, either through the police or the Director of Public Prosecutions. Thus criminal proceedings may be taken against firms and their officials, e.g. for tax evasion, breaking certain trade regulations and fraud.

If disputes or offences are between one individual and another, e.g. for breach of contract, it is a civil case which has to be decided in a *civil* court. Most actions concerning firms are civil cases (see pp. 75–7).

Functions of the courts   Law must be obeyed. Courts have therefore been set up to:

(1) try persons accused of breaking the law;

(2) impose appropriate penalties on those proved guilty of doing so;

(3) decide disputes between citizens;

(4) restrain any persons who interfere illegally with the rights of others, e.g. by injunctions; and

(5) award damages to an offended party to redress for grievances suffered, e.g. by breach of contract.

In carrying out their work, the courts should have three main attributes.

First, they must be *efficient*, the procedure being exhausted as quickly as possible given adequate time to collect evidence and summon witnesses.

Second, they must preserve *impartiality*, the prosecution and defence having equal opportunities to present their case before an impartial judge and jury. It follows that nobody, even a government body, shall be a judge in its own case. In Britain, therefore, the administration of justice is kept as distinct as possible from the other functions of government, a principle known as the 'separation of powers'. Such impartiality is fostered by giving judges a large measure of independence, e.g. they can only be removed by an 'Address to the Sovereign' by both Houses of Parliament, and by choosing juries randomly from a broadly based list.

Third, they must uphold *certainty* in the administration of justice in that they uphold the rule of law, insisting that penalties can only be imposed for a breach of the law which has been established by recognised and accepted rules of procedure. In this way Britain avoids 'political' trials.

III Criminal jurisdiction

The work of the criminal courts is divided according to the importance of the case: lesser cases are tried mostly by summary jurisdiction in magistrates' courts the more serious before a jury at the Crown Courts (see Figure 6.1).

**Fig. 6.1
Organisation of
criminal justice**

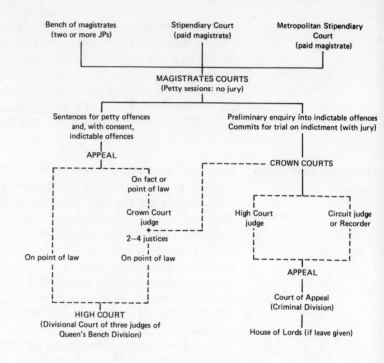

Magistrates' courts

Most magistrates' courts consist of a bench of magistrates – two to seven JPs – assisted by a clerk. In London and large boroughs where the work is particularly heavy full-time paid magistrates may be appointed by the Lord Chancellor to replace or supplement the JPs. A *stipendiary magistrate,* who is a qualified lawyer, sits alone and has slightly wider powers than a bench of magistrates.

Magistrates' courts have three main functions:

(1) to hear and sentence for petty offences;

(2) with the consent of the accused, to hear certain indictable offences; and

(3) to conduct preliminary hearings to see whether there is sufficient evidence to justify committing the accused for trial before a higher court.

Crown courts

On an indictable offence the accused can elect for trial by jury at a Crown court, held in most major towns. Criminal cases are classified into first, second and third tier according to the seriousness of the alleged offence, and Crown courts are similarly divided.

Appeals

Appeals from a magistrates' court usually go to a Crown court. On a point of law an appeal can go to a Divisional court of the Queen's Division.

Appeals from Crown courts or Assizes go to the Criminal

Division of the Court of Appeal. This is presided over by the Lord Chief Justice or a Lord Justice of Appeal, and a quorum is three judges.

An appeal may be taken to the House of Lords if any appeal court or the House of Lords itself considers that the case involves a point of law of 'general public importance'. With criminal cases, however, such appeals are rare.

An appraisal of the jury system

Criticism of criminal procedure is often directed at the jury system, especially in trials involving commercial matters. Although there used to be a property qualification, today nearly everyone who is on the Register of Electors and under the age of 65 can be called upon to act as a juror. To avoid instances where immigrants have understood court procedure only imperfectly because of language difficulties, jurors must have been resident in the UK for at least five years since the age of 13, while a judge has power to dismiss any person from serving as a juror whom he feels has inadequate command of English. Otherwise juries are a representative cross-section of society.

This serves to make juries a safeguard of individual liberty and a protection from oppression by the government. Moreover, in reaching their decision they tend to reflect the commonsense of the everyday man in the street and also current sentiment on such matters as 'reasonable force', 'an offensive weapon' and 'obscene material' which defy precise legal definition. Although the police and lawyers complain that present trial procedure often misleads the jury into favouring the accused, this is at least a safeguard against the conviction of an innocent person. In addition jury service gives citizens an opportunity to participate in the processes of government.

On the other hand it has to be asked whether the average person, even though assisted by the judge in his summing up, is able to follow and assimilate complicated and technical evidence in trials, such as fraud cases, which might extend over many weeks.

IV Civil jurisdiction

More frequently firms are involved in disputes with other firms or with the public. Such civil cases are decided either in the County Court or in the High Court, depending mainly on the sum involved (see Figure 6.2).

**Fig. 6.2
Organisation of civil
jurisdiction**

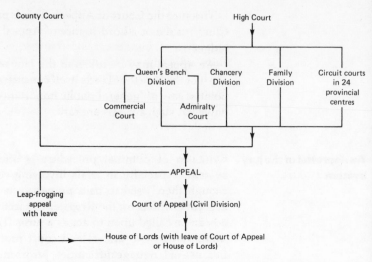

Also: (1) Certain cases dealt with by Courts of Summary Jurisdiction
(2) Restrictive Practices Court

The County Court

There are nearly 375 County Courts which are held regularly in many provincial towns throughout England and Wales. They deal mostly with cases where relatively small amounts of money are involved. For instance, the limit in actions concerning contracts is £2,000. The tendency has been to make the County Courts responsible for hearing the new types of case which arise as a result of the development of the welfare state – the adoption of children, disputes under the Rent Acts, claims for farm improvements, disputes over hire-purchase agreements, and undefended divorce cases.

A large increase in the work of County Courts is likely to result from two changes in the law. The first is the Supply of Goods (Implied Terms) Act, 1973 (see p. 129), which should encourage dissatisfied customers, previously unsure of their rights, to take County Court action. The second is that consumers with small claims (maximum £75) arising from faulty goods can apply to the County Court for *informal arbitration* by a judge or registrar.

The High Court

The High Court hears mostly those cases which are above the County Court's monetary limits, but a plaintiff may start a High Court action in order to intimidate a defendant or where proceedings are in the nature of a test case.

The Court consists of three divisions, with its judges usually specialising in the work of a particular division.

The *Queen's Bench Division* is the largest division and its President is the Lord Chief Justice. It hears common law cases, chiefly claims for damages for injury to persons or property and commercial disputes. Certain cases, e.g. defamation and fraud, may be heard before a jury, but today little use is made of juries.

The jurisdiction of the *Chancery Division* is concerned with equity matters, such as the estates of deceased persons, the wardship of infants, trusts, mortgages, bankruptcy, partnerships and company business.

The *Family Division* deals with all domestic matters (including divorce and guardianship) as well as probate (the proving of a will). Most of the work is on divorce, despite the transfer in 1969 of undefended cases to certain divorce county courts.

The Restrictive Practices Court

Restrictive trading agreements and resale price conditions have to be registered with a Registrar of Restrictive Trading Agreements. If the Registrar thinks an agreement cannot be justified by any of the specified 'gateways', he refers it to the Court. The case is heard by a judge and two lay assessors, and their decision is on a majority basis (see p. 171).

Appeals

Appeals against a County Court or High Court decision go to the Court of Appeal, Civil Division. Permission to take an appeal further to the House of Lords may be granted by the Court of Appeal or the House of Lords.

V Administrative justice

What is administrative justice?

The welfare state has meant that citizens are in frequent contact with government officials. Disputes are bound to occur as individuals allege that they are being deprived of their rights: A house stands in the way of a road-widening scheme; farmland is wanted for an airport; a site is required by the local authority for a school; insurance benefit is refused on the grounds of insufficient contributions; a taxpayer challenges the local Inspector of Taxes' view that certain expenditure is not a legitimate expense.

Sometimes, too, welfare legislation gives rise to disputes between individuals. Thus an employee may complain of unfair dismissal, while a tenant may claim that his landlord is overcharging on rent.

For reasons which will be given later the courts are not suitable for deciding such disputes. Instead they are heard by:

(1) *Statutory inquiries.* These are normal when planning decisions or the compulsory purchase of land are in dispute. An inspector from the Ministry concerned (usually the Department of the Environment) holds a local inquiry at which each side can present its case. The inspector reports to the Minister stating where he considers the balance lies between the private and public interests concerned. The Minister usually accepts the recommendations, but he is not bound to do so.

(2) *Administrative tribunals.* Apart from the statutory inquiry, which is an investigating body to hear a particular matter, there are some 2,000 permanent tribunals for deciding types of dispute which are likely to occur fairly regularly. Thus we have Special Commissioners of Income Tax, Supplementary Benefits Appeal Tribunals, Rent Assessment Committees, Pensions Appeal Tribunals, Area Traffic Commissioners (for public and heavy-vehicle licensing), Valuation Courts (rating assessment), Industrial Tribunals (complaints of unfair dismissal), and the Lands Tribunal (values of freeholds, etc.). Members are often laymen, but the chairman is usually qualified in some way.

In addition there are courts of professional bodies, e.g. the General Medical Council and the Law Society, which have statutory powers relating to the professional conduct of members. These are not appointed by a Minister.

Since inquiries and tribunals are dealing with cases arising through the administration of certain services, their decisions are known as *administrative justice.*

Reasons for administrative tribunals

The main reason for referring disputes to tribunals is that the courts could not cope with the number of cases involved. In any case it would be uneconomic to appoint judges and court officials, for many disputes are of a comparatively trivial nature.

More than that, tribunals have certain advantages over courts of law. In essence the type of case is different: tribunals have to reconcile the rights of the individual with a policy aimed at securing benefits for society as a whole. Decisions, therefore, have to be flexible according to different circumstances. The courts, on the other hand, are inclined to emphasise private-property rights and to follow precedents established by previous decisions.

In their composition and procedure, too, tribunals are more appropriate for certain types of dispute than are courts of law. Where technical knowledge is involved, e.g. the Lands Tribunal, experts can be included. Local tribunals, e.g. Rent Assessment Committees, are helped by knowledge gained of local conditions. Since tribunals are located as conveniently as possible, people find them accessible, and cases can be heard fairly quickly. Procedure, too, is less formal than in a court of law. Strict rules of evidence do not apply and a person feels free to state his case. Legal representation is rarely necessary. As a result decisions are quicker and cheaper than in a court.

Criticisms of administrative tribunals

Some people object to administrative tribunals on the grounds that they offend basic principles. When tribunals contain members responsible for administering schemes (for example, employees of the Board of Inland Revenue are Special Commissioners for Income Tax), they clash with the rule of law and the principle of the separation of powers as it applies to judicial decisions.

The difficulty is that tribunals cannot be constituted in the same way or follow the same procedures as courts of law without destroying many of their advantages. All the same, once administrative tribunals are recognised as being desirable, they should be seen to be open, fair and impartial. Moreover, if they are to pay due regard to the rights of the individual, hearings should conform to the rules of 'natural justice'. This means that: (a) tribunals should usually be composed of persons independent of both sides; (b) opportunities should exist for adequate presentation of the case; and (c) decisions should, as far as possible, be based on established principles in order that the citizen can assess his position.

To achieve these objectives the system has been tightened up as regards composition, procedure and appeals. The chairman is now usually legally qualified and, while some tribunals still contain officials interested in the dispute, most are composed of laymen.

Moreover, procedure has been regularised without destroying informality. The citizen is now notified of his right to present his case to a tribunal, and is given time to prepare it. Hearings are in public except where intimate personal details are involved, and tribunals are expected to follow rules of procedure laid down by the Council on Tribunals. Reasons are given for decisions and parties are advised on their right to appeal.

Finally, while the appeal procedure varies with the particular tribunal, the general rule now is that appeals should always lie with an appellate tribunal which should endeavour to establish a body of 'case law' by informing the lower tribunals of the grounds of its decisions. On points of law appeal is to the High Court and, if necessary, to the Court of Appeal.

Control of administrative justice

The courts can review the decisions of tribunals in two main circumstances. First, they can prevent a tribunal from exceeding its jurisdiction, and may quash decisions already given. Second, they can intervene if a tribunal's proceedings do not follow the rules of natural justice. This is because tribunals are making what are virtually judicial decisions and thus, as inferior courts, are subject to the jurisdiction of the High Court.

The weakness of the courts is that their control tends to be negative. To secure the better functioning of tribunals, therefore, the *Council on Tribunals* was set up to advise on their composition and procedure. To do this it has to observe proceedings, and is therefore now regarded as the supervising body. Not only does it consult with government departments about rules of procedure but it also considers complaints from citizens who think they have not been given a fair hearing. Here the Council can investigate with the department concerned and, if necessary, report to the Lord Chancellor.

VI Arbitration

In certain cases parties may agree to settle their dispute by arbitration. This can be the most appropriate method when a compromise solution is possible (e.g. a trade union's demand for higher wages).

Alternatively, recourse to arbitration may be prompted by the high cost and delays of litigation through the courts. Thus certain institutions, e.g. insurance companies, may stipulate in their contracts that arbitration shall be used to decide disputed claims. Usually the arbitrator is an expert, and the atmosphere friendly. Compared with a court of law the proceedings are quicker, with written evidence being accepted, and as far as possible arranged to suit the parties concerned. Being in private, damage is not done, say, to the good name of a firm in the way that allegations in open court might.

Procedure is governed by the Arbitration Act, 1950. The hearing must conform to the rules of natural justice, and if not the High Court can intervene. Provision is sometimes made for parties to go to the High Court if dissatisfied with the arbitrator's decision or for clarification of a point of law.

VII Forms of firms' legal liability

As we have seen, the responsible directors of firms can be prosecuted for *criminal* offences. This applies both in the private and public sectors. Thus where a firm makes fraudulent statements the directors may be subject to a criminal charge, for any director who does not wish to be associated with the statement should have resigned. Similarly, the responsible chairman of the Board of a nationalised industry may be prosecuted. Thus a chairman of the Yorkshire Electricity Board was given a prison sentence for wilfully exceeding the building licences granted for the Board's headquarters. With government departments sanctions are mainly political, the responsible Minister possibly being forced to resign.

Parliament decides what breaches of the law by firms shall be treated as criminal offences. Normally those against society are subject to criminal proceedings, but in economic matters affecting the 'national interest' only civil penalties are imposed through fines being imposed on the company, e.g. for restrictive trade practices. Most *civil* cases involve disputes between firms or individuals. Here a useful distinction is between strict liability, fault and vicarious liability.

Strict liability arises without the necessity of proving fault; that is, the defendant need have acted neither intentionally nor negligently. The basic rule is provided in *Rylands v. Fletcher, 1865*. Here *B*, a mill-owner, employed independent contractors to construct a reservoir on his land to provide water for his mill. In doing so the contractors came across some old shafts and passages on *B*'s land which, unknown to them, communicated with the mines of *A*, a neighbour of *B*. When the reservoir was filled with water it burst through the old shafts and flooded *A*'s mines. Although *B* had not been negligent, but the contractors had, he was still held to be liable. The judgment defined the classic exposition:

> We think that the true rule of law is, that the person who for his own purposes brings on his lands and collects and keeps there anything likely to do mischief if it escapes, must keep it in at his peril, and, if he does not do so, is *prima facie* answerable for all the damage which is the natural consequence of its escape. . . .
> The person whose grass or corn is eaten down by the escaping cattle of his neighbour, or whose mine is flooded by the water from his neighbour's reservoir, or whose cellar is invaded by the filth of his neighbour's privy, or whose habitation is made unhealthy by the fumes and noisome vapours of his neighbour's alkali works, is damnified without any fault of his own.

This principle that for certain wrongs there can be no defence of 'reasonable' care has been applied by Parliament in recent legislation to prevent undesirable results of modern industrial processes. These cover safety at work (Health and Safety at Work Act, 1974) and environmental hazards which may result from nuclear incidence (Nuclear Installations Act, 1965), oil pollution (Merchant Shipping Act, 1971), keeping a species of dangerous animal (Animal Act, 1971) and the deposit of poisonous waste (Control of Pollution Act, 1974).

Most civil actions are concerned with *fault* – the defendant can claim in defence that he had acted reasonably or had not been negligent in that he had covered his duty of care with regard to his neighbour, e.g. by the erection of a fence to prevent children trespassing on a railway.

Vicarious liability is where a person may be held liable for a tort committed by another, usually his servant or an independent contractor employed by him. Such liability tends to ensure that: (a) there is a financially responsible person as defendant; and (b) a firm provides standards of safety in its operations.

A master is liable for all torts committed by his servants *in the course of his employment.* A master and servant relationship can be presumed to exist if the employee is subject to the control and direction of his employer in respect of the manner in which the work is to be done. But this is not the only test, the court having to decide on the factual evidence.

A tort is committed by the servant if it is a wrongful act or omission: (a) expressly or implicitly authorised by the master; or (b) performed in an unauthorised manner but sanctioned by the master; or (c) subsequently ratified by the master. There is no liability if the servant were acting solely for his own and not the master's purposes (sometimes described as being 'on a frolic of his own').

An employer is even liable for the torts of an independent contractor employed by him if the task is in fulfilment of a legal duty but is performed negligently by the contractor, or if it had to be done at the employer's peril, or if the employer provided defective equipment. However, an employer is never liable for what is either the collateral or casual negligence of an independent contractor since the latter controls how his servants work, not the employer. Thus if a council employs a contractor to dig a hole in the road it would be responsible for his negligence in not fencing it since this is a necessary part of the street excavation, but not for his negligence in carrying materials to and from the excavation site.

Justification for making the employer, although not personally negligent, responsible for the torts of his employees, rests on grounds of both expediency and reasonableness. The employer is likely to be the wealthier and also likely to be insured against such acts by employees. Moreover, the employee has been recruited by the employer and the latter should take responsibility for any error of judgement. Finally, in what he does the employee is representing the employer.

VIII Making contracts

The nature of a contract

In their everyday life individuals are frequently making contracts, though they do not often think of what they are doing in legal terms. Thus the housewife who takes in the three pints of milk from her doorstep each morning has entered into a contract with the dairy. Its part of the bargain is to supply the milk; her part is to pay the bill at the end of the week. If she does not, the County Court judge can compel her to do so.

Similarly, in its operations a firm enters into contracts, e.g. in buying or renting premises, engaging labour (see p. 193), purchasing machinery, raw materials and components, stipulating a price and delivery date for the finished product, and giving guarantees.

A contract is an agreement which binds the parties by being legally enforceable. Many agreements, e.g. to take your wife out to dinner, are not contracts because they were not intended to be legally binding. Moreover, in practice courts rarely enforce performance of the contract, awarding damages instead to the suffering party.

Types of contract

To be enforceable at law an agreement to do or to refrain from doing something must be either made by deed under seal or given for a consideration (i.e. in return for something). Thus there are two types of contract:

1 Contracts made by deed under seal   A formal contract by deed under seal is necessary when a person unilaterally assumes an obligation to another or in the few cases where the constitution of a company requires it to contract under seal even though it is receiving a consideration.

A deed is a document signed by the parties and to which each has attached his seal (a small red paper wafer). Today the mere signature of the party executing the deed, coupled with an intention to seal and deliver is sufficient. But to be used in evidence in court proceedings it must be stamped (usually 50p), though for conveying real property and certain other property the stamp varies with the purchase price.

Today one of the most common forms of deed is the 'deed of covenant' by which a person agrees to devote an annual sum to a specified charity for a minimum period of seven years. The charity benefits additionally by being able to claim any income tax at the standard rate paid by the donor on the sum involved.

A right of action for breach of a contract under seal lasts for twelve years, compared with six years for a simple contract.

2 Simple contract   The basis of a simple contract is that there is a bargain whereby rights and duties arise which are intended to be legally enforceable. For a bargain to amount to a contract, certain essentials are required.

Essentials of a valid contract

1 Agreement   Agreement is brought about in two stages: (i) offer, and (ii) acceptance. Both are necessary to complete the circle of agreement and both must be communicated, either by words or conduct. Thus a bus company serving a particular route offers by implication to carry passengers if they pay the proper fare, and a person who takes a seat accepts by implication the bus company's offer. It is necessary to distinguish a true *offer* from an 'invitation to treat'. The display of goods in a shop is merely an invitation to treat, not an offer to sell. Similarly, it is usual today for a person wishing to buy land or buildings to offer a certain figure 'subject to contract'. This is merely an offer to enter into a preliminary agreement on the understanding that it shall not be binding until the terms are embodied in a subsequent contract. Nor is the request of a person to tradesmen to submit tenders or estimates for supplying particular goods or services an offer; the offer comes from the tradesmen in the form of the tender or estimate. An offer can be revoked at any time before it is accepted.

The offer may be made by direct contact, telephone, letter or even advertisement. With the latter the offer is usually open to anyone, e.g. the offer of shares by public subscription, or it may be restricted, e.g. a 'rights' issue to existing shareholders.

The *acceptance* must be absolute, unqualified, in accordance with the terms of the offer, and within the prescribed time. In short it must fit the offer exactly. Thus it can only be accepted by the person to whom the offer was made, while if the response to an offer shows an inclination to contract on different terms, that response is a counter-offer and it destroys the offer.

Generally the acceptance of the offer must be communicated to the offeror. This can be by direct contact, either face to face or by telephone, telegraph or telex. If it is sent by post, the acceptance operates from the *time of posting* provided the letter has been correctly addressed. This is simply a rule of convenience, for otherwise it could not be assumed that a contract had been agreed until the acceptor had proof that his letter had arrived. But it also means that if the offer is revoked, notice of this must be received by the acceptor before he posts his acceptance.

2 Intention to create legal relations   While every contract is an agreement, not every agreement is a contract. The agreement must: (a) be intended to affect; and (b) actually affect the legal relationship of the parties concerned.

The basic question is whether the parties have shown an intention to be bound. Thus if a person agrees to act as best man at a friend's wedding and incurs expense in hiring a morning suit, there is no redress in a court of law should the wedding be called off since it was never contemplated that the arrangement should be legally binding. While an intention to create legal relations will normally be inferred in commercial matters, it will not for social and domestic agreements even though a consideration is present.

Thus a husband's maintenance provision might well be a binding contract, but where a husband left his wife and agreed to pay her £15 per week *as long as he could manage it*, the Court of Appeal held that there was no contract because the uncertainty of the terms indicated that there was no intention to create legal relations (*Gould v. Gould, 1969*).

As regards agreements between trade unions and employers, section 18 of the Trade Union and Labour Relations Act, 1974, provides that a collective agreement is conclusively presumed not to have been intended by the parties to be a legally enforceable contract unless it is in writing and expressly provides that it is so intended.

3 Consideration   A consideration having value is essential to the validity of every contract that is not under seal. Such a consideration has been defined as 'some right, interest, profit, or benefit accruing to the one party, or some forbearance, detriment, loss, or responsibility given, suffered or undertaken by the other' (*Currie v. Misa, 1875*). In short a consideration is some benefit accruing to one party or some detriment suffered by another. A *promise* to do or not to do something is a valuable consideration in the eyes of the law. For instance, if a grocer promised to deliver groceries on a Saturday, and the customer promised to pay on delivery, the customer can sue the grocer if he does not deliver the goods since he can point to his promise to pay as being the consideration for the grocer's promise to deliver. The promise to pay is a detriment to the customer and a benefit to the grocer.

The consideration may not necessarily be an adequate return for what has been done or promised, but it must have some value, e.g. an agreement to postpone the bringing of an action. On the other hand an act or promise is not a consideration if it is one which the person is bound to do by the general law, or already legally bound to do for the other person. For example, if A makes a contract with B, and then A in return for a promise of further consideration undertakes to B that he will fulfil the original contract, A cannot claim the further consideration. The exception to this rule is where a creditor agrees to accept a smaller sum in settlement of a larger one, for this will give the debtor a good discharge provided it was not agreed under duress.

4 Required formalities   In common law there is no basic difference between an oral and a written contract. But, as we have seen, certain contracts are required by statute to be by deed under seal while others have to be in writing. The latter cover:
    (a) credit sale agreements;

(b) negotiable instruments, contracts of marine insurance and assignment of copyright;

(c) contracts of guarantee (where a person promises to answer for the debt, default or miscarriage of another); and

(d) contracts for the sale or other disposition (e.g. a lease) of land or any interest in land.

5 Capacity   All persons over 18 years of age have full legal rights, and thus *sole traders* are bound by contracts made. *Partnerships,* too, are similarly bound if the contract is within the scope of their ordinary business. *Companies* are given legal status by being incorporated, but they can only make contracts within the objectives set out in their Articles of Association. However, under EEC law, if an outsider has dealt in good faith with a company in the normal course of business but without knowing its precise objectives, he can sue on a contract made.

Infants (persons under 18 years of age) are limited in their ability to contract. While they are bound by contracts for supplying *necessaries* or for stipulating *conditions of service or apprenticeship*, they may repudiate during infancy, or within a reasonable time of attaining majority, a contract which gains an interest in property of a permanent nature or which involves continuous or recurring obligations, such as leases, shares in companies or partnerships. *Other contracts* made by infants – for loans or goods which are not necessaries – are absolutely void.

6 No invalidating factors   Contracts are void if they are *illegal* by contravening: (a) statutes, e.g. price-fixing agreements contrary to the Resale Prices Act, 1976, and insurance contracts where the insurer has no insurable interest in the life of the person insured; (b) common law, e.g. agreements to commit a crime or tort (i.e. a civil wrong, such as trespass), to pervert the course of justice, to produce corruption in public life, to defraud the Inland Revenue, to obstruct public policy, for example by excluding the jurisdiction of the courts or by restraining trade where the terms cannot be regarded as normal contractual provisions.

In the course of negotiations statements are made to induce a person to enter into a contract, e.g. regarding the profits of a business, the age of an antique, the distance from the sea of a hotel. *Misrepresentation* occurs when these *facts* are not true. But it does not apply to the expression of an *opinion*, while 'puffing statements', such as 'as good as new', are not normally regarded as representations. Mere non-disclosure of facts is generally not sufficient, but if something is said which is true but silence is kept about something else this is misleading and can be regarded as being misrepresentation.

While the representation need not be the sole cause of the

injured party making the contract, it must materially have affected his decision. However, where a purchaser employs an accountant to investigate the business or a surveyor to examine a building before entering into the contract, he relies on their reports and thus cannot complain subsequently of misrepresentation by the vendor. It does not matter whether misrepresentation occurs innocently, negligently or fraudulently: all can make the contract voidable and may give rise for liability for damages.

In the course of negotiating a contract *mistakes* can occur. Some mistakes do not affect the validity of a contract, others do. Ignorance of the law, failure to read the small print of a document or simply a bad bargain for one of the parties concerned do not make the contract void. Thus if a builder's tender is accepted but proves to have been too low, he has to be the loser. On the other hand where the parties are in agreement but there is a mistake about the subject-matter of the contract there is no contract because there is nothing to make a contract about.

A mistake in the identity of the other party is more complicated. Such identity must be important to the contract. Thus if a rogue is impersonating somebody to obtain goods, e.g. by use of a stolen credit card, he obtains no entitlement to those goods and so anyone he may have subsequently sold them to can be required to hand them over to the injured party. In practice the owner of the credit card or bank usually stands the loss.

Sometimes, through a mistake, the parties may not in fact have reached agreement, though they think they have. Here the court may exercise its equitable jurisdiction to allow the written document to be rectified so as to represent truly the parties' intentions.

Duress renders a contract voidable by the person coerced. It means actual or threatened violence upon the person (not goods) of one party or members of his family by the other party or by someone acting with his knowledge and to his advantage.

Undue influence is an equitable concept, wider than duress. While it does not put a person in fear, it covers any form of pressure which impairs the exercise of a person's free judgement, thereby resulting in him concluding a bad bargain. There are two categories: (a) where the parties are in such a relationship that one reposes confidence in, or is under the authority of, the other (e.g. parent and child, guardian and ward, doctor and patient, solicitor and client, trustee and beneficiary), undue influence will be presumed, and the contract will be voidable unless the party seeking to uphold it can show that it was the result of the free exercise of independent will; and (b) other cases, where the party attacking the contract must prove undue influence.

The inadequacy of contract rules

The law of contract simply deals with the legal relationship between the parties concerned. It tends to assume that the agreement is reached between two willing parties of equal bargaining strength. In practice, however, this is often not so.

First, one party may have *inadequate knowledge* of what should be a fair market price for the type of good or of the quality of the merchandise being sold. In comparison with the specialist dealer they are in a weak position. Thus in the past antique furniture has been sold by private persons at ridiculously low prices, while others have been persuaded to buy seriously defective cars. The legal rule that goods should be inspected before purchasing cannot always be applied because, for instance, delivery may be from a central warehouse or by post. In any case lack of knowledge often takes the form of the layman failing to appreciate when he should take expert advice and even of knowing where to go for an opinion. Alternatively it may simply be the inability to recognise the 'sales talk' of the plausible salesman or the embellishments of the glossy advertisement.

Second, the terms of the agreement may be weighted in favour of the seller. Being a specialist he can have standard forms which allow him to take full advantage of the current state of the law. Such forms set out the terms of the deposit to be paid when placing the order or making a booking and the conditions of any refund (e.g. when buying furniture or arranging a holiday abroad). With credit sales the provisos contained in the small print often come to light only when the purchaser starts to complain.

Finally, the seller may be virtually the sole supplier of a particular good or service, e.g. the Post Office for telephones, car firms for spare parts. Alternatively one buyer may be able to play off a number of separate sellers against each other. Thus small farmers have had to form co-operatives to deal with wholesale merchants. Above all this has been the situation in the labour market with one employer being able to take advantage of unorganised labour.

These basic weaknesses have meant that Parliament has had to legislate to redress the balance, in particular to protect the interests of the consumer and the worker. The nature of this intervention is examined in Chapters 8 and 11.

Part III

The Market Economy

7 The Operation of the Free Market

I Markets

Value and price

In the market economy a want is significant only when a person is prepared to give up something in order to satisfy it. As the strength of the different wants varies, so will the amounts which people are willing to give up. In other words different goods have a different *value* to them, value being the rate at which a particular good or service will exchange for others.

In modern economic systems the values of goods are expressed in terms of money as a *price.* By comparing prices we can see the *rates* at which different goods may be exchanged.

Changes in *relative* prices, if supply conditions have not changed, indicate a relative shift in the importance of those goods. Thus price changes signal changes in what people want. We must therefore examine the mechanism by which these signals are flashed. We begin by looking at the 'market'.

What is a 'market'?

'I am offered £350 for this heifer. No more offers? For the last time of asking, any advance on £350? Going at £350, going, gone.' Down comes the hammer: 'Sold at £350 to Mr Giles on my right.'

This is the local cattle market. On his stand above the cattle ring is the auctioneer. Inside the ring, a black-and-white heifer is appraised by local farmers and dealers. Some are buyers, some sellers. The market fixes the price at which those who want something can obtain it from those who have it to sell.

Note that it is only exchange value which is significant. The farmer selling the heifer may have considered that it ought to have made more than £350. Or, as it was the first calf reared by his son, it may have had great 'sentimental value' to him. Such niceties, however, mean little in the market economy.

Of course prices are not always fixed by auction. This is the method usually employed where there are many buyers but the seller only comes to the market infrequently or wishes to dispose of his goods quickly. If there are few buyers and sellers, e.g. in the purchase of a house or a second-hand car, the final price may be arrived at by 'higgling' the seller meeting the prospective buyer personally and bargaining with him.

But where goods are in constant demand the above methods would take too long. Thus most goods, such as foodstuffs, clothing, household utensils and new books, are given a definite price by the shopkeeper. But buyers will still influence this price. If it is too high, the market will not be cleared; if it is too low, the shopkeeper's stocks will run out.

A market need not be formal or held in a particular place. Second-hand cars are often bought and sold through newspaper advertisements. Second-hand furniture may be disposed of by a card in a local shop window. Foreign currency, gold, base metals, raw cotton and other goods which can be accurately described are dealt in over the telephone.

However, in studying the market economy our major interest is in how price is determined. Since this takes place in the market we can define the market simply as *all those buyers and sellers of a good who influence its price.* Within the market there is a tendency for the same price, allowing for costs of transport, to be established for the same commodity.

World markets

Today modern transport allows many commodities to have a 'world' market – a change in one part of the world affects the price in the rest of the world. Examples of such commodities are wheat, vegetable oils, basic raw materials (such as cotton and rubber), gold, silver and base metals. What conditions must such commodities fulfil?

First, there must be a wide demand. The basic necessities of life (e.g. wheat, frozen meat, wool, cotton) answer this requirement. In contrast such goods as national costumes, books translated into little-used languages, souvenirs and post-cards of local views have only local demand.

Second, commodities must be capable of being transported. Land and buildings are almost impossible to transport. Personal services are limited by the distance the consumer can travel. Labour, too, is particularly immobile, workers showing reluctance to move to a different country (see Chapter 11). Closely connected with this is the action of governments who, by import taxes and quotas, may effectively prevent the entry of certain commodities into the country.

Third, the costs of transport must be small in relation to the value of the commodity. Thus the market for diamonds is world-wide, whereas that for bricks is small. Similarly wheat and oil are cheap to transport compared with coal because they are more easily handled, though as sea transport is relatively cheap coal mined near the coast can be sent long distances.

Last, the commodity must be durable. Goods which perish quickly, such as milk, bread, fresh cream and strawberries, cannot be sent long distances. Nevertheless modern developments such as refrigeration, canning and air freight transport are extending the market.

Perfect and imperfect markets

In any market the price of the commodity in one part affects its price in another part. Hence the same price tends to be established. Where price differences are eliminated quickly, we say the market is a 'perfect' market. (Note: this is not quite the same as 'perfect competition' (see Chapter 9).)

For a market to be perfect certain conditions have to be fulfilled. First, buyers and sellers must have exact knowledge of the prices being paid elsewhere in the market. The development of communications, particularly the telephone, has facilitated this. Second, both buyers and sellers must base their actions solely on price, and not favour one particular person out of loyalty or mere inertia. Thus, if one seller puts up the price of his good, his customers immediately go to another in the market who is cheaper. Alternatively if he lowered his price, customers would so flock to him that he would sell out quickly unless he raised his price to that asked elsewhere.

Examples of perfect markets are the precious stones market at Hatton Garden and, above all, the organised produce markets and the Stock Exchange (see pp. 215–18). In these markets the two essential conditions are fulfilled for prices are watched closely by professional dealers. As a result variations in price are quickly eliminated.

But such conditions are rarely satisfied in other markets. Buyers and sellers have neither perfect knowledge nor act solely on the basis of price. The ordinary housewife, for instance, cannot afford the time to go from one shop to another in order to compare the prices of her everyday purchases, though she is usually much more careful when spending on the more expensive goods bought at infrequent intervals. Similarly shopkeepers do not always know what other shopkeepers are charging for similar goods. Moreover, purchasers may be influenced by considerations other than price. Thus they may continue to deal with one particular trader even though he is charging a slightly higher price because he has given them good service in the past. It is this personal relationship which is the basis of the 'goodwill' built up by a business. Moreover, although two goods may be virtually the same physically, by 'product differentiation' and advertising the merits of his own brand a producer may convince the consumer of its superiority. Such 'persuasive' advertising, which accounts for over one-half of present advertising expenditure, makes the market less perfect, and must be contrasted to 'informative' advertising which increases knowledge and thus helps to make the market more perfect.

Where price differences persist, markets are said to be 'imperfect'. As we have already hinted, such markets are often found in retailing.

Organised produce markets

As explained above, the market for certain commodities can be world-wide. Moreover, many of these commodities are in constant demand, either as a basic raw material or as a main food or beverage for a large section of the world's people. They therefore figure prominently in international trade, and are the subject of the following discussion.

England's foreign trade commenced with the export of raw wool in the thirteenth century, and it was extended by the subsequent development of the Chartered Companies. These were based in London, and it was here that merchants gathered to buy and sell the produce which the companies' ships brought from abroad.

The big change, however, came about with the expansion of international trade following the Industrial Revolution. The UK became the greatest importing and exporting nation in the world. London, her chief port and commercial city, not only imported the goods which were required for the people of her own country but, assisted by the fact that British ships were the carriers of world trade, built up an important *entrepôt* business, acting as a 'go-between' in the distribution of such commodities as tea, sugar, hides, skins and wool to many other countries, particularly those of Western Europe.

Hence formal 'organised markets' developed. These markets are distinctive in that buying and selling takes place in a recognised building, business is governed by agreed rules and conventions, and often only special persons are allowed to engage in transactions. Generally the public are excluded, even from watching. They are thus a highly developed form of market, and today London has exchanges or auction centres for buying and selling such commodities as rubber, wool, tea, coffee, furs, metals (tin, copper, lead and zinc), grain and shipping freights (the Baltic Exchange). It must not be thought, however, that such organised produce markets exist only in London. Liverpool has exchanges for cotton and grain, while most of the large trading countries have exchanges. Although today much of the goods goes directly to other countries, profits of London dealers forms part of the UK's 'invisible exports' (see p. 334).

Broadly speaking, organised markets fulfil three main functions. First, they enable manufacturers and wholesalers to obtain supplies of commodities easily, quickly and at the competitive market price. Because they are composed of specialist buyers and sellers, prices are sensitive to any change in demand and supply. Thus they are 'perfect markets'.

Second, 'futures' dealings on these markets enable persons to protect themselves from heavy losses through price changes. Thus a cotton grower prefers to know what price he will receive before his output is actually delivered to the market. On the other hand a cotton spinner has to protect himself from a rise in the price of raw cotton between the time of quoting a price for his yarn and its actual manufacture. Where a good is bought today for delivery today, the deal is known as a 'spot' transaction and the price is the 'spot price'. With many goods, however, it is possible to buy today for delivery in the future. The good may not even be in stock but the seller contracts to obtain and deliver the good at the agreed time. The price agreed upon is the 'future' or 'forward' price. For a commodity to be dealt in on a 'futures' market certain conditions must be fulfilled: (a) the commodity is durable, thereby enabling stocks to be carried; (b) the commodity can be described by grades which are internationally uniform; (c) dealings are sufficiently frequent to occupy professional dealers; and (d) the commodity is one which is subject to price fluctuations.

Where futures dealings take place the market is usually divided between brokers and dealers. The broker merely carries out the wishes of his client, whereas the dealer is the person who uses his expert knowledge to make a profit on what he considers will be the future price of the commodity. At any time a dealer will quote a price (according to the view he takes of the future movement of prices) at which he is prepared to buy or sell at some future date. Thus a cotton grower can cover himself against a possible fall in price by selling his produce forward, while a cotton spinner can quote a weaver a price for yarn and guard himself against loss by buying the raw cotton forward.

Such dealing usually performs the third function of organised markets – evening out price fluctuations. At a time when an increase in supply would cause the price to fall considerably, the dealer adds his demand to the normal demand in order to build up his stocks, and thereby keeps the price up. On the other hand when the good is in short supply he releases stocks and so prevents a violent rise in price. The difficulty is that speculation on the future price may dominate the real forces which influence it, prices fluctuating violently in response to changes in optimism and pessimism.

II   Forces determining price

Demand and supply

'That animal was cheap,' remarks Dan Archer as the auctioneer's hammer falls. 'And no wonder,' replies Fred Barrett, 'this has been a long winter. We're now in the middle of April, and the grass is hardly growing. Hay is running short, and breeders are being forced to sell quicker than they expected. Old Giles is about the only farmer who will take the risk of buying extra cattle.'

What can we learn from Fred Barrett's observations? Simply that the £350 at which the heifer was sold was not really determined by the final bid. The real factors producing the relatively low price were the reluctance of farmers to buy and the number of young animals being offered for sale. In short the price was determined by the interaction of the forces of demand and supply. We shall examine each in turn.

Preliminary assumptions

First, we must see how these forces work in an imaginary market – for eggs. To simplify, we shall assume:

(a) all eggs are exactly the same in size and quality;

(b) no transport costs within the market;

(c) the market consists of so many small buyers and sellers that there is keen competition;

(d) a *perfect market* – price differences are quickly eliminated because buyers and sellers: (i) have complete knowledge of prices and conditions in other parts of the market, and (ii) act solely on the basis of price; and

(e) no interference by the government in the operation of market forces, e.g. by price control, regulating supply, etc.

Demand

Demand in economics is the desire for something *plus* the willingness and ability to pay a certain price in order to possess it. More specifically, it is how much of a good people in the market would buy at a given price over a certain period of time.

It is helpful if we separate the factors affecting demand into: (1) price; and (2) the conditions of demand.

1 Price, the conditions of demand remaining unchanged
Normally a person will demand more of a good the lower its price. This is because once you have some units of a good your want is partially satisfied, and so you will only buy more if less has to be given for them. This conforms to our everyday observations. 'Winter sale, prices slashed,' announce the shops when they wish to clear their stocks of clothing.

We can draw up a table showing how many eggs a person would be willing to buy at different prices. If they are very expensive, other foodstuffs will, as far as possible, be substituted; if they are cheap, persons may even pickle them. By adding up the demand of all buyers of eggs in the market at different prices for a given period of time it is possible to obtain a *market-demand schedule* (see Table 7.1).

Table 7.1 *Demand schedule for no-such market for the week ending 27 January 1979*

Price (pence per egg)	Eggs demanded* (thousands)
12	3
10	9
8	15
6	20
4	25
2	35

*What buyers would take at each price.

Note that this schedule does not tell us anything about the actual market price or how much is in fact sold. It is an 'if' schedule. All it says is: 'If the price is so much, then this quantity will be demanded.' Plotting this schedule on a graph and assuming that demand can be obtained for intermediary prices gives the demand curve D in Figure 7.1.

Fig. 7.1 Quantity demanded and price

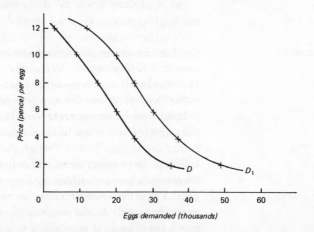

2 The conditions of demand Something may occur to cause housewives to demand more eggs at a given price. In other words the demand schedule alters. Suppose, for instance, farmers unite in an advertising campaign describing tasty egg dishes. As a result more eggs are demanded at all prices (see Table 7.2).

Table 7.2 *An increase in demand*

Price (pence per egg)	*Eggs demanded* (thousands)
12	12
10	20
8	25
6	30
4	37
2	49

Plotting this revised demand schedule gives curve D_1 to the right of D. Had conditions so changed that demand decreased the new demand curve would have been to the left.

The influence of both (a) price, and (b) the conditions of demand on the quantity demanded, is thus shown on the graph. The former determines the shape of the demand curve – its slope downwards from left to right; the latter determines its position within the axes – an increase in demand shifting the curve to the right, a decrease shifting it to the left. To assist clarity of exposition a change in demand resulting from a change in price will in future be referred to as an *extension or contraction* of demand; a change in demand due to new conditions of demand will be described as an *increase or decrease* in demand.

(a) *A change in the prices of other goods.* Goods compete for our limited income and are thus, to some extent, substitutes for each other. When the prices of other goods fall, the particular good under discussion becomes *relatively dearer*, and therefore less of it is demanded. When the prices of other goods rise, it becomes relatively cheaper, and so more of it is demanded.

But the effect on the demand for a particular good is more pronounced when the price of a close substitute changes. If now the price of tomatoes falls, housewives will tend to buy them rather than eggs. Thus although there has been no initial increase in the price of eggs, demand for them has decreased. Similarly, where goods are complementary, a change in the price of one good has a pronounced effect on the demand for the other. For example, a fall in the price of cars results in more cars being purchased, leading eventually to an increase in the demand for petrol and tyres.

(b) *A change in tastes and fashion.* A campaign advertising eggs would increase demand; a scare that eggs were the source of infection would decrease it.

(c) *Expectations of future price changes or shortages.* The fear that the price of eggs may rise considerably the following week will induce people to increase their demand now in order to have eggs in stock.

(d) *Government policy*. A tax on eggs paid by the consumer would raise the price and lead to a decrease in demand; a rebate paid to the consumer would have the opposite effect (see Chapter 19).

In *the longer period,* the conditions of demand may change through:

(e) *A change in real income.* If there was an all-round increase in income, people could afford more eggs, and demand would probably increase. On the other hand it might now be possible to afford mushrooms for breakfast, and these would take the place of eggs.

(f) *Greater equality in the distribution of wealth.* The wealth of a country may be so distributed that there are a few exceptionally rich persons whereas the remainder are exceedingly poor. If many poor persons felt they could not afford eggs, greater equality of wealth would be likely to increase the demand for eggs.

(g) *A change in the size and composition of the population.* Additional people coming into the market increase demand, especially if eggs figure prominently in their diet.

Supply

Supply in economics refers to how much of a good will be offered for sale at a given price over a given period of time. As with demand, this quantity depends on (1) the price of the good, and (2) the conditions of supply.

1 Price, the conditions of supply remaining unchanged
Normally more of a good will be supplied the higher its price. The real reason for this is explained in Chapter 9. But even a brief consideration of how the individual farmer reacts to a change in price will show that it is likely to be true. If the price of eggs is high, he will probably consume fewer himself in order to send as many as possible to market. Moreover, the higher price would allow him to give his chickens more food so that they would lay a few extra eggs. When we extend our analysis to the market supply it is obvious that a higher price for eggs would enable other farmers – the less efficient – to go in for egg production.

Hence we are able to draw up a *market supply schedule* for eggs. This consists of the total amounts supplied at different prices by all the sellers in the market for a given period of time (see Table 7.3 for an example).

Table 7.3   *Supply schedule for no-such*
market for the week ending
27 January 1979

Price (pence per egg)	*Eggs supplied** (thousands)
12	40
10	32
8	25
6	20
4	13
2	7

*What sellers would offer at each price.

Once again it must be noted that this is an 'if' schedule, for all it says is: 'If the price is so much, then this quantity will be offered for sale.' We can plot this schedule (see Figure 7.2) and, assuming supply can be obtained for all intermediate prices, obtain a supply curve S.

**Fig. 7.2
Quantity supplied and
price**

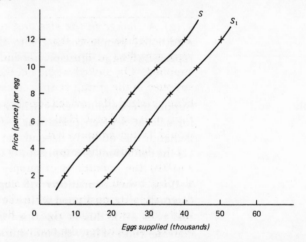

However, there is a fundamental difference between demand and supply. Whereas demand can respond almost immediately to a change in price, a period of time must usually elapse before supply can be fully adjusted. For the first day or two the only way in which the farmer can send more eggs to market is by eating fewer himself. By the end of the week he may have increased output by giving the hens more food or by leaving the light on in the hen-house all night; the higher price covers the extra cost. But to obtain any sizeable increase the farmer must add to his hens; if all farmers are following the same policy, this will take about five months, the period required to rear laying hens from chicks.

These different periods of time are dealt with more fully in Chapter 9. There we see that each period of time produces a supply curve of a different slope.

2 The conditions of supply   The number of eggs supplied may change even though there has been no alteration in the price. In the spring, for instance, chickens lay more eggs than in winter. Thus more eggs will be supplied at all prices in the spring, and fewer in winter. A new supply schedule for the spring could read as shown in Table 7.4.

Table 7.4 *An increase in supply*

Price (pence per egg)	Eggs supplied (thousands)
12	50
10	43
8	36
6	30
4	25
2	19

This schedule shows that, whereas in winter only 25,000 eggs were supplied at 8p each, during the spring 36,000 would be supplied. Or looked at in another way, 25,000 eggs can be supplied in the spring at 4p each compared with 8p in the winter. When plotted, the revised supply schedule gives a curve S_1, to the right of the old one. Had supply decreased the new supply curve would have been to the left.

Like demand, therefore, supply is influenced by both (a) price, and (b) the conditions of supply. The former determines the shape of the curve – its upward slope from left to right. The latter determines its position within the axes – an increase in supply shifts the curve to the right, a decrease shifts it to the left. To distinguish between the two we shall refer to a change in supply resulting from a change in price of the commodity as an *extension* or *contraction* of supply; a change in supply due to new conditions of supply will be described as an *increase* or *decrease* in supply.

In general conditions of supply may change fairly quickly through:

(a) *A change in the prices of other goods, especially when it is easy to shift the resources which produce those goods.* Suppose there is a considerable increase in the price of chicken meat, including boiling-fowls. It may now pay the farmer to kill some of his laying pullets. Thus fewer eggs are supplied at the old price.

(b) *A change in the prices of factors of production.* A fall in the cost of pullets or of their food would reduce the cost of egg production. As a result more eggs could be supplied at the old price, or, looked at in another way, the original quantity could be produced at a lower price per egg. A rise in the wages of workers on chicken farms would have the opposite effect.

(c) *Changes resulting from nature,* e.g. the weather, floods, drought, pest, or from *abnormal circumstances,* e.g. war, fire, political events.

(d) *Government policy.* A tax on the output of eggs or an increase in the amount employers have to pay in workers' national insurance would result in fewer eggs being offered for sale at the old price. That is, the supply curve moves to the left. On the other hand a subsidy, by decreasing costs, would move the supply curve to the right (see Chapter 19).

Other changes in supply take longer, occurring through:

(e) *Improved techniques.* Technical improvements reduce costs of production, shifting the supply curve to the right. Thus automatic feeding devices might be developed, as might selective breeding produce hens which lay more eggs over a given period.

(f) *The discovery of new sources of raw materials, or the exhaustion of existing sources.*

(g) *The entry of new firms into the industry.*

III The determination of price: market-clearing

The demand and supply curves can be combined in a single diagram (see Figure 7.3). Let us see how this analysis helps as a

Fig. 7.3
The determination of equilibrium price

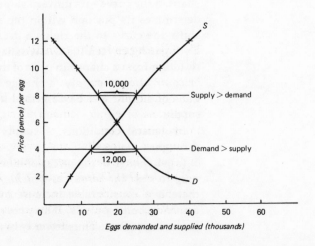

Eggs demanded and supplied (thousands)

first approach to understanding how the market is cleared. The assumptions we have made so far are:

(1) many buyers and sellers;

(2) keen competition between buyers, between sellers, and between buyers and sellers;

(3) more will be demanded at a lower price than at a higher price; and

(4) less will be supplied at a lower price than at a higher.

Given assumptions (3) and (4), the two curves slope in opposite directions. Thus they cut at a single point – in our example where the price is 6p. It can be predicted that in no-such market, where these conditions of demand and supply exist, the price of eggs will move towards and eventually settle at 6p. We call this price the *market* or *equilibrium price*.

This proposition can be proved as follows. Suppose that initially the price of eggs is fixed at 8p. Here 15,000 will be demanded but 25,000 supplied. There is thus an excess supply of 10,000. But some sellers will want to get rid of their surplus supplies, and therefore reduce the price being asked. As this happens some supplies are withdrawn from the market, and there is an extension of demand. This continues until a price of 6p is reached, when 20,000 eggs are both demanded and offered for sale. Thus 6p is the only price at which there is harmony between buyers and sellers: given existing demands and supply the market is 'cleared'.

Similarly, if the initial price is 4p, 25,000 will be demanded but only 13,000 offered for sale. Housewives queue to buy eggs, and sellers see that their supplies will quickly run out. Competition among buyers will force up the price. As this happens more eggs are supplied to the market, and there is a contraction of demand. This continues until a price of 6p is reached, when demand equals supply at 20,000 eggs.

IV Changes in the condition of demand and supply

The equilibrium price will persist until there is a change in the conditions of either demand or supply. Let us begin with our market price of 6p.

Suppose tastes alter, and people eat more eggs. The conditions of demand have now changed, and the demand curve shifts to the right from D to D_1 (see Figure 7.4). At the original price of 6p we now have an excess of demand over supply – 30,000 eggs are demanded, but only 20,000 are supplied. As explained in the previous section, competition between buyers will now force up the price to 8p, where 25,000 eggs are both demanded and supplied.

Fig. 7.4
The effect on price of a change in the conditions of demand

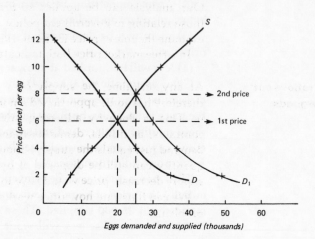

Similarly a decrease in demand, resulting, for instance, from a significant fall in the price of tomatoes, would cause the curve to shift to the left and the price of eggs to fall.

Alternatively a change may occur in the conditions of supply. At any given price more eggs can be produced during the spring, when the supply curve shifts to the right from S to S_1 (see Figure 7.5). At the original price of 6p we now have an excess supply over demand – 30,000 eggs are supplied, but only 20,000 are demanded. Here competition amongst sellers will mean that the price falls to 4p, where 25,000 eggs are both demanded and supplied.

Fig. 7.5
The effect on price of a change in the conditions of supply

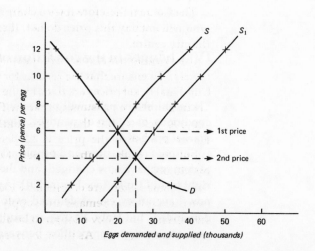

V The functions of price in the free market

Our analysis can be applied to practical problems, especially those relating to government policy. First, however, we use it to examine the role of price in the market economy.

In a free market price both indicates and motivates.

1   It 'rations out' scarce goods

At any one time the supply of a good is relatively fixed. It therefore has to be apportioned among the many people wanting it. This is done by adjusting price. As price rises, demand contracts; as it falls, demand expands. At the equilibrium price demand just equals the supply. Should supply increase, the total quantity can still be disposed of by lowering the price; should supply decrease, price would have to be raised.

We can illustrate how price works by considering two current problems:

(a) *Who shall be allowed to park his car in a congested area?* Car-parking is causing traffic congestion in the centre of Barthem City. This is because it costs motorists nothing to park their cars at the kerbside. The Council decides to limit car-parking to one side of the road and to 800 places, each with a parking meter. The demand schedule for two-hour parking is estimated to be as follows:

Price (pence)	Demand
30	450
20	800
10	1200
0	1800

The Council therefore fixes a charge of 20p. The 1000 motorists who will not pay this price do not, therefore, bring their cars into the city centre.

(b) *Why do ticket touts obtain such high prices for Cup Final tickets?* To ensure that the regular football supporter can afford a Cup Final ticket prices are fixed by the Football Association (FA). Let us simplify by assuming that the FA has one price, £1, for the 100,000 tickets, but that a free-market price would be £3. In Figure 7.6 when the price is £3 demand equals the available supply but, at the controlled price of £1, demand exceeds supply by 150,000.

But some tickets are obtained by touts who resell at a profit in a free market where demand and supply determine price. Keen club supporters, not lucky enough to be allocated a ticket, are willing to pay more than £1. As the price rises, some persons possessing

Fig. 7.6
Excess demand for
Cup Final tickets

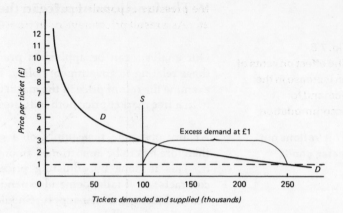

tickets may be induced to sell them to the touts. Thus the demand and supply curves are roughly as shown in Figure 7.7, giving a 'black-market' price of £10.

Fig. 7.7
The black-market price
of Cup Final tickets

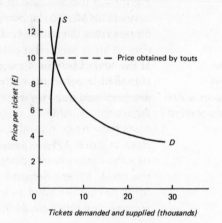

An important conclusion can be drawn from this example: where price is controlled below the market price, only some form of rationing can ensure that everybody gets a share of the limited supply. Thus, after allocating so many tickets to each finalist, the FA normally limits each affiliated club to approximately two. The alternative would simply be a 'first-come, first-served' method of distribution, penalising those who could not queue and increasing the scope for black-market activity.

2   It indicates
changes in wants

Prices are the signals by which households indicate the extent to which different goods are wanted, and also any changes in those wants.

Consider how the demand for owner-occupied houses in South-east England has increased over the last ten years through the pressure of population, higher real incomes, tax concessions, etc. As a result prices have risen from OP to OP_1 (see Figure 7.8).

Fig. 7.8
The effect on rents of an increase in the demand for accommodation

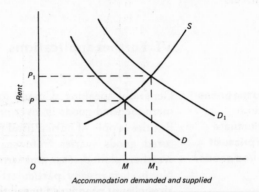

Accommodation demanded and supplied

3   It induces supply to respond to changes in demand

When demand increases, price rises and supply extends; when demand decreases, price falls and supply contracts. Thus in Figure 7.8 the increase in price has made it profitable for extra houses, MM_1, to be supplied by new building, transferring houses from the rented sector, etc.

4   It indicates changes in the conditions upon which goods can be supplied

If the cost of producing a given commodity rises, this should be signalled to consumers who can then decide to what extent they are prepared to pay these higher costs by forgoing other goods. Again this is achieved through price. Assume in Figure 7.9 that costs have risen in producing good x because raw materials have risen in price. Where demand is depicted by D most consumers pay the higher costs (price rises by PP_1) rather than do without the good. Where demand is depicted by D_1 consumers tend to forgo having the good as its price rises (demand falls by MM_1), substituting other goods for it.

Fig. 7.9
The effect of a change in the conditions of supply on price and quantity traded

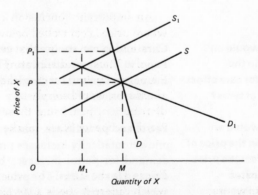

Quantity of X

5   It rewards the factors of production

Payments for factors of production give their owners spending power. The relative size of this spending power determines the division (usually termed 'distribution') of the cake produced. If the price of a good rises, producers can afford to offer higher rewards in order to attract factors from other uses.

VI Further applications

1   Why do the prices of agricultural products fluctuate more than prices of manufactured goods?

Generally speaking demand for both agricultural products and manufactured goods is, over not too long a period, fairly stable. But the supply of agricultural products, unlike that of manufactured goods, varies from season to season, and, because of weather, plant disease and farmers' decisions, from year to year. Nor is storage easy, particularly of foodstuffs. Thus the supply of agricultural products fluctuates considerably, and so do prices. The difference between agricultural products and manufactured goods can be seen by comparing tomatoes and carpets (see Figure 7.10). Whereas the price of tomatoes varies between OP_1 and OP_2, that of carpets remains steady at OR.

Fig. 7.10
Fluctuations in the prices of tomatoes and carpets

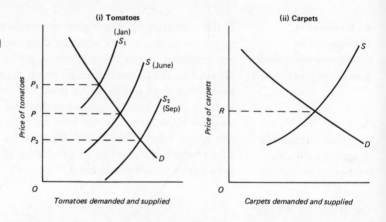

2   How would an increase in the demand for cars affect the price of tyres?

Cars and tyres are 'jointly demanded'. With such goods prices move in the same direction. This can be seen in Figure 7.11. The increased demand for cars leads to an increased demand for tyres, and the prices of both rise.

3   How would an increase in the price of petrol affect the price of paraffin?

Petrol and paraffin are 'jointly supplied'; increased production of one automatically increases production of the other. Suppose that demand for petrol increases but that there is no change in the demand for paraffin. The price of petrol rises from OP to OP_1, and supply expands from OM to OM_1 (see Figure 7.12). But this means that the supply of paraffin increases, though there has been no change in price. Thus the supply curve for paraffin moves from S to S_1, and the price of paraffin falls from OR to OR_1.

**Fig. 7.11
Joint demand**

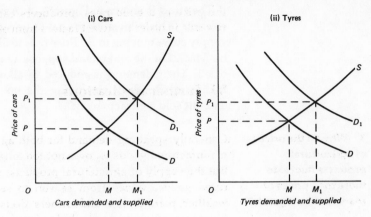

(i) Cars

Cars demanded and supplied

(ii) Tyres

Tyres demanded and supplied

**Fig. 7.12
Joint supply**

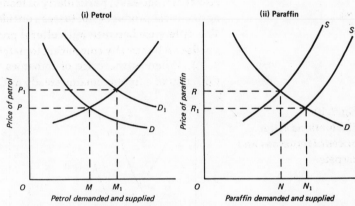

(i) Petrol

Petrol demanded and supplied

(ii) Paraffin

Paraffin demanded and supplied

**Fig. 7.13
The effect on quantity
bought of a subsidy
and tax**

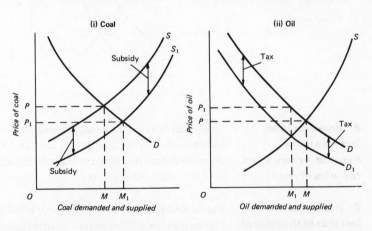

(i) Coal

Coal demanded and supplied

(ii) Oil

Oil demanded and supplied

**4 How could the
government secure
greater use of coal in
order to conserve the
stock of North Sea oil?**

Here the government must operate to alter the relative prices of
coal and oil, reducing the former and increasing the latter. To
reduce the price of coal it could give the producer, the National
Coal Board (NCB), or consumers, like the Central Electricity
Generating Board, a subsidy. In contrast a high tax could be
imposed on the producers or consumers of oil.

The effect is shown in Figure 7.13. Assume the NCB is given a subsidy. This allows more coal to be supplied at all prices, the supply curve moving to S_1. Price falls to OP_1 and demand expands by MM_1. On the other hand suppose a tax is levied on consumers of oil. Their demand is reduced to allow for the tax, the curve falling to D_1. Price, including the tax, rises to OP_1, and the amount sold contracts by MM_1.

8 The Firm and its Customers

Organisations assemble resources to produce the goods and services wanted by the community. In the private sector production is based on demand, and the ability and willingness to pay a given price. In the public sector production is mainly for needs, both individual and social. We shall consider such needs and how they are assessed in Chapter 14. Here we are concerned with the relationship between private-sector firms and their customers.

I The role of the firm

Objectives of the firm

In a market economy a firm has to cover its costs if it is to stay in business. Thus regard must be paid to 'profitability'. But in practice are firms always single-minded in seeking to *maximise money* profits? The answer is 'no'; there is a range of possible objectives.

Personal motives may be important, especially where the manager is also the owner of the firm. Thus emphasis may be placed on good labour relations, the welfare of the workers, the desire for power, political influence, approbation or simply a 'quiet life'. To cover such objectives 'profit' would have to be interpreted in a wider sense than 'money profit'.

With major companies there is in practice a gap between the ownership and its administration. The business is run by professional managers, and is too complex for shareholders to be able to exert effective control. This applies even to the institutional shareholders who avoid being directly involved in the running of the business. Thus the motives of the full-time executive managers tend to override the shareholders' desire for maximum return on capital invested. Managers may emphasise security of their own jobs and, instead of taking the calculated risks necessary to earn maximum profits, adopt a 'play-for-safety' attitude. More likely they will be motivated by their personal desire for status.

Provided they achieve a level of profit which is satisfactory in the sense that it keeps shareholders content, their positions and salaries can be enhanced by expanding the firm to where it *maximises sales* rather than profits.

Even when there is an emphasis on money profit, a firm may stress its long-term position rather than immediate maximum profit. Security of future profits may be the dominating motive for mergers and takeovers as an alternative to developing new products and techniques. Moreover, where there is an element of monopoly a firm can follow its own pricing policy rather than having it determined by competitive market conditions (see Chapter 10). In such circumstances it may not adjust prices to short-term changes in demand and supply conditions. For one thing there are the administrative costs of printing and distributing new price lists. For another frequent changes in price tend to offend retailers and customers.

Again, a producer enjoying a degree of monopoly has always to assess what effect the pursuit of maximum profit may have on his over-all position in the long term. Will a high price attract new entrants or encourage the development of a rival product? Will it lead to adverse publicity and eventually to government intervention by a reference to the Office of Fair Trading or possibly by nationalisation?

Finally, a firm has often to modify its objectives to pressure from a government pursuing its own economic, social and political aims. Thus the firm may be expected to follow government guidelines regarding wage increases, to have regard to the environment in the disposal of its waste products, and even to retain surplus workers for a time rather than add to an already high level of unemployment.

Yet, while we must take account of these other objectives, our analysis cannot proceed far if any of them are adopted as the main motive force of the firm. In any case they merely supplement the profit objective, for profits have to be made if the firm is to survive. Thus it is useful to start with the broad assumption that firms seek to maximise profits. We can then establish principles concerning how resources should be combined and what output should be produced.

The decisions of the firm

The firm has to decide on policies to secure its profit objective. In broad terms these cover assessing demand from its potential customers and organising production accordingly. If it is seeking to maximise its profits, a firm will have to produce that output which secures the largest possible difference between total receipts and total costs. It will therefore always have an incentive to keep the cost of producing a given output to a minimum. This means that the following questions have to be answered:

(1) What to produce?

(2) What techniques shall be adopted, and what shall be the scale of its operations?

(3) How shall resources be combined?

(4) What shall be the size of output?

(5) How shall it deal with its employees?

(6) How is the necessary capital to be obtained?

(7) Where shall production be located?

We consider how the firm approaches the first problem in the remainder of this chapter; the rest are examined in Chapters 9–13.

II What to produce: marketing strategy

The firm's 'market'

So far we have used the term 'market' to denote the mechanism by which buyers and sellers contact one another to exchange goods and services. When, however, the firm refers to the 'market' for its goods it has in mind the aggregate of customers, both at home and overseas, who are possible purchasers of its products. In short the term 'market' in this context refers to 'potential demand'.

What we now have to ask is: How does the firm decide what to produce? How does it try to identify its market?

Initial guidelines

Other things being equal a firm will produce those goods which enable it to make the greatest return on capital. However, in practice this usually means that it has to choose a line of production within the limited range of its specialist knowledge. Let us assume that the firm is manufacturing light farm machines and that it is contemplating producing lawn-mowers.

Since it is likely that some firms are already producing lawn-mowers, the market economy throws up two guidelines. First, there is the current price of mowers. The firm would have to estimate its own costs for producing similar mowers, the extent to which it can cut price, and the number it could expect to sell at this price by creating new demand and cutting into the sales of existing producers. From this it can calculate its likely profit, and is thus in a position to compare the rate of return on capital with possible rates of return in other lines of production. Second, the accounts of companies have to be filed with the Registrar of Companies, while the profit earned by public companies is publicised in the financial pages of leading newspapers and specialist journals. If existing producers of lawn-mowers were shown to be earning a high rate of profit, the prospects for a new competitor would look favourable.

The broad determinants of the firm's market

When the proposed good is new or different from existing goods, less use can be made of the above indicators. The risk which the firm faces arises from the fact that it has to produce in advance for an uncertain demand (see p. 134). Thus the more precisely it can estimate the demand for its product, the more it reduces this risk.

Market research proceeds in three main stages: (1) desk research; (2) field studies; and (3) test marketing.

Desk research examines the broad determinants of the market and, by using published material or the firm's own sales records, quantifies demand as accurately as possible. For a consumer good these main determinants are:

(a) the total population;

(b) the proportion of the total population likely to be interested in the firm's product;

(c) the income level of these potential customers;

(d) the attitudes, customs or habits of people which might affect their demand for the product, e.g. preferences for houses as opposed to flats, 'keeping up with the Joneses' lawn care;

(e) government policy affecting the income of people in the group, e.g. the level of direct taxation, or indirect taxes, such as VAT, or subsidies, such as income-tax relief on house mortgages, which might directly affect the product;

(f) the production of complementary products, e.g. houses with gardens;

(g) the extent of existing or possible competition;

(h) the relative importance of packaging, delivery dates and after-sales service;

(i) the degree to which a change in price affects demand (see below under 'elasticity of demand');

(j) the possibility of overseas markets, when the same factors would have to be considered.

Government statistical sources for the above information include census returns and population projections, the *National Income and Expenditure* Blue Book, *Housing and Construction Statistics, Economic Trends, Social Trends*, the *Family Expenditure Survey*, labour statistics covering earnings and hours worked, and similar figures for relevant foreign countries including those produced by the United Nations Organisation, the European Economic Community and the Organisation for Economic Co-operation and Development.

More specialist facts can be obtained from relevant periodicals and trade journals, e.g. *Gardeners' World*, especially its circulation figures, while Royal Horticultural Society membership would indicate the number of keen gardeners likely to require a high-quality mower.

Field research. The initial field research will probably be undertaken by the firm's own salesmen and distributors. Thus a firm already manufacturing light agricultural machines may have a feedback from its salesmen, wholesalers or retailers that many people are dissatisfied with existing models and have indicated the features they are looking for (see below). Such suggestions can be cross-checked with distributors in other parts of the country.

For forecasting sales figures of a current project, the opinions of sales staff can be used as follows. Obtain from each salesman his personal forecast for the next sales period, and check whether this was within 5 per cent of his sales for the previous year. If not, ask him the reasons for the variance. If it comes within the prescribed parameter, find the weighted average percentage forecasting error of the individual over as many periods as possible, and apply this correction to his new forecast. Aggregating results for all salesmen gives the company prime forecast. This is then adjusted for: (a) factors within the company's control, e.g. contemplated marketing effort, new bonus or incentive schemes; (b) external information, e.g. NEDO or Treasury estimates, government policy changes, etc.

More precise and consumer-orientated information on potential sales can be obtained from a specific and planned *market-research programme.* Usually a specialist market-research organisation is employed. Its study would cover many aspects of market behaviour, particularly consumer reaction to the type of product, its quality, packaging, delivery dates, after-sales service and price cuts. There are three main stages:

(1) *Selecting the sample.* The sample must be representative of the whole market, selected as far as possible on a random basis in order to give all potential customers an equal chance of being included in the sample. The method chosen must avoid bias, such as would result, for example, if an opinion on lawn-mowers were sought from every tenth house in an urban area where gardens were small.

Sometimes people are scattered or rarely available when interviewers call, and the omissions which can result upset the randomness of the sample. Thus the sample can be chosen on a *quota* basis: that is, the interviewer is told to question a given number of individuals who reflect the characteristics, e.g. as regards sex, age, income and ethnic origin, and relative importance in the whole market, but it is left to him to find the actual persons who match the specification.

(2) *Obtaining information.* Various methods are available for obtaining information relevant to the purposes of the research. *Questionnaires* can be attached to products (with incentives to answer) or sent through the post. Whichever method is used care must be taken to avoid bias in the questions asked. Questionnaires are more appropriate to surveys where only common

characteristics of persons are required, for there may be a low response from certain groups. Alternatively, questions can be asked by telephone, but subscribers may resent replying to unknown callers and, in any case, the method is only suitable where being able to afford a telephone does not affect the validity of the sample.

Personal interviews are the most reliable method but tend to be expensive, time-consuming and really require standardised interviewing as regards both the personality and techniques of the interviewer.

(3) *Presenting the results.* The raw data have to be classified (often by computer), and statistical methods can be applied to draw out the significant results. The conclusions should then be presented in plain English for the attention of the firm's decision-makers, being illustrated by graphs, histograms, pie diagrams, etc., as appropriate. Any unavoidable shortcomings of the research programme ought to be included in the report.

Test marketing. Before a national or major sales campaign is undertaken some form of test marketing would probably be carried out so that modifications can be made to correct any deficiences revealed. The exercise can cover all marketing activities – the sales organisation, advertising, distribution outlets, promotional devices and after-sales service. Obviously it is important to hold the other factors constant while the one being tested for is varied.

Like the market-research programme, the test marketing must be carefully standardised as regards the area and methods chosen (e.g. for personal and income characteristics of the residents), the over-all level and types of employment, the sales organisation and effort, and the degree of competition. The test should also be spread over a period which covers changes in the weather and seasons.

Test marketing may reveal that certain features of the product are unnecessary, thus permitting greater standardisation. It may also uncover unanticipated psychological reactions. Thus one manufacturer who added scent to his carbolic soap found that sales were poor simply because in the predominantly manual-worker district being tested the men thought they might be branded as effeminate by their fellows.

The importance of the customer

Persuading people to buy the product is one of the absolute conditions for the success of the business, for receipts from sales must cover expenses. Initially inadequate sales lead to cash-flow difficulties. If continued, the business fails and shareholders lose capital invested. Thus the customers' preferences have to be considered as regards the type of product, quality, price, information by advertising and through salesmen, and convenience of purchase.

As regards the type and quality of the product market, research is an on-going process. Consumers' wants change, e.g. shortages of labour may mean that people have to do their own lawn-mowing, and so switch from roller-mowers to the quicker rotary-mower. Or, as incomes increase or customers grow older, a sit-on mower may be preferred. Thus most products have what is known as a 'product life-cycle' (see Chapter 10). It is essential, therefore, that products are restyled, modified and improved as regards materials, reliability, durability, colour, packaging, storage, etc. If some form of market research is not maintained, the changes demanded will not be revealed, and there may be a sudden collapse in sales and extreme difficulty in regaining them.

Not all the customers in the market may have identical preferences. The firm must therefore consider (a) a 'marketing mix', producing different models at different prices, and (b) varying sales' methods and channels of distribution. The 'marketing mix' may involve producing different products and for different markets, e.g. home and overseas.

Somehow the consumer has to be informed of the product. TV advertising gives the most extensive coverage, but for specialist goods, e.g. antiques, sewing machines and fishing tackle, advertising outlays might be better spent on advertising in newspapers and, particularly, in specialist journals.

Since products must be accessible to the consumer, choosing the method of distribution most convenient to him is important. Does he prefer to deal with a retailer, and even a particular form of retailer? Or would he feel happier being in direct contact with the manufacturer, either through showrooms or the post? Against this the firm has to consider the costs of different methods of distribution (see pp. 121–8).

Producer goods and the customer

Most of the above discussion has been concerned with markets for consumer goods. With producer goods there is much more direct contact between the manufacturer and the client. But, in general, the same considerations will tend to apply.

III Elasticity of demand

Measurement of elasticity of demand

Consider Figure 8.1. At price OP demand for both commodities A and B is OM. But when the price of both falls by PP_1, demand for A expands by only MM_1, whereas that for B expands by MM_2.

Responsiveness of demand to a change in price is of obvious importance to a firm which has some control over the price it charges. In economic terms it is interested in its 'elasticity of demand'.

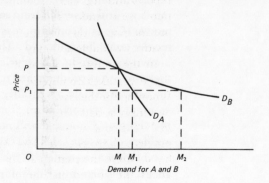

Fig. 8.1
Elasticity of demand

Elasticity of demand always refers to the elasticity at a particular price, and in what follows when we talk about 'elasticity' it will be assumed that there is some price in mind.

Elasticity of demand is defined by comparing the *rate* at which demand expands to the rate at which price falls. If the former is greater than the latter, we say that demand is *elastic*; if it is smaller, we say that demand is *inelastic*. When they are equal elasticity of demand is said to be equal to unity. Using this definition elasticity of demand can be measured in two ways. One is direct, showing the degree of elasticity; the other is indirect, merely indicating whether the demand for the good is elastic or inelastic.

(1) Elasticity of demand is the proportionate change in the amount demanded in response to a small change in price divided by the proportionate change in price. That is:

$$\text{Elasticity of demand} = \frac{\text{Proportionate change in demand}}{\text{Proportionate change in price}}$$

$$= \frac{\text{Change in quantity demanded} \,/\, \text{Original quantity demanded}}{\text{Change in price} \,/\, \text{Original price}}$$

$$= \frac{\text{New quantity} - \text{Old quantity} \,/\, \text{Old quantity}}{\text{New price} - \text{Old price} \,/\, \text{Old price}}$$

We can illustrate from Table 7.1 on p. 97. When price falls from 10p to 8p demand for eggs expands from 9000 to 15000. Elasticity of demand is thus equal to:

$$\frac{6000\!\!\Big/9000}{2\!\!\Big/10} = \frac{2\!\!\Big/3}{1\!\!\Big/5} = 3\tfrac{1}{3}$$

(2) If the proportionate expansion in demand is greater than the proportionate change in price, the total amount spent on the good will increase. In other words demand is elastic when, in response to a fall in price, total outlay increases; or, in response to a rise in price, total outlay decreases. Similarly demand is inelastic when, in response to a fall in price, total outlay decreases; or, in response to a rise in price, total outlay increases. Demand is equal to unity when, as price changes, total outlay remains the same. Thus, using the same demand schedule, we have:

Price of eggs (pence)	Demand (thousands)	Total outlay (pence)	
10	9	90000	Elastic demand
8	15	120000	
6	20	120000	Inelastic demand
4	25	100000	

Between 8p and 6p, elasticity of demand equals unity.

Factors determining elasticity of demand

1 The availability of substitutes at the ruling market price As a good falls in price, so it becomes cheaper relative to other goods. People are induced to buy more of it to replace goods which are now relatively dearer. How far they can carry out this replacement will depend upon the extent to which the good in question is, in their own minds, a substitute for the other goods. Goods within a particular class are easily substituted for one another. Beef is a substitute for mutton. Thus if the price of beef falls, people will buy more beef and less mutton. Between one class and another, however, substitution is more difficult. If the price of meat in general falls, there will be a slight tendency to buy more meat and less fish, but this tendency will be very limited because meat is not nearly so perfect a substitute for fish as beef is for mutton.

The success of supermarkets has been based on the high elasticity of demand for their products, people switching to them when prices of processed goods are cut, for they can recognise packages and tins as being almost perfect substitutes for those being sold for higher prices in other shops.

2 The proportion of income spent on a good   When only a very small proportion of a person's income is spent on a good, as (for example) with pepper, salt, shoe polish, newspaper and toothpaste, no great effort is made to look for substitutes when its price rises. Demand for such goods is therefore, relatively inelastic.

On the other hand when the expenditure on a good is fairly large (as, for example, with most groceries) a rise in price would provide considerable incentive to find substitutes.

3 The period of time   Since it takes time to find substitutes or to change spending habits, elasticity may be greater, the longer the period of time under review. In practice many firms try to overcome the ignorance or conservatism of consumers by advertising, giving free samples, or making special offers.

4 The possibility of new purchasers   In discussing the possibility of substitution above we have looked at elasticity of demand solely from the point of view of the individual consumer. But when we are considering market demand we must allow for the fact that, as price falls, new consumers will be induced to buy the good. In fact with many goods, such as cars, TV sets, washing machines, etc., of which people require *only one*, it is the fall in price bringing the good within the reach of new consumers which leads to the increase in demand. Hence a fall in price which induces people in a numerous income group to buy will produce a high elasticity of demand, whereas a fall in price which affects only the higher and smaller income groups will not produce many new customers and hence the market demand schedule tends to be inelastic in this price range.

Uses of the concept of elasticity of demand

The concept of the elasticity of demand figures prominently in the economist's analysis and in the practical decisions of the businessman and government.

Thus a trade union will find it more difficult to obtain a wage increase for its members without creating unemployment where the elasticity of demand for the product they help make is high (see p. 191).

British Rail, too, have to consider elasticity of demand when fixing fares. Should they, for example, raise fares in order to reduce losses? If, at existing fares, the demand is relatively elastic, then a fare increase would mean that total revenue would fall. Losses would only be reduced if operating costs (through carrying fewer passengers) fell more than revenue.

Finally, the Chancellor of the Exchequer must take account of elasticity of demand when imposing a selective tax on a particular good. The demand may be so elastic that the increase in price might cause such a falling-off in sales that the total tax recouped was less than originally received.

Income-elasticity of demand

An increase in real income usually increases the demand for goods, but this occurs to a varying degree. Thus it is possible to speak of *income-elasticity of demand* – the proportionate change in demand divided by the proportionate change in real income which has brought it about. If demand increases by 20 per cent, for instance, as a result of a 10 per cent increase in real income, the income-elasticity of demand equals 2. Which goods have a high income-elasticity of demand depends upon current living standards. In Western Europe today it is demand for such goods as cars, washing-machines, dish-washers, central-heating appliances, new houses and personal services which expands most as income increases. In contrast necessaries, such as potatoes, salt, eggs and soap, have a low income-elasticity of demand.

IV The distribution of goods to the consumer

The scope of production

A manufacturer has to decide how to get his finished goods to the consumer. He may undertake the task himself. But if he does so, he must employ salesmen, run delivery transport, carry stocks, advertise his product, organise exports, advise customers, establish servicing centres and give credit. Experts for these highly specialised functions can only be employed if output is large enough. Moreover, the manufacturer's main ability lies in organising production rather than selling.

Fig. 8.2
The role of the wholesaler and retailer in the 'production' of chocolate

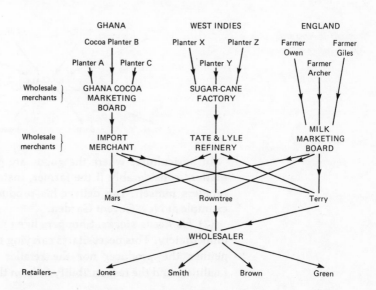

Thus the principle of the division of labour is usually applied. Just as the manufacturer buys raw materials and components from other producers, so specialist firms get his goods to the consumer – there is *forward* vertical disintegration (see p. 135). We will simplify this selling process by grouping such firms into 'wholesalers' and 'retailers'. Figure 8.2 shows how they fit into the various stages in the production of chocolate.

The wholesaler

The wholesaler buys goods in bulk from producers and sells them in small quantities to retailers. In doing so he helps the production process.

(1) *He economises in distribution.* Because shops usually stock a variety of goods they can order supplies only in small quantities. Thus it is not economical for each producer to sell directly to them, for this would mean employing many salesmen, packing separate parcels and making deliveries to each shop in turn. Thus in Figure 8.3(a) sixteen contacts and deliveries are necessary if four chocolate firms supply directly four retailers, whereas in Figure 8.3(b) each producer deals only with a wholesaler, reducing the total journeys to eight.

Fig. 8.3
Economising in distribution through the wholesaler

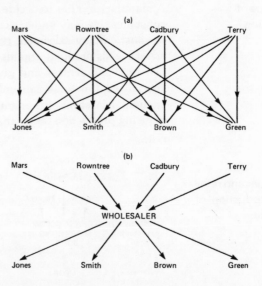

In agriculture, where the goods are perishable, it simplifies matters considerably if the farmer, instead of trying to contact retailers himself, can deliver his produce to a wholesaler, for example at New Covent Garden.

(2) *He keeps stocks.* Shoppers like to be able to obtain goods immediately. This necessitates carrying stocks. Often, however, neither the producer nor the retailer has extensive storage facilities, and the responsibility falls on the wholesaler.

Moreover, he bears other costs of storage. By buying and holding stocks he relieves manufacturers and retailers of the risk of a fall in demand, e.g. through fashion changes.

The holding of stocks is in itself a valuable economic function, evening out price fluctuations resulting from temporary changes in demand and supply (see p. 95).

(3) *He arranges imports from abroad.* Foreign manufacturers can rarely be bothered to ship small parcels to individual retailers abroad or to undertake the foreign currency transactions involved. They prefer to deal with a wholesaler, an import merchant with established trade connections.

(4) *He carries out certain specialised functions.* Not only does the wholesaler advertise goods but, in order to make selling easier, he may process goods – pasteurising milk, cooking beetroot, blending tea, refining sugar and grading commodities such as wheat and cotton.

(5) *He is a channel for information and advice.* Suggestions which customers make to the retailer are passed on to the wholesaler, who, if he sees that they reflect the general view, conveys them to the manufacturer. Thus the latter can improve his product and anticipate fashion changes.

(6) *He assists in the day-to-day maintenance of the good.* With many products, particularly vehicles and machinery, the wholesaler relieves the manufacturer of the task of providing an efficient maintenance, repairs and spare-part service.

The retailer

The retailer performs the last stage of the productive process, for it is he who puts the goods in the hands of the actual consumer. His work is 'to have the right goods in the right place at the right time'.

(1) *He stocks small quantities of a variety of goods.* What is the 'right good' depends on the customer, for different people have different tastes. It is therefore necessary to stock a variety of different goods so that customers can choose and take delivery there and then. Thus the retail shop is basically a showroom, particularly where goods are bought infrequently.

The size of the stocks carried will depend on many factors: the popularity of the product, the possibility of obtaining further supplies quickly, the perishability of the good or the likelihood of its going out of fashion, the season, the possibility of future price changes and, above all, the cost of carrying stocks, chiefly bank interest charges.

(2) *He takes the goods to where it is most convenient for the customer.* Taking the goods to the customer usually means that the retailer sets up his shop within easy reach, e.g. in the town centre. However, with goods in everyday use, such as groceries, small shops are often dotted around residential districts. Where

customers are very dispersed the retailer may be a 'travelling shop'.

While customers take most goods away with them, the retailer arranges delivery if transport is essential, e.g. furniture, or if the customer likes the extra convenience of delivery, e.g. morning milk and newspaper.

(3) *He performs special services for customers.* In the course of his main business the retailer performs many services which help to build up customer goodwill. Where the good is not in stock he will order it and, in other matters where contact with the manufacturer is necessary, he often acts for the customer, e.g. returning the good for repair.

With many goods, too, such as fishing tackle, photographic equipment, musical instruments and machinery, he can often provide special advice.

Finally, goods may be sent on approval or credit facilities arranged through hire purchase, special credit accounts, etc.

(4) *He advises the wholesaler and manufacturer of customers' preferences.*

Types of retail outlet   Retailing might be widely defined to include all shops, mail-order firms, garages, launderettes, betting shops or indeed any business selling products or services to the consumer. However, it is usual to confine retailing to shops and mail-order outlets. These can be classified as follows (see also Figure 8.4).

Fig. 8.4
Retail sales, Great
Britain, 1971 (% of total
value)

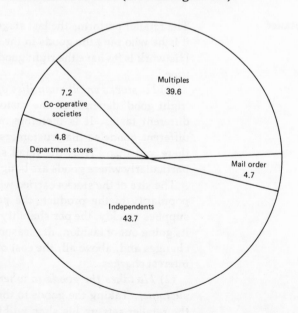

Multiples
39.6

7.2
Co-operative
societies

4.8
Department stores

Mail order
4.7

Independents
43.7

1 Independents These are mainly small shops with no branches, and they account for nearly 50 per cent of total shop sales. Yet, in spite of their advantages of individual attention to customers, handy locations for quick shopping trips, and the willingness of owners to accept a lower return to be their own boss, these independents are steadily losing ground to the larger stores.

A major bid to avert the decline has come through the voluntary chains, such as Spar, Mace and Wavy Line, of which over a third of independents are members. While retaining their independence, members buy in bulk from the wholesaler and use common advertising and display techniques.

2 Multiples   These can be defined arbitrarily as organisations of ten or more shops. Some, such as Mothercare and Dixon's Photographic, sell a particular type of good. Others, such as Woolworth, Boots, and Marks & Spencer have a fairly extensive range of products. Together multiples account for about 40 per cent of all retail sales. Their chief advantages are: economies of bulk-buying and centralised control, the elimination of the wholesaler, quick recognition through standardised shop fronts and a reputation established through brand names.

3 Supermarkets   These may be defined as self-service shops with a minimum selling area of 2000 sq. ft. While in their organisation they would count as multiples, their share of the food trade warrants separate attention. In 1977 they accounted for half the grocery trade and nearly a third of total food sales.

The field is led by the four retail grocery chains: Tesco, Sainsbury, Allied Suppliers and Fine Fare. They thus enjoy economies of scale, low labour costs, an attractive display of merchandise, bulk-buying and selling under their own labels (e.g. Sainsbury's cornflakes and Tesco coffee). As a result they have gained ground rapidly through highly competitive prices. Indeed many have extended their activities to self-service selling of goods showing higher profit margins, e.g. clothing and hardware.

4 Hypermarkets   Urban congestion, inadequate parking space and rising rents have made High Street sites increasingly expensive. The American and, to an increasing extent, the European answer to these problems has been the large (over 40,000 sq. ft) 'out-of-town' shopping or hypermarket to cater for the car-borne weekly shopper.

However, in the UK this development has been slow, largely because planning consents have not been readily given since out-of-town shopping may have an environmental cost in 'downtown' decay or intrusion on the countryside.

5 Department stores Competition from multiples has forced department stores to vary their traditional pattern of separate departments under the control of a responsible buyer (often described as 'many stores under one roof') in favour of bulk-buying by central office. This, together with extended credit facilities, has allowed them to retain nearly 5 per cent of the market.

The main groups are Debenhams, the House of Fraser, the John Lewis Partnership, Great Universal Stores and United Drapery Stores.

6 Co-operatives (see pp. 10–11).

7 Mail order During the 1960s mail-order business secured an increasing share of retail sales. Since then, however, much higher postal charges have reduced the rate of expansion. In 1977 mail-order business accounted for nearly 5 per cent of the retail market.

The five major companies – Great Universal Stores, Littlewoods Mail Order, Grattan Warehouses, Freemans, and Empire Stores – sell by agency and illustrated catalogues, purchases usually being arranged through weekly interest-free payments. Over one-half of all sales are accounted for by women's clothing and household goods.

Factors determining the retail outlet

The trend away from the small, independent shop towards the larger organisation, notably the multiples and supermarket chains, reflects a greater emphasis on competition through price rather than by better service. The larger firms are in a strong position to cut prices. Not only do they obtain the advantages of bulk purchase but they may induce manufacturers to supply goods under the retailer's own brand label at a price below that of the national brand. Moreover, large retailers catering for a whole range of shopping, e.g. food, can attract customers into their stores by 'loss-leaders'.

Economic factors helping this trend are:

(1) *Increased income*, which has led to a swing in expenditure towards the more expensive processed foods and consumer-durable goods.

(2) *An increase in car ownership*, which has enabled people to move from the city centre to the outer suburbs. Shops have followed, not only to be near their customers, but also to obtain larger sites with parking facilities, lower rents and less congestion. The car has also made customers more mobile, enabling them to travel to good shopping centres where they can purchase all their requirements at a single stop.

(3) *An increase in married women going to work*, which has

promoted the demand for convenience foods and labour-saving devices. It has also led to a reduction in the number of shopping expeditions, a trend helped by the wider ownership of refrigerators and freezers.

These factors are likely to remain important in the future. It seems probable, therefore, that new supermarkets will take the form of discount stores or hypermarkets selling a wider range of products, the profit margins of which are larger than those on groceries. Moreover, the more favourable response to planning applications is enabling new stores to be developed outside towns, while cash-and-carry warehouses are now available to consumers who can buy in quantity.

Such changes are likely to be at the expense of the medium-sized business, for the smaller local retailers can offer 'convenience' services.

The future of the middleman

Wholesalers and dealers who come between the manufacturer and the retailer or consumer are often referred to as 'middlemen'. They are frequently criticised on the grounds that they take too large a share of the selling price. It is argued that if the manufacturer sold direct to consumers, prices could be reduced.

But, as we have seen, wholesalers relieve producers of performing essential functions, allowing them to obtain the advantages of specialisation in marketing products. Such forward vertical dis-integration is the cheapest way of getting goods to the consumer.

However, this does not mean that all criticism of middlemen is unjustified. Sometimes their profit margins may be too high. This may occur through the perpetuation of antiquated methods or by a single middleman playing off one small producer, such as a farmer, against another (hence the formation of producers' co-operatives).

In recent years a tendency for the wholesaler to be eliminated has been due to: (i) the growth of large shops which can order in bulk; (ii) the development of road transport, which reduces the necessity of holding large stocks; (iii) the desire of manufacturers to retain some control over retailing outlets in order to ensure that their products are pushed or a high standard of service is maintained; and (iv) the practice of branding many products, which eliminates many specialised functions. In other cases, however, the elimination of the wholesaler has been confined to those goods which are of high value, such as furniture and TV sets, to circumstances where the producer and retailer are close together (as with the market gardener who supplies the local shop), and cases where the manufacturer does his own retailing.

To some extent the wholesaler has responded to this challenge by developing in two main directions: (a) the cash-and-carry warehouse, sometimes called 'the retailers' supermarket'; and

(b) becoming the organiser of a voluntary chain of retailers, who are supplied, and to some extent controlled, by him.

Selling direct to consumers by the manufacturer occurs chiefly where: (a) he wishes to push his product (e.g. beer and footwear) or to ensure a standard of advice and service (e.g. sewing machines); (b) the personal-service element is important (e.g. made-to-measure clothing); (c) he is a small-scale producer/retailer, often selling a perishable good (e.g. cakes and pastries) or serving a local area (e.g. printing); (d) so wide a range of goods is produced that a whole chain of shops can be fully stocked (e.g. Maynard sweets, Manfield shoes); (e) the good is highly technical or made to individual specification (e.g. machinery).

V Consumer protection

Protection of consumers takes three main forms: criminal sanctions, civil remedies and administrative safeguards.

Criminal sanctions

Largely to discourage cheating in the sale of goods, Parliament has passed a variety of Acts imposing penalties.

Thus under the *Food and Drugs Act, 1955*, it is an offence to sell unsound food or to use a label which falsely describes the quality or nutritional value. Similarly the *Weights and Measures Act, 1963*, deals with short weight or measure, and requires many prepacked goods to be marked with their quantity. Both Acts are enforced through the inspectors of local authorities.

The *Mock Auctions Act, 1961*, forbids 'mock auctions' in a variety of specified goods, e.g. china, glass, books, jewellery and articles of household use. A mock auction occurs where: (a) goods are sold to a bidder at less than his highest bid; or (b) the right to bid is restricted to previous purchasers; or (c) if any articles are given away.

The *Trade Descriptions Act, 1968*, prohibits the use of false or misleading trade descriptions about goods or known false statements about services, accommodation or facilities. For instance, where a good is described as 'non-shrinkable' or 'waterproof' it must be exactly so; while if a hotel is described as 'only one mile from the beach' this must be literally true. Some kinds of false price 'mark downs' are also an offence; any indicated higher price must have been charged for twenty-eight days continuously in the preceeding six months, unless expressly stated otherwise. The *1972 Trade Descriptions Act* also provides that imported goods must not have a name or mark which could imply a UK origin. These Acts were designed chiefly to protect retail consumers but they also cover transactions between businesses. Again it is the local authority which prosecutes and, apart from other penalties, damages can be awarded to the complainant.

Civil remedies   A contract for the sale of goods requires no special formality to be enforceable. It may be in writing or by word of mouth or be implied by the conduct of the parties. The bulk of the law relating to such contracts is contained in the *Sale of Goods Act, 1893* (as amended by the *Supply of Goods (Implied Terms) Act, 1973*), and the *Unfair Contract Terms Act, 1977*.

Where there is a sale of goods by description or one based on the examination of a sample, there is an implied condition that the goods shall correspond with that description or sample. Furthermore, if the dealer is selling in the course of business (as opposed to a private seller), there are also implied conditions that: (a) the goods are of merchantable quality unless the buyer's attention is drawn to any defect or the buyer examines the goods and ought to have seen defects; and (b) the goods are reasonably fit for the purpose for which they are required. The latter, for instance, would cover the sale of a second-hand car by a dealer or where the buyer relied on the seller's expertise for advice.

The above conditions and warranties can be excluded where reasonable. The *Unfair Contract Terms Act, 1977*, covers what is 'reasonable'; for example, where there have been regular dealings between the buyer and seller, a wide choice of suppliers, customs of the trade, buyer and seller having equal bargaining power, special orders or obvious bargain prices are all factors to be taken into account.

The *Resale Prices Act, 1964*, made minimum resale price maintenance illegal, except for goods approved by the Restrictive Practices Court. To be approved the resulting benefits to consumers must outweigh any detriments, an example of this being book sales.

Legislation also deals with credit and hire-purchase agreements. The *Hire Purchase Act, 1964*, as strengthened by the *Consumer Credit Act, 1974*, covers transactions of under £2000. The agreement has to be in writing with a special signature box printed in red warning the purchaser not to sign unless prepared to be bound by law. Where payments cannot be maintained after one-third of the total price has been paid, the goods can only be reclaimed on a court order.

The *Unsolicited Goods and Services Act, 1971*, provides that an unsolicited good may be treated as an unconditional gift if the sender fails to collect it within six months, or within thirty days if the recipient has given written notice to the sender. This protects people from having unsolicited goods sent through the post and thereafter being pressed for payment by threats of legal action.

Administrative safeguards

The *Fair Trading Act, 1973,* set up a Director General of Fair Trading, whose functions includes consumer protection as well as investigation of restrictive practices. His *Office of Fair Trading* has a Consumer Affairs Division, concerned with matters directly affecting consumers. While the Director may prosecute for persistent offences, usually adverse publicity acts as a deterrent to traders. The Division investigates trading activities affecting consumers, e.g. methods of selling and guarantees, and has negotiated *codes of practice* with trade associations.

As already shown, *Weights and Measures Inspectors* and *Health Inspectors* of local authorities have administrative functions, backed by criminal proceedings, with regard to consumer protection.

Furthermore, the *Consumers' Association*, a private body which publishes *Which?*, examines and reports on a variety of goods to subscribers, copies being available in most public libraries.

9 How to Produce: General Principles

In organising resources to produce for the wants of consumers the firm will have to pay attention to the advantages of specialisation, the economies of producing on a large scale, its own internal organisation, and combining resources in order to obtain as much output as possible from its limited means.

I The division of labour

Advantages of specialisation

Specialisation is the fundamental principle upon which modern production is organised. Here we examine it with particular reference to labour, though, as we shall see, it is equally applicable to machines, the distribution of goods to the consumer, localities and even countries.

Where workers are organised so that each specialises on a particular task, increased production results. This is because:

(1) *Each man is employed in the job in which his superiority is most marked.* Suppose that, in one day, Smith can plane the parts for twenty tables *or* cut the joints for ten, whereas Brown can either plane ten tables *or* cut the joints for twenty. If each do both jobs and spend the same amount of time on them, their combined production in a day will be fifteen tables planed *and* fifteen table joints cut. But Smith is better at planing, while Brown is better at cutting joints. If they specialise on what they can do best, their combined production will be twenty tables planed *and* twenty table joints cut – an increase in output of a third. Even if initially workers were equally proficient at the different jobs, it might still pay to specialise.

(2) *Practice makes perfect, and so particular skills are developed through repetition of the same job.*

(3) *Economy in tools allows specialised machinery to be used.* This is illustrated in Figure 9.1, where in part (b) division of labour has been introduced. Not only are specialised tools in

constant use but their output is much greater. Thus division of labour sets free talented men for research – and allows their inventions to be used profitably.

(4) *Time is saved through not having to switch from one operation to another.*

(5) *Less time is taken in learning a particular job.*

(6) *The employer can estimate his costs of production and output more accurately.*

**Fig. 9.1
Economy in tools
through specialisation**

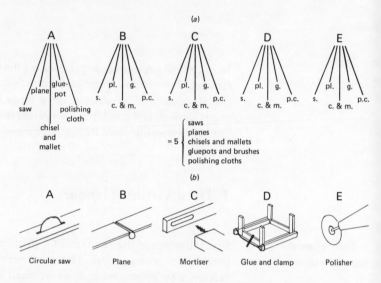

(a)

A   B   C   D   E

= 5 {
saws
planes
chisels and mallets
gluepots and brushes
polishing cloths

(b)

A   B   C   D   E

Circular saw   Plane   Mortiser   Glue and clamp   Polisher

Disadvantages of the division of labour

While the division of labour leads to lower costs of production, it may have disadvantages both to the worker and to society. The worker may find his job monotonous, while with some occupations such as paint-spraying there is a risk of occupational disease. Moreover, the skilled specialist may face redundancy if demand falls, while a strike by a few key workers can lead to widespread unemployment. Finally, standardised products tend to replace individual craft work.

Limitations to the division of labour

Naturally the scope for the division of labour varies from one industry to another. Countries like Switzerland having too few workers to permit a high degree of specialisation concentrate on manufacturing a narrow range of products. Again, in industries such as agriculture and building where the same operations are not taking place each day many 'Jacks of all trades' are required. Moreover, an exchange system is essential: we must first unite in exchange before we can divide in production. Finally, the division of labour has to be related to current demand for the product. It is no use specialising in making something which nobody wants, while minute division of labour requires a large demand. The complex organisation of car production, for instance, is possible because there is a mass demand for a standardised product made up from a multitude of small parts.

II The advantages of large-scale production

As a firm's output increases, costs per unit may fall as a result of the advantages of large-scale production. These are often referred to as 'internal economies' to distinguish them from 'external economies' which arise indirectly from the growth of the *industry* (see p. 135).

Internal economies

Internal economies are of five main kinds:

1 Technical economies   In making a good, as distinct from its distribution, increased output permits more division of labour, greater specialisation of machines, the economy of large machines (e.g. a double-decker bus can carry twice as many passengers as a single-decker, though neither the initial cost nor the running costs are doubled) and the linking of processes (e.g. in steel-making, where reheating is avoided).

Generally technical economies fix the size of the unit actually producing, e.g. a supermarket, rather than the size of firm, which may consist of many units, e.g. Tesco. Where technical economies are great, the size of the typical unit will tend to be large as, for example, in the production of cars, sheet steel, gas and electricity. Where, however, increased output merely means duplicating and reduplicating machines, the tendency will be for the unit to remain small. For instance, in farming at least one combine harvester is necessary for about 400 acres. Thus farms tend to remain small, for as yet there are no great technical economies to be derived from large machines. Where few technical economies can be gained and yet the firm is large, consisting, as with chain stores, of many operating units, it is usually because other types of economy are possible.

2 Managerial economies   When output increases division of labour can be applied to management. For example, in a shop owned and run by one man the owner, although having the ability to order supplies, keep his books and sell the goods, has yet to do such trivial jobs as sweeping the floor, weighing articles and packing parcels, tasks within the capability of a boy who has just left school. His sales, however, may not warrant employing a boy. The large business overcomes this difficulty: a brilliant organiser can devote all his time to organising, the routine jobs being left to other workers.

The function of management can itself be divided, e.g. into production, sales, transport, personnel (see later). These departments may be further subdivided – sales, for instance, can be split into sections for advertising, exports and customers' welfare.

3 Commercial economies   If a bulk order can be placed for materials and components, the supplier will usually quote a lower price per unit since this enables him also to gain the advantages of large-scale production.

Economies can also be achieved in selling the product. If the sales staff are not being worked to capacity, the additional output can be sold at little extra cost. Moreover, the large firm often manufactures many products and then one acts as an advertisement for the others. Thus Hoover vacuum-cleaners advertise their washing-machines, dish-washers and steam-irons. In addition a large firm may be able to sell its by-products, something which might be unprofitable for a small firm.

Finally, when the business is sufficiently large, the division of labour can be introduced on the commercial side, with expert buyers and sellers being employed.

The above commercial economies represent real gains to the community, lowering prices through better use of resources. On the other hand, where a large firm uses its muscle to *force* suppliers into granting it favourable prices, it will simply result in higher prices to other buyers.

4 Financial economies   In raising finance for expansion the large firm is in a favourable position. It can, for instance, offer better security to bankers and, because it is well known, raise money at lower cost since investors have confidence in it and prefer shares which can readily be sold on the Stock Exchange.

5 Risk-bearing economies   Here we can distinguish three sorts of risk. First, there are risks which can be insured against, enabling large and small firms alike to spread risks. Second, certain businesses usually bear some risk themselves, saving some of the profits made by the insurance company. Here the large firm has a definite advantage. London Transport, for instance, can cover its own risks, while a large bank can call in funds from other branches when there is a run on the reserves in a particular locality. The third kind of risk is one that cannot be reduced to a mathematical probability and thus cannot be insured against – risk arising from changes in demand for the product or in the supply of raw materials, usually referred to as risks arising from 'uncertainty'. To meet changes in demand the large firm can diversify output (e.g. the Imperial Tobacco Company) or develop export markets. On the supply side materials may be obtained from different sources to guard against crop failures, strikes, etc.

External economies

While the firm can plan its internal economies, it can only *hope* to benefit from external economies which arise as the *industry* grows.

First, the concentration of similar firms in an area may produce mutual benefits: a skilled labour force; common services, such as marketing organisations; better roads and social amenities; technical schools catering for the local industry; product reputation; ancillary firms supplying specialised machinery, collecting by-products, etc. The firm must take into account such economies when deciding where production shall take place, for the lower costs may outweigh any diseconomies which arise through traffic congestion, smoke, etc. (see p. 198).

Second, external economies can take the form of common information services provided either by associations of firms or even by the government.

Finally, as an industry grows in size, specialist firms may be established to provide components for all producers. Since such firms can work on a large scale these components are supplied more cheaply than if the original producer had to manufacture his own.

III The size of firms

Horizontal and vertical combination

The advantages of large-scale production provide firms with a strong impetus to combine.

Horizontal integration occurs where firms producing the same type of product combine. Thus British Motor Holdings merged with Leyland Motors to form British Leyland.

Vertical integration is the amalgamation of firms engaged in the different stages of production of a good. Thus British Motor Holdings took over Fisher & Ludlow, a producer of car bodies. Vertical integration may be 'backward' towards the raw material, or 'forward' towards the finished product (see Figure 9.2).

Both the above can lead to lower costs per unit, and therefore to increased profits. Thus horizontal integration can allow greater specialisation, commercial economies and a saving on administrative overheads. Vertical integration facilitates linked processes and reduces risk by more direct control over the supply and quality of raw materials and components. Moreover, all parts can be manufactured to an integrated design, e.g. cars, and there is direct control over the distribution of the final product (see Chapter 8).

Lateral integration occurs where a firm increases the range of its products. Concentration on one product may expose a firm to a

Fig. 9.2
Horizontal and vertical
integration

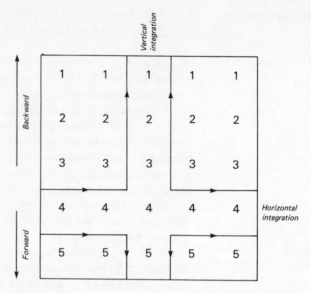

change of fashion, a switch in government policy or a recession.
Thus the firm diversifies, often in completely different products.
Imperial Tobacco, for instance, includes among its interests
Golden Wonder crisps, while P & O is engaged in road transport
and construction through its subsidiary companies.

Apart from increasing profits through economies of scale,
integration can achieve other objectives, such as security of
profits and prestige. One other aim, however, must not be
overlooked – monopoly power. This is discussed in Chapter 10.

Integration may result from internal development or by combination with existing firms. Combination may be secured by a
complete takeover, when a company buys all the shares of a
smaller firm and absorbs it completely, or by the formation of a
holding company in which the parent company owns sufficient
shares of a subsidiary company to give it effective control, though
the smaller company preserves its identity and enjoys considerable independence of action. Many large companies, e.g. Unilever, GEC and Great Universal Stores, hold such controlling
interests in subsidiary companies.

**The predominance of
the small firm**

In spite of the advantages enjoyed by the large firm we must not
conclude that every firm must be large to be competitive. Indeed
the small firm still predominates in all forms of production. In
agriculture two-thirds of all holdings are less than fifty acres in
size, while in retailing nearly three-quarters of all firms consist of
only one shop. Even more remarkable it is true of manufacturing,
where it would seem that technical economies of scale would be
all-important. Table 9.1, which shows the size of the establishment – the factory or workshop – in manufacturing, reveals two

important features: (a) the small establishment is typical of manufacturing in the UK, over four-fifths employing less than 100 persons; and (b) these small units employ only one-fifth of the labour force.

Table 9.1 *Size of manufacturing establishments in the UK, 1973*

Employees	Number of firms	Percentage of total firms	Number of employees (000's)	Percentage of total employed
1–10	50,000 (est.)	45	250 (est.)	3
11–99	45,888	42	1,487	20
100–999	12,740	12	3,487	46
Over 1,000	1,113	1	2,402	31
Total	109,741	100	7,626	100

Any explanation of this predominance of the small firm has to deal with two salient facts: (i) small firms are especially important in certain industries, such as agriculture, retailing, building and personal and professional services; and (ii) variations in the size of firms exist even within the same industry. Both result from the nature of the conditions of demand or supply.

Demand   Large-scale production may be only *technically* efficient; it is not *economically* efficient unless a large and regular demand justifies it.

The market may be small because demand is local (e.g. personal services and the village store), or limited to a few articles of one pattern (e.g. highly specialised and individually designed machine-tools) or because transport costs are high (e.g. perishable market-garden produce and bricks), or product differentiation divides it artificially (see Chapter 10).

Where demand fluctuates (e.g. in construction) the overhead cost of idle specialised equipment is heavy, but the smaller the firm, the less the burden.

Supply   Even if demand is large, factors on the supply side may make for small firms. While in certain industries, e.g. retailing and building, it is possible to start with only a small amount of capital, the difficulty of obtaining further funds and the taxation of profits are obstacles to expansion. Furthermore, government monopoly policy may prevent mergers (see Chapter 10). Alternatively, where vertical disintegration is possible, firms need not expand internally but simply employ specialist firms for advertising, research, supplying components and selling by-products.

Important, too, is the fact that many small owners have not got the drive to expand or the ability to manage a large concern. Or, as in farming and retailing, they will work long hours (that is, accept a lower rate of profit) simply to be their own boss.

Above all, as the size of the firm increases, management difficulties occur. If management is vested in heads of department, problems of co-ordination arise and rivalries develop. This means that one person must be in over-all command – yet such persons are in very limited supply. In certain industries these difficulties may soon occur. Rapid decisions are required where demand changes quickly (e.g. in the fashion trades) or supply conditions alter (e.g. through the weather in agriculture). Or care may have to be given to the personal requirements of customers (e.g. in retailing and services). This may require the close super-vision of management, and thus the firm has to be small (see Figure 9.3).

Fig. 9.3
Factors influencing the size of the firm

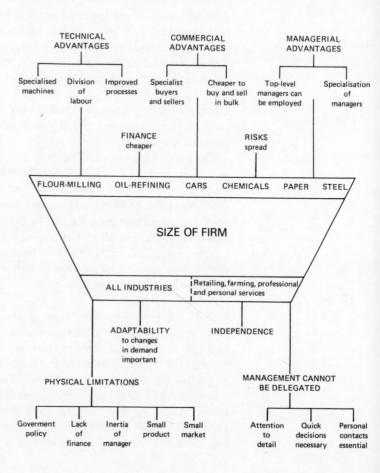

IV The functional organisation of the firm

**The basic
requirements**

All firms have to recognise consumers' demand, organise resources to produce for that demand and sell what is produced.
With small firms, e.g. a farmer, builder or shop-keeper, the
owner makes the appropriate decisions and carries out these
broad functions.

However, as the firm grows in size, it is possible to obtain the
advantages of the division of labour and the economies of large-
scale production in management. On the other hand this necessitates a more formal organisation providing a recognised chain of
authority, a breakdown of the firm's activities into separate
functions under different departments, and a means of co-
ordinating the decisions and work of these individual departments. Naturally each company will have its own particular
organisation depending on its size and the nature of its operations, but a typical arrangement for a company of medium size or
above is shown in Figure 9.4.

Fig. 9.4
The functional
organisation of a
company

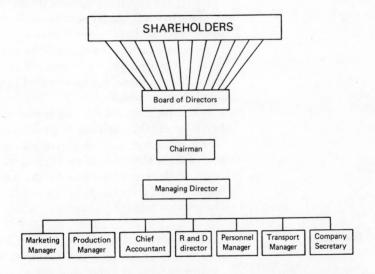

The Board of Directors

A company is owned by the shareholders, who elect a Board of
Directors at a general meeting. Some directors may only function
on a part-time basis, giving advice at meetings of the Board and at
other times if required according to their special interests and
qualifications. But to ensure that the Board has first-hand knowledge of the company's operations when reaching its decisions,
there must be executive directors, usually the managing director
and the managers of the most important departments.

The Board is responsible for the general policy of the company,
formulating precise plans to achieve its objectives but taking into

account its legal obligations under the Companies Acts and other legislation, e.g. the Health and Safety at Work Act, 1974. It has to harmonise the work of the functional departments, review progress, ensure adequate finance for proposed operations and plan the future development of the company, e.g. regarding expansion or amalgamation with other firms. To a large extent the company's success and the morale of its workers is dependent upon the leadership shown by the Board of Directors.

The Board chooses a *Chairman*. He may simply chair meetings of the Board and deliver the annual report, in which case a separate managing director will be appointed. Or he may be an executive Chairman, spending the whole of his working time on the affairs of the company and thus fulfilling the role of a managing director.

The *managing director* sees that the decisions of the Board of Directors are carried out, is responsible for the day-to-day running of the business and initiates proposals to be considered by the Board. Moreover, he plays a key role in co-ordinating the work and views of the departmental managers.

Under the managing director there is a horizontal organisation of departmental heads, with these further subdivided vertically under section heads (see Figure 9.4). If there are subsidiary companies, each company may be similarly divided, but with certain departments, e.g. insurance and finance, servicing all of them. Multinational companies are likely to have an organisation divided geographically.

It will be observed that departments are organised on a functional basis, thus helping large-scale economies to be obtained while achieving administrative efficiency. But, as explained below, if the objectives of the organisation are to be achieved, the work of departments must be dovetailed. This will probably require regular meetings of the heads of department under the chairmanship of the managing director.

Marketing

The task of the marketing department is to sell the products of the firm. This, as we saw in Chapter 8, means concentrating on consumer demand, producing what appeals to consumers rather than mere selling of goods produced. In short the firm must be market-orientated rather than production-orientated. This means that the marketing department must have a major influence on the form which products take as regards type, price, quality, size, packaging, presentation, delivery dates, and after-sales and complaints service. It therefore has to work closely with other departments, particularly with the production department and the costing section of the finance department.

The first task of the marketing department will be to research markets thoroughly before full production is undertaken (see

Chapter 8). Subsequently the marketing department must watch for changes in demand and, through contact with the research and development department, anticipate such changes so that the necessary modifications can be put in hand by the production department. Not only does this involve intimate knowledge of the specialist markets for the firm's products and continuous monitoring of competitors' policies, but also some assessment has to be made of likely future changes in the level of economic activity both in the UK and also in those countries to which the firm exports.

Once the nature of the product has been determined the marketing department will have to consider the form and timing of advertising, the sales organisation, the channels of distribution and, unless there is a separate transport department, the method of transport.

The effectiveness of different methods of advertising varies with the type of product. Thus a special cash-and-carry offer would be advertised in local newspapers or on local radio, whereas a national product, such as cornflakes, will be covered by the national press, TV, etc. Goods having a high income-elasticity of demand figure prominently in the Sunday newspaper supplements and the more exclusive journals. An estimate would also have to be made of the value of exhibiting at trade fairs, both as regards direct sales and indirectly through 'showing the flag' and fostering good public relations.

Export markets present their own particular problems. Often a start in developing export business is made by choosing the market which seems to have the best potential, using the experience gained there to extend activities later. Initially it is likely that export agencies will be used, and, in order to guard against non-payment, insurance can usually be arranged through the Export Credits Guarantee Department (ECGD) of the Department of Trade.

Attention must be paid to the efficiency of the selling process, for example by comparing calls with orders received and assessing the effectiveness of incentive schemes on the success achieved by salesmen. Distribution may be through a wholesaler and retailer (see Chapter 8), but even so the form of transport will vary with the product (oil, for instance, relying considerably upon pipeline). Moreover, it may be necessary for the firm to have strategically placed warehouses and depots. As the firm grows in size the marketing department may recommend the establishment of its own distribution organisation which eliminates the wholesaler and, in some cases, even the retailer.

Production
Forecasts of expected sales provide the production department with output targets regarding quantity, quality and delivery

dates. Failure to meet these targets can result in lost orders, reducing profits and undermining the morale of salesmen.

Attention has therefore to be paid to production control, the aim being to make the most efficient use of the firm's resources. As we saw earlier, economic efficiency depends upon the size of demand as well as on the technical conditions of supply, and this will affect the production process. Thus a car manufacturer is likely to produce by the 'flow method', whereas the local repair garage remains small and labour-intensive. This applies even to the provision of services. On the one hand we have multiple national companies running chains of hotels and, on the other, a seaside landlady taking in a few people for bed and breakfast. However, forecasts of sales from the marketing department may influence changes in production methods.

The production department will have to work closely with other departments also. Although the R & D department will initiate new or better products, the production department may suggest modification of design to achieve technical economies or to allow production by existing methods and equipment. It will also have to liaise with the purchasing department to ensure that adequate supplies of raw materials and machines are available as required, and with the personnel department in the recruitment of labour.

Finally, the department will have to cover the regular maintenance of buildings and the replenishment of stocks of spare parts for machines in order to ensure that there is no halt in the chain of production.

Accounting

Accounting records the operations of the business in financial terms, supplying figures to guide the policy decisions of the Board of Directors and departmental heads.

First, the Board of Directors will have to ensure that sufficient finance is available for the firm's proposed operations. Thus attention has to be given to cash flow – the difference between receipts from sales and the amount spent on raw materials, wages, etc. (see p. 206). The company has to work within the budget determined by its cash flow and borrowing possibilities: an expanding company can easily run into difficulties by embarking on an over-ambitious production programme.

Second, breaking down figures under selected cost headings allows the Board of Directors to assess production performance and the profitability of different products. Such cost control would seek to calculate the cost of producing each product. While this is relatively simple for raw materials and piece-work labour, administrative items, such as clerical staff, rent, heating and lighting, have to be apportioned arbitrarily, e.g. according to the relative time taken in producing the given product. Once a *standard* cost per unit has been obtained, any variance from this standard will be revealed, and measures can then be taken to improve efficiency.

The accounting department also ensures that a check is kept on payments for goods sold and raw materials purchased through delivery notes, invoices and statements. Furthermore it advises on possible action to secure the maximum benefits for the company from existing tax legislation.

Research and development

R & D is concerned with the continuous updating of the firm's products by improving existing models and initiating new products. Much of this is achieved by testing products scientifically.

A part of its work may consist in applying science and technology to improving methods of production including work study and energy conservation. Indeed it may be required to advise on organisation and management structure.

Purchasing

If production is to flow smoothly and production targets met, the purchasing department must arrange adequate supplies of raw materials and components to be available when required. While ordering in bulk from a central supplier is likely to yield advantages in price terms, failure in the delivery of a raw material can be costly in production delays. Hence the purchasing department may opt for various sources of supply rather than 'put all its eggs in one basket' by concentrating on a single supplier.

Personnel

Other departments will indicate their staff requirements to the personnel department, which will be responsible for recruiting staff having the requisite qualifications and experience.

Emphasis must be placed on the motivation of employees. Obviously they will expect current wage and salary rates, possibly with the addition of fringe benefits. But provision also has to be made for systematic training, overcoming monotony of the job, social and sports clubs and family welfare.

Above all, to avoid misunderstanding, there must be liaison with the recognised trade unions regarding pay and conditions of work. This is particularly important should redundancies be necessary. Treatment of surplus employees must be seen to be fair if the morale of those being retained is not to suffer. The keynote regarding staff relations is taking care to promote good communications between the company, managers and employees (see also Chapter 11).

Secretarial

The company secretary is responsible for the legal aspects of the firm's activities under the Companies Acts – arranging the Annual General Meeting, giving the required twenty-one days' notice to shareholders, and sending the annual report and statutory accounts to the Registrar of Companies.

The department also initiates and services meetings of the Board of Directors, records share transfers, and administers the company's pension scheme.

V Combining resources

Classification of factors of production

In order to examine the problems connected with employing resources it is helpful to classify them according to particular characteristics.

Land refers to the resources provided by nature, e.g. space, sunshine, rain and minerals, which are fixed in supply.

Labour refers to the effort, physical and mental, made by human beings in production. It is this 'human' element which distinguishes it from other factors, for it gives rise to problems regarding psychological attitudes and unemployment.

Capital as a factor of production consists of producer goods and stocks of consumer goods not yet in the hands of the consumer. While consumer goods directly satisfy consumer's wants, e.g. a loaf, a bicycle, a TV set, producer goods are only wanted for their contribution to making consumer goods, e.g. buildings, machines, raw materials. Capital is treated as a separate factor of production in order to emphasis: (a) the increased production which results from using it; (b) the sacrifice of present enjoyment which is necessary to obtain it (see Chapter 1); and (c) the fluctuations of economic activity which may result from changes in its rate of accumulation (see Chapter 18).

Enterprise is the acceptance of the risks of uncertainty in production, risks which, as we saw earlier, cannot be insured against. They arise because the firm spends in advance on raw materials, labour and machines, and the extent to which such costs are covered depends on the demand for the product when it is sold. Tastes may have changed or a rival may be marketing the good at a lower price than anticipated. The reward for uncertainty-bearing is profit – but this may be negative, i.e. a loss may be incurred. Whoever accepts such a risk is the true entrepreneur – the farmer working on his own account, the person who buys ordinary shares in a company or the citizens of a state who ultimately have to bear any losses made by a nationalised industry.

The problem of combining resources

The problems peculiar to the different types of factors of production are considered in Chapters 11–13. Here we are concerned with the more general problem of how much of each a firm will hire. In other words how will the firm allocate its spending in order to obtain the greatest possible output from a given outlay? For example, the same amount of concrete can be mixed by having many men with just a shovel apiece or by having only one man using a concrete mixer. Can we discover any general principle governing its decision? We can begin by seeing what happens to output when one factor is held fixed while the amount of another factor is increased.

The law of diminishing (or non-proportional) returns

Assume: (a) production is by two factors only, land and labour; (b) all units of the variable factor, labour, are equally efficient; (c) there is no change in techniques or organisation.

Table 9.2 shows how the output of potatoes varies as more labourers work on a fixed amount of land. Until three men are

Table 9.2 *Variations in output of potatoes resulting from a change in labour employed*

Number of men employed on the fixed unit of land	Total output	Yield (cwt) Average output	Marginal
1	1	1	1
2	8	4	7
3	27	9	19
4	40	10	13
5	$47\frac{1}{2}$	$9\frac{1}{2}$	$7\frac{1}{2}$
6	54	9	$6\frac{1}{2}$
7	60	$8\frac{4}{7}$	6
8	65	$8\frac{1}{8}$	5
9	69	$7\frac{2}{3}$	4
10	71	$7\frac{1}{10}$	2
11	71	$6\frac{5}{11}$	0
12	66	$5\frac{1}{2}$	−5

Notes:
(a) *Total output* is the total yield (cwt) from all factors employed.
(b) *Average output* refers to the average yield per man. It therefore equals

$$\frac{\text{Total output}}{\text{Number of men employed}}$$

(c) *Marginal output* refers to the marginal yield (cwt) to labour, and equals the addition to total output which is obtained by increasing the labour force by one man. That is, marginal output equals total output of $(n+1)$ men – total output of n men.
(d) There is a fundamental relationship between average output and marginal output. Marginal output equals average output when

Table 9.2 – *Notes continued overleaf*

employed the marginal product of labour is increasing, the third labourer, for instance, adding 19 cwt. Here there are really too few labourers to the given amount of land. Thereafter the marginal product falls, the fourth labourer only adding 13 cwt, and so on; total output is still increasing but at a diminishing rate. The maximum return per labourer occurs when there are four labourers to the plot. If we increase the number of labourers to eight, the maximum return per labourer can only be maintained by doubling the amount of land. When eleven labourers are employed they start to get in one another's way, and from then on total output is declining absolutely (see also Figure 9.5).

Again it must be emphasised that units of the variable factor are homogeneous. The marginal product of labour does not fall

Fig. 9.5
The relationship between the number of labourers employed, average output and marginal output

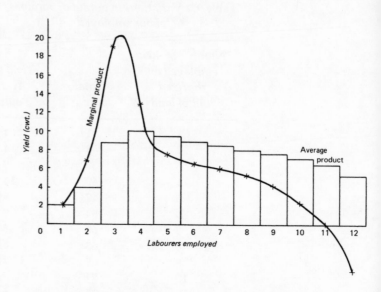

the latter is at a maximum (see also Figure 9.6). This relationship is bound to occur. So long as the marginal output is greater than average output, the return to an additional labourer will raise the average output of all labourers employed. On the other hand, as soon as the marginal output falls below average output, the additional labourer will lower the average output. Hence when average product is neither rising nor falling, that is, at its maximum, it is because marginal product equals average product. This relationship can be made clearer by a simple example. Suppose Boycott has played twenty innings and that his batting average is 60 runs. Now if in his next innings he scores more than 60, say 102, his average will increase – to 62. If, on the other hand, he scores less than 60, say 18, his average will fall – to 58. If he scores exactly 60 in his twenty-first innings, his average will remain unchanged at 60.

because less efficient labourers have to be employed. Diminishing returns are the result of more labourers being employed on a fixed amount of land.

Nor does the law formulate any *economic* theory; it merely states physical relationships. While the physical productivity of an extra labourer is important to a farmer in deciding how many men to employ, it will not *determine* his decision. He must also know the relative costs of factors: that is, he requires economic data as well as technical facts.

The practical application of the law of diminishing returns

The law is significant both in our everyday life and in the theoretical analysis of the economist.

First, it helps to explain the low standard of living in many parts of the world, particularly the Far East. Increasing population is cultivating a fixed amount of land. Marginal product, and thus average product, are falling; and so, therefore, is the average standard of living.

Second, it shows how a firm can adjust the marginal physical products of factors by altering the proportion in which they are combined. Thus few labourers to the plot gave a high return to labour; after four labourers the average product began to fall. So the law is more generally referred to as 'the law of varying proportions'. The firm will choose that proportion which yields the maximum output from a given outlay, as follows.

The optimum combination of variable factors

So far we have assumed that there are just two factors, land and labour, and that land is fixed. But suppose that there is another variable factor, say capital. Now the farmer will have to decide how he will combine labour with capital.

How much of each he employs will depend upon its productivity relative to its price, since he will alter the combination until, for the last pound spent on both labour and capital, he obtains the same amount of product. Suppose, for instance, the last pound's worth of labour is yielding more potatoes than the last pound spent on capital. It will obviously pay the farmer to transfer this pound from capital to buying more labour, for this will increase his total physical yield.

But labour and capital are obtained in different units, their units being different in price. Thus we cannot compare directly the productivity of one man with that of one unit of capital, say a mechanical hoe; we must allow for their respective prices. If the cost of one man is only one-third of the cost of a mechanical hoe, then the marginal product of a man need only be one-third of the hoe's to give the same yield for a given expenditure. Thus the farmer will be in equilibrium in combining factors when:

$$\frac{\text{Marginal product of labour}}{\text{Price of labour}} = \frac{\text{Marginal product of capital}}{\text{Price of capital}}$$

A corollary of this is that, like the housewife in purchasing her goods, the entrepreneur will tend to buy more of a factor as its price falls, and less as it rises. Suppose the wage rate rises but the marginal product of labour remains unchanged. The fundamental relationship stated above has now been destroyed. To restore the position it is necessary to raise the marginal product of labour and to lower that of capital by combining less labour with more capital: in short a rise in wages without a corresponding increase in the productivity of labour will tend to bring about a replacement of labour by machines.

VI The costs of production

Opportunity costs and profits

Suppose a man sets himself up as a shopkeeper selling sweets. He invests £1000 of his savings in the business, and in the first year his receipts are £20,000 and his outgoings £11,000. The accountant would say that his profits over the year were £9000. The economist, however, would disagree.

The reason for this is that the economist is not so much concerned with money costs as with 'opportunity cost' – what a factor could earn in its best alternative line of production. This concept of cost has a bearing on: (a) the economist's concept of 'profit'; and (b) how long production should continue when total costs are not being covered.

'Implicit costs'

The £11,000 money outgoings of the shopkeeper above can be regarded as 'explicit costs'. But when we look at costs as alternatives forgone we see immediately that the shopkeeper has certain 'implicit costs' – the rewards his own capital and labour could earn elsewhere. If, for instance, his capital could be invested at 12 per cent, there is an implicit cost of £120 a year. Similarly with his own labour. His next most profitable line, we will assume, is as a shop manager earning £5880 a year. Thus a total of £6000 implicit costs in addition to the explicit costs should be deducted from his receipts.

Normal and super-normal profit

But we have not finished yet. The shopkeeper knows that even in running a sweet shop some risk arises through uncertainty – a risk which he avoids if he merely works for somebody else. The shopkeeper must therefore anticipate at least a certain minimum profit, say £1000 a year, before he will start his own business. If he does not make this minimum profit, he feels he might as well go into some other line of business or become a paid shop manager. Thus another type of cost (which we call 'normal profit') has to be allowed for – the minimum return which keeps a firm in a particular industry after all other factors have been paid their opportunity cost. Normal profit is a cost because, if it is not met, the supply of entrepreneurship to that particular line of business dries up.

We have, therefore, the following costs: explicit costs, implicit costs, normal profit. Anything left over after all these costs have been met is 'super-normal' profit. In terms of our example we have:

	(£)	(£)
Total revenue		20 000
Total costs: explicit	11 000	
implicit	6 000	
normal profit	1 000	
	———	18 000
Super-normal profit		2 000

Fixed costs and variable costs

For the purposes of our analysis we shall classify costs into *fixed costs* and *variable costs*.

Fixed costs are those costs which do not vary in direct proportion to the firm's output. They are the costs of indivisible factors, e.g. buildings, machinery, vehicles. Even if there is no output fixed costs must be incurred, but for a time as output expands they remain the same.

Variable costs, on the other hand, are those costs which vary directly with output. They are the costs of the variable factors, e.g. operative labour, raw materials, fuel for running the machines, wear and tear on equipment. Where there is no output variable costs are nil; as output increases so variable costs increase.

In practice it is difficult to draw an absolute line between fixed and variable costs: the difference really depends on the length of time. When current output is not profitable the entrepreneur will have to contract production. At first overtime will cease; later workers will be paid off. In time more factors, e.g. salesmen, become variable and, if receipts still do not justify expenditure on them, they too can be dismissed. A factor becomes variable when a decision has to be taken on whether it shall be replaced, for then its alternative uses have to be considered. Eventually machines need renewing; even they have become a variable cost. A decision may now be necessary on whether the business should continue.

The distinction between fixed and variable factors and costs is useful in two ways. First, in economic analysis it provides a means of distinguishing between differences in the conditions of supply which result from changes in the time period. The *short period* is defined as a period when there is at least one fixed factor. While, therefore, supply can be adjusted by labour working overtime and more raw materials being used, the time is too short for altering fixed plant and organisation. Thus the firm cannot achieve its best possible combination for a given output. In the *long period* all factors are variable; they can therefore be combined in the best possible way. Thus supply can respond fully to a change in demand.

Second, as we shall see later, the distinction is fundamental when the firm is considering whether or not to continue producing. In the long period all costs of production, fixed and variable, must be covered if production is to continue. But in the short period fixed costs cannot be avoided by ceasing to produce; they have already been paid for simply because it was necessary to have some 'lumpy' factors even before production could start. Only variable costs can be saved; and so, provided these are covered by receipts, the firm will continue to produce. Anything that it makes above such costs will help to recoup its fixed costs.

Changes in costs as output expands

In our discussion of the law of non-proportional returns we referred to quantities of factors and yields in physical terms. But in deciding how to maximise profit the firm will be concerned with those quantities translated into money terms. It can then see directly the relationship between costs and receipts at different outputs and is thus able to decide what output will give the maximum profit (see Table 9.3). Our first task, therefore, is to consider how costs are likely to change as output increases. We shall assume perfect competition in buying factors of production – the demand of each firm is so small in relation to total supply that any change in demand will not directly affect the price of those factors.

In the short period there are, by definition, bound to be fixed factors. And, in the law of non-proportional returns we found that when a variable factor was added to a fixed factor for a time the marginal product might increase but eventually would diminish. How will this affect costs as output expands?

Let us assume that two factors are being used, one of them fixed. If each additional unit of the variable factor costs the same, but the output from additional units is increasing, the firm is obtaining an increasing amount of output for any given addition to expenditure. In other words the cost of each additional unit of output is falling as output expands. On the other hand, if the marginal product of the variable factor is diminishing, the cost of an additional unit of output is rising. This cost of an additional unit of output is known as *marginal cost (MC)*.

The above conclusions can be represented diagrammatically (see Figure 9.6).

Cost schedules

Table 9.3 *Costs of Rollermowers Ltd (£)*

Output per week (units)	Fixed cost (FC)	Total variable cost (TVC)	Total cost (TC)	Marginal cost (MC)	Average fixed cost (AFC)	Average variable cost (AVC)	Average total cost (ATC)
0	1000	—	—	—	—	—	—
				20			
10	1000	200	1200		100	20	120
				14			
20	1000	340	1340		50	17	67
				10			
30	1000	440	1440		$33\frac{1}{3}$	$14\frac{2}{3}$	48
				10			
40	1000	540	1540		25	$13\frac{1}{2}$	$38\frac{1}{2}$
				$13\frac{1}{2}$			
50	1000	675	1675		20	$13\frac{1}{2}$	$33\frac{1}{2}$
				$18\frac{1}{2}$			
60	1000	860	1860		$16\frac{2}{3}$	$14\frac{1}{3}$	31
				24			
70	1000	1100	2100		$14\frac{2}{7}$	$15\frac{5}{7}$	30
				30			
80	1000	1400	2400		$12\frac{1}{2}$	$17\frac{1}{2}$	30
				39			
90	1000	1790	2790		$11\frac{1}{9}$	$19\frac{8}{9}$	31
				51			
100	1000	2300	3300		10	23	33
				66			
110	1000	2960	3960		$9\frac{1}{9}$	$26\frac{8}{9}$	36
				84			
120	1000	3800	4800		$8\frac{1}{3}$	$31\frac{2}{3}$	40

Notes:
(1) *TC* of *n* units = *FC* + *VC* of *n* units.
(2) *MC* is the extra cost involved in producing an additional unit of output. That is, *MC* of the *n*th unit = *TC* of *n* units − *TC* of *n*−1 units. Here output is shown in units of 10, so that this difference in total costs has to be divided by 10.
(3) AFC of n units $= \dfrac{FC}{n}$
(4) AVC of n units $= \dfrac{TVC \text{ of } n \text{ units}}{n}$
(5) $ATC = \dfrac{TC \text{ of } n \text{ units}}{n}$

Table 9.3 above illustrates this relationship between output and costs. The figures, which have been kept as simple as possible, are for an imaginary firm, Rollermowers Ltd, manufacturers of lawn-mowers. Fixed costs (*FC*) amount to £1000 and, as variable

**Fig. 9.6
The relationship
between returns and
costs**

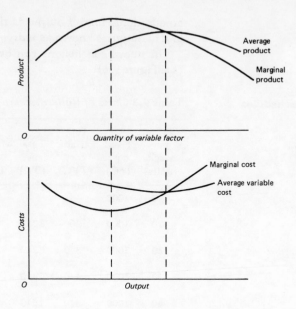

**Fig. 9.7
Cost curves**

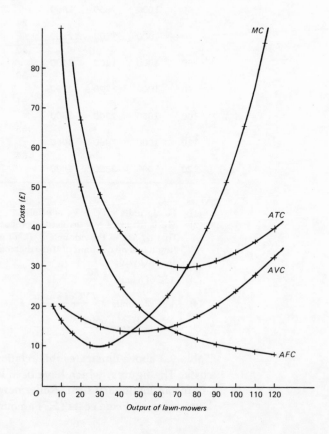

factors are added, output expands. At first there is an increasing marginal product; as a result MC is falling. This has its effect on average total cost (ATC) until approximately 75 units are being produced. From then onwards, as the fixed factors are being worked more intensively, diminishing returns cause the ATC curve to rise.

These figures can be plotted on a graph (see Figure 9.7). The following relationships between the curves should be noted:

(a) AFC and AVC added vertically give ATC; and

(b) the MC curve cuts both the AVC and ATC curves when they are at a minimum, the same reason applying as in Table 9.2, note (d).

10 The Firm's Output: How Much to Produce

In order to ascertain whether a firm is maximising profits we have to know:

(a) the price at which it can sell different outputs and the price at which it can buy different quantities of factors; and

(b) whether it is free to enter another industry where it can make higher profits.

Both involve us in a study of the extent to which competition prevails.

The degree of competition can vary. But to begin with we shall make the theoretical assumption that the conditions of 'perfect competition' – the highest form of competition – apply. Later these conditions can be modified to examine imperfect competition, forms of which prevail in real life.

I Output under perfect competition

The conditions necessary for perfect competition

For perfect competition to exist the following conditions must hold:

(1) *A large number of relatively small sellers and buyers.* If there are a large number of sellers relative to demand in the market any one seller will know that, because he supplies so small a quantity of the total output, he can increase or decrease his output without it having any significant effect on the market price of the product. In short he takes the market price as given, and can sell any quantity at this price.

This is illustrated in Figure 10.1, where part (a) shows market price OP determined by the demand for and supply of the goods of the industry as a whole. But the industry supply, we will assume, comes from a thousand producers, each of about the same size. Each producer therefore sells such a small proportion of the total market supply that he can double his output from ON to OM or halve it from OM to ON without affecting the price (see Figure 10.1(b)).

Fig. 10.1
The firm's demand
curve under perfect
competition

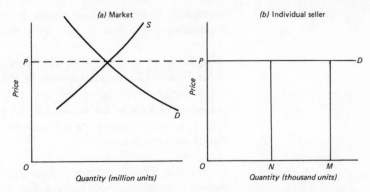

In other words in perfect competition a seller is faced with an infinitely elastic demand curve for his product. If, in our example, he charges a higher price than *OP*, nobody will buy from him; if he charges less than *OP*, he will not be maximising his revenue, for he could have sold all his output at the higher price, *OP*.

In contrast the producer in Figure 10.2(b) sells such a large proportion of the market supply that a change in his output affects the price he receives for his product. When he supplies *OM*, the price is *OP*. If he increases his supply to M_1, the price falls to OP_1. Similarly, if he decreases his supply to OM_2, the price rises to OP_2. Alternatively such a producer can decide on the price he charges, leaving it to the market to determine how much is sold at that price. But he cannot fix both price and quantity at the same time.

Fig. 10.2
The firm's demand
curve under perfect
and imperfect
competition

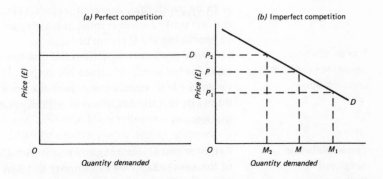

(2) *Homogeneous product*. Buyers must regard the product of one producer as being a perfect substitute for that of another, and purchase solely on the basis of price, switching to a competitor if one producer raises his price.

Such identity of product does not exist where there is a real or imaginary difference (e.g. a special wrapping or brand name) or where reasons other than price (e.g. goodwill) influence buyers. Here an individual producer can raise his price without necessarily losing all his customers. In short product differentiation leads to some downward slope in the demand curve.

(3) *Perfect knowledge of market conditions.*

(4) *Free entry of new firms into the market.*

(5) *Perfect mobility of the factors of production in the long period.* A change in the demand for a product must, in the long period, result in factors of production being transferred from one line of production to another.

In practice these conditions never apply simultaneously, and perfect competition must be regarded primarily as an analytical device which enables us to arrive at some fundamental conclusions.

Maximising profit

Since the objective of the firm, we have assumed, is to maximise its profits, it will seek to produce that output where the difference between total revenue and total costs is greatest. The firm, therefore, will be concerned with two broad questions: (a) How much will it obtain by selling various quantities of its product? (b) How much will it cost to produce these different quantities?

At first sight it may seem that maximum profit will occur at the minimum average cost output. But this is unlikely to be so. The real question which the entrepreneur will be continually asking is: 'If I produce another unit, will it cost me less or more than the extra revenue I shall receive from the sale of it?' That is, he concentrates his attention at the margin: if an extra unit of output is to be profitable, *marginal revenue* (the revenue received from the last unit of output) must at least equal *marginal cost* (the cost of producing the last unit of output).

Under perfect competition the producer will obtain the market price for his good, whatever his output. In other words, marginal revenue (*MR*) equals price, with the price line horizontal (Figure 10.2(a)). But the *MC* curve eventually rises because of diminishing returns.

The equilibrium output of Rollermowers

Let us return to our imaginary firm. Assume that the market price of mowers is £45. We can impose this *MR* curve on the cost-curve diagram (Figure 10.3).

Now at any output where *MR* (price) is above *MC* Rollermowers can increase profits by expanding output. Or, if *MC* is above *MR*, contracting output will increase profits. The equilibrium output, therefore, is where *MR* (price) equals *MC* (that is, 90 lawnmowers), provided total revenue covers current costs. 'Current revenue' is simply the number of goods currently produced times their price. But, as we have seen, 'current costs' depends upon whether we are dealing with the short or the long period.

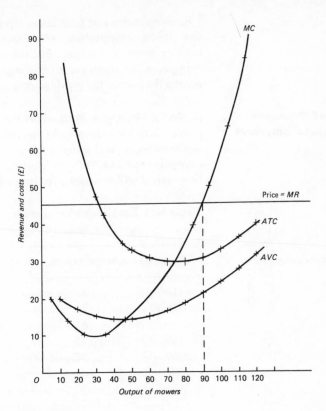

Fig. 10.3
The equilibrium output
of the firm under
perfect competition

The short-period
'shut-down' price

A firm will only *start* to produce if it expects that total revenue will be sufficient to cover:

(a) the cost of fixed factors;

(b) the cost of variable factors, e.g. labour, raw materials; and

(c) normal profit.

We will imagine that the firm does think it can make a 'go' of it. It buys highly specific machinery (fixed costs) which, we will assume for the sake of simplicity, has no value to any other firm, together with labour and raw materials (variable costs), and starts producing.

But as time goes by it finds that the original expectations are not being fulfilled. Although the cost of variable factors is being covered, the firm sees that unless the price rises the margin is too small to replace machines when they wear out. In other words the business as a whole will prove unprofitable.

But what will our firm save by stopping production forthwith? Obviously its variable costs, for these vary directly with output. But what of its machines, which, since they have no alternative use, have no resale price? These are fixed factors which have already been paid for, and ceasing to use them now cannot recoup past expenditure.

Consequently our firm takes a philosophic view of the situation. It has some perfectly good machines which, if used, will add nothing to costs. So, provided the cost of the variable factors is being covered, it goes on producing. Anything above will help to recoup the cost of the fixed factors.

The firm's short-period supply curve

A firm's *MC* curve is its short-period supply curve. Consider Table 10.1, for example. At any price below £13.50 per mower, Rollermowers will stop production, because *TVC* are not covered; thus £13.50 is its 'shut-down' price. At higher prices, however, it will produce an output where price equals *MC*.

Table 10.1 *The firm's short-period supply schedule*

Price (£)	Outputs (units)
13·50	45
18·50	55
	65
30	75
39	85, and so on

The industry's short-period supply curve

In the short period, no new firms can enter the industry because, by definition, they cannot obtain fixed factors. The supply curve of the industry, therefore, is obtained simply by adding the output of all existing firms at each given price.

Suppose, for the sake of simplicity, that the industry consists of four firms, the other three being less efficient than Rollermowers. Their outputs (starting from minimum *AVC*) are given under *A*, *B* and *C* in the following schedule:

Price (£)	Output (units)				
	Firm A	Firm B	Firm C	Roller-mowers	Total
13·50	—	—	—	45	45
18·50	—	—	45	55	100
24	—	45	55	65	165
30	50	55	65	75	245
39	55	65	75	85	280

This is shown graphically in Figure 10.4. The *MC* curves of the four firms are summed horizontally to obtain the short-period supply curve of the industry. This rises from left to right, showing that when more is supplied the higher the price. It will be

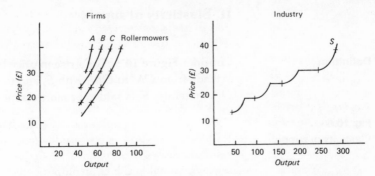

Fig. 10.4
The short period
supply curve of the
industry

observed that the supply curve derived above is not smooth, but is
stepped instead. This is because we have taken only four firms. If
there had been many firms, each differing only slightly in efficiency, we should have had a much smoother curve.

**Supply in the long
period**

In the long period a firm will still produce where $MR = MC$, but
total costs must now be covered.

As regards the industry, however, super-normal profits will
attract new firms since they can now obtain plant. Moreover,
competition will force all firms to achieve the most efficient size.
As supply expands, the price of the product falls and super-
normal profits are eliminated (see Figure 10.5).

Fig. 10.5
The effect of
competition on the
super-normal profits
and output of
Rollermowers Ltd

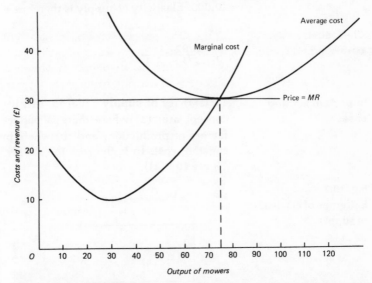

Now while there may be some external economies as the
industry expands, there is a major diseconomy – higher rewards
will have to be paid to factors to attract them from other industries. The situation, therefore, is that, even in the long period,
there is likely to be an upward-sloping supply curve. The extent
to which this happens is indicated by the elasticity of supply.

II Elasticity of supply

Consider Figure 10.6. For a rise in price from OP to OP_1 supply extends from OM to OM_1 with S_1 and to OM_2 with S_2. At price OP, therefore, S_2 is said to be more elastic than S_1.

Fig. 10.6
Elasticity of supply

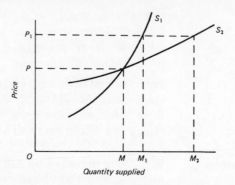

More precisely the elasticity of supply of a good at any price or at any output is the proportional change in the amount supplied in response to a small change in price divided by the proportional change in price. In Table 7.3 on p. 100, for instance, when the price of eggs rises from 10p to 12p, supply expands from 32,000 to 40,000. Elasticity of supply is therefore equal to:

$$\frac{8/32}{2/10} = \frac{5}{4}$$

Important limiting
cases

1 Elasticity of supply equal to infinity   The main uses of this concept are: (a) where there is perfect competition in buying factors of production; and (b) where production takes place at constant cost. In both cases the supply curve is horizontal (see Figure 10.7(a)).

Fig. 10.7
Extremes of elasticity
of supply

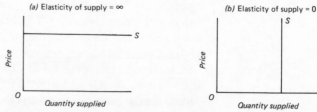

2 Supply absolutely inelastic   Here a good is fixed in supply whatever the price offered (see Figure 10.7(b)). It applies to rare first editions and Old Masters, and, by definition, to fixed factors in the short period (see p. 157).

Factors determining elasticity of supply

Elasticity of supply is determined by: (1) the period of time under consideration; (2) the relationship between the individual firms' minimum supply points; and (3) the cost of attracting factors from alternative uses. We shall consider each in turn.

1 Time   We distinguish three main periods:

(a) *Momentary equilibrium.* Here the supply is fixed, and elasticity of supply = 0. An example is Christmas trees on Christmas Eve. With many goods some increase in supply can take place by (i) drawing on stocks, or (ii) switching factors of production from one product to another (where a firm makes two or more different products).

(b) *Short-period equilibrium.* Usually varying supply requires a change in the factors of production employed. But this takes time – and the period differs between one factor and another. In the short period, as we have seen, it is possible to adjust supply only by altering the variable factors (raw materials, labour, etc.).

(c) *Long-period equilibrium.* Other factors, the fixed factors (e.g. land already sown, capital equipment, etc.), can be altered in the long period, allowing supply to adjust fully to a change in price. Thus elasticity is greater in the long period. For example, in Figure 10.6 S_1 could well represent the short-period supply curve, and S_2 the long.

2 The relationship between the firms' minimum supply points   The supply curve is obtained by aggregating the supply of individual firms. If these firms each offer a supply to the market at more or less the same minimum price, then supply will tend to be elastic at that price. Similarly as price rises, the greater the number of firms coming in, the greater the elasticity of supply.

3 The cost of attracting factors of production   In order to expand production additional factors have to be attracted from other industries. For an industry as a whole, this means that higher rewards will have to be paid. What we have to ask, therefore, is: How much of a factor will be forthcoming in response to a given price rise? In other words what is the elasticity of supply of factors of production? And, of greater significance what are the influences determining this elasticity?

In answering this question we can first consider what happens when one particular industry, e.g. office-building, wishes to expand. Let us concentrate on one factor, labour. With increased demand for building labourers, wages rise. But they rise not only to the office-building industry but to all other industries employing such labourers – house-building, road construction, public works, etc. How will it affect these industries?

First, they will try to substitute other factors (e.g. cement-mixers, bulldozers, etc.) for the labour which now costs more. Is such substitution physically possible? If so, how elastic is the supply of these alternative factors? Will their prices rise sharply as demand increases? If physical substitution is fairly easy, and the supply of alternative factors is elastic, it will mean that a small rise in wages will release much labour for the office-building industry.

Second, higher wages will lead to increased costs in building houses, constructing roads, etc. The supply curve of these products, therefore, moves to the left and, the higher the proportion of wages to total costs, the further will it move. The extent to which it leads to a reduced production of these alternative goods will depend upon the elasticity of demand for them. If elasticity is high, the small rise in the price of the good will cause a considerable contraction of demand, and labour will be released for office-building. If, on the other hand, demand is inelastic, even a considerable rise in wages will have little effect on the output of houses, etc., and the increase in the supply of labour to office-building will be correspondingly small.

We see, therefore, that the two main influences affecting the elasticity of supply of a factor to a particular industry are: (a) the substitutability of other factors; and (b) the elasticity of demand for the alternative goods it produces.

Practical uses of the concept of elasticity of supply

(1) *The elasticity of supply of a good is a major factor in determining how much its price will alter when there is a change in the conditions of demand.* This can be seen by considering how the price of cane sugar is likely to be affected in the short and long periods if the demand for sugar increased.

We can assume a fairly inelastic demand curve for sugar. The original price is *OP* (see Figure 10.8). Demand then increases from *D* to *D₁*. The supply of cane sugar in the short run is

Fig. 10.8
Changes in the price of
cane sugar over time in
response to a change
in demand

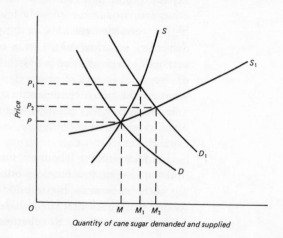

Quantity of cane sugar demanded and supplied

inelastic, for supply can be expanded only by adding labour, fertilisers, etc. Price therefore increases to OP_1. But in the long period more land can be planted with sugar cane. Supply is therefore more elastic, and is represented by the curve S_1. The long-run price falls to OP_2.

(2) *The elasticity of supply is significant with regard to taxation.* First, where the supply of a good is inelastic, the Chancellor of the Exchequer can impose a tax on the producer without it having a great effect on the amount of the good offered for sale. Suppose, for instance, that a man owns a field which is suitable only for sheep-grazing, and that the most any farmer will pay him for the use of this field is £10 a year, which the owner accepts. Now suppose that the government puts a tax of £5 a year on this type of land. This means that the owner will have to pay the tax out of his own pocket, for the farmer will pay no more, and the land cannot be put to any other use. In fact the government could tax almost all the rent away before it would make any difference to the number of sheep being grazed on it; but, if all the rent went on tax, the owner might leave the land standing idle.

Second, the relative elasticities of demand and supply determine the proportion of a selective indirect tax borne by the producer as compared with the consumer (see pp. 318–19).

III Monopoly

Imperfect competition Where any of the conditions of perfect competition are not fulfilled, some form of 'imperfect competition' results. Thus where one seller is so large that the quantity he supplies to the market affects the price, the demand curve for his product is downward-sloping.

Again, products may not be homogeneous, product differentiation or goodwill allowing a producer to raise his price somewhat while still retaining some customers.

Finally, lack of knowledge, barriers to entry or immobility of factors of production result in demand or supply not being perfectly elastic. Consumers, for instance, may not have complete knowledge of prices ruling elsewhere, as, for example, in retail markets. Thus sellers can raise their price without losing all their custom.

There are many 'shades' of imperfect competition. At one extreme we have a single producer of a product, e.g. British Oxygen; at the other, the only difference from perfect competition is that firms each produce a slightly different brand, e.g. toothpaste. The first we call 'monopoly', the second 'monopolistic competition'. In between we can have just a few sellers of the same or of a slightly different product – 'oligopoly'. In this case each seller has to take into account the reactions of rivals to his own pricing policy (see below).

The broad market forms are shown in Figure 10.9. We begin by examining monopoly.

Fig. 10.9
Market forms

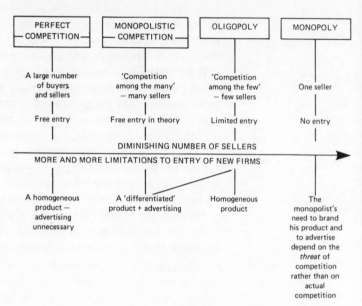

Sources of monopoly power

While to some extent all goods are substitutes for one another, there may be essential characteristics in a good or group of goods which give rise to gaps in the chain of substitution. If one producer can so exclude competitors that he controls the supply of a good, he can be said to be a 'monopolist', a single seller.

In real life there is seldom complete monopoly. But one producer may dominate the supply of a good or group of goods. In the UK any firm which accounts for a quarter (in value) of the market supply is considered to be a monopoly (see p. 171).

Possible sources of a monopolist's power to exclude competitors are:

1 Immobility of the factors of production Such immobility means that existing suppliers cannot be challenged by new entrants. It may arise through:

(a) *Legal prohibition of new entrants*, as with public utilities where many firms would create technical difficulties, e.g. gas, electricity, water and telephone services.

(b) *Patents, copyrights, trade marks, etc.* (see pp. 226–7).

(c) *Government policy of establishing single buying and selling agencies*, e.g. marketing boards.

(d) *Control of the source of supply by one firm,* e.g. minerals, specialist workers (e.g. Dior dress designers), trade unions and professional associations.

2 Ignorance   A monopoly may persist largely through the ignorance of possible competitors. They may not know the supernormal profits being made by the existing firm, or they may be unable to acquire the necessary 'know-how', e.g. for involved technical processes.

3 Indivisibilities   Whereas the original firm may have been able to build up its size gradually, new firms may find it difficult to raise the large capital required to produce on a scale which is cost competitive, e.g. cars, drugs, computers.

In some cases, too, the efficient scale of plant may be so large relative to the market that there is only room for one firm. This applies to many of the public utilities, e.g. transport, water, electricity generation.

4 Deliberate policy to exclude competitors   Restriction of competition falls into two main groups. Monopoly power described so far has been derived from sources which have arisen indirectly rather than by any deliberate action of producers. Such 'spontaneous' monopolies must be contrasted with 'deliberate' monopolies, those which are created specifically to restrict supply.

It is essential to distinguish between the two when formulating policy. While the 'spontaneous' monopolies may still abuse their fortunate position in order to make high profits, to a large extent they are inevitable, and usually policy should seek to control rather than to destroy them. On the other hand monopolies designed to follow restrictive practices detrimental to the consumer should, where possible, be broken up. In practice, however, it is often difficult to draw a distinct line between the two. While firms may increase production or combine in order to reduce costs through economies of scale, the effect may still be that competitors are forced out.

Deliberate action to exclude competitors takes various forms. Firms producing or selling the same good may combine, or a competitor may be subject to a 'takeover' bid. Monopolies are often formed in the sale of services. Trade unions are primarily combinations of workers formed with the object of obtaining higher wages (see Chapter 11). Certain professions, such as medicine and the law, have their own associations which regulate qualifications for entry, professional conduct, and often the fees to be charged.

Some practices to exclude competitors are highly questionable

– vicious temporary price-cutting, agreements in submitting tenders, intimidation of rivals' customers by threats to cut off the supply of another vital product, etc.

The effect of the downward-sloping demand curve on marginal revenue

Consider Figure 10.10 In part (a) the producer is selling under conditions of perfect competition. His marginal revenue is equal to the full price, since all units sell at this. Thus for the fourth unit *MR* is the shaded area *A*.

Fig. 10.10
Marginal revenue under conditions of perfect and imperfect competition

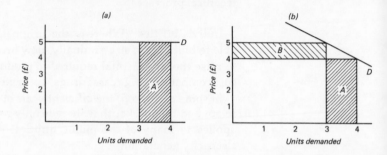

In part (b), however, the producer is selling under conditions of imperfect competition. If he wishes to sell a fourth unit, he must lower his price from £5 to £4. But this lower price applies not only to the fourth unit but also to the first three units. Thus his net addition to receipts is equal to what he gets for the fourth unit, *A*, less what he loses on the three previous units, *B*. Under imperfect competition, therefore, *MR* is always less than price at any given output.

The relationship between costs, revenue and the output of a monopolist

Let us consider another imaginary manufacturer of lawnmowers, Airborne Mowers Ltd. To simplify we shall assume that it has identical cost curves to Rollermowers, but differs in that it has a patent for its particular mower, thereby excluding competitors. In short Airborne Mowers is a monopolist. Since its output is also the market supply, the number of mowers which it puts on the market affects the price. Thus if it produces only twenty mowers a week, each will sell at £79; if total output is increased to ninety mowers, the price drops to £44.

Airborne Mowers has the same problem as Rollermowers – to decide which output yields maximum profit. But it has an extra complication on the revenue side – as output increases, price falls for the *whole* of the output. The result can be seen in marginal receipts (see Table 10.2).

These figures are plotted in Figure 10.11.

By inspection we can see that the maximum profit is made when sixty-five Airborne mowers are produced each week. At this output *MR* = *MC* (both £24), as in perfect competition. But *MR* is no longer equal to, but is less than price (£56.50). Total

Table 10.2 *Costs, receipts, and profits of Airborne Mowers (£)*

Output per week (units)	Costs Total	Average total	Marginal	Price per unit	Receipts Total	Marginal	Profits
0	1000	—	—	—	—	—	−1000
			20			84	
10	1200	120		84	840		−360
			14			74	
20	1340	67		79	1580		240
			10			64	
30	1440	48		74	2220		780
			10			54	
40	1540	38½		69	2760		1220
			13½			44	
50	1675	33½		64	3200		1525
			18½			34	
60	1860	31		59	3540		1680
			24			24	
70	2100	30		54	3780		1680
			30			14	
80	2400	30		49	3920		1520
			39			4	
90	2790	31		44	3960		1170
			51			−6	
100	3300	33		39	3900		600
			66			−16	
110	3960	36		34	3740		−220
			84			−26	
120	4800	40		29	3480		−1320

weekly receipts are £3672.50 and total costs £1982.50 (by interpolation), giving a maximum profit of £1690.

Alternatively we can use the price and *ATC* at an output of 65 units to calculate profit. In Figure 10.11 total receipts equal the rectangle *OMCP* (output times price), which equals 65 times £56.50; total cost equals the rectangle *OMAD* (output times average cost), which equals 6.5 times £30.50. Thus profit is the difference between the two, the rectangle *DACP*, which equals 65 times £26, i.e. £1690.

Monopoly and perfect competition as policy objectives

Monopoly is an emotive word so that it is often assumed that in seeking to maximise his profit the monopolist will always follow policies inimical to the consumer. The argument runs as follows.

Where there is perfect competition output for all firms in the

Fig. 10.11
The equilibrium output
of a monopolist

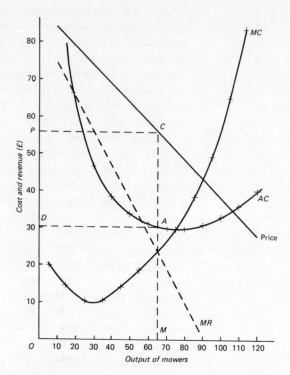

industry will take place where price equals *MC,* i.e. at *OM* (Figure 10.12). In other words production is carried to the point *OM* where the cost of producing an extra unit *MP* just equals the value which consumers place on that extra unit in the market.

Fig. 10.12
Output under perfect
competition and
monopoly

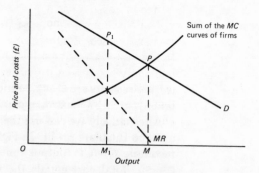

Now suppose a cartel formed from all the individual firms becomes responsible for selling the product. In order to maximise profits the cartel will sell an output where *MC = MR,* i.e. *OM₁,* at price *P₁.* Thus consumers get less of the product and at a higher price than under perfect competition. In short factors of production are not fully allocated according to the wishes of consumers.

Yet, although it may contain much truth, the argument is not infallible.

First, it rests on the implicit assumption that the competitive industry's supply curve will be the same as the MC curve of the monopolist. But this is unlikely to be so. A single firm may be able to obtain economies of scale not open to the comparatively small firms which comprise the competitive industry. In addition its investment may be higher since it need not fear over-capitalisation of the industry as similar investment is carried out by rival firms.

It is probable, therefore, that the monopolist will, at the relevant market output, have lower costs than firms producing under perfectly competitive conditions. Indeed, even though the monopolist is maximising profits, the consumer may obtain more of the product and at a lower price than under perfect competition.

Second, the argument ignores influences on the growth of firms over time, especially investment in research and innovation. Thus we have to ask the question: 'Are firms more likely to spend on research and innovate if, by giving them monopoly powers, they can be assured of the rewards?' In short is monopoly more conducive to growth than perfect competition? We cannot develop the argument here, but the mere existence of patents suggests there is some truth in it. On the other hand there have been instances where monopolies have bought up patents so that they could *not* be developed in competition with them.

Third, if a monopolist can keep separate the parts of his market where elasticities of demand differ, he may, by charging different prices, supply certain clients which a single price would eliminate, e.g. lower surgery fees to poor persons, and students' concessionary rail fares.

The control of monopoly

The division of monopolies into (a) spontaneous and (b) deliberate does not make the first group 'white' or the second 'black'. In the first place our analysis has shown that no matter how the monopoly has arisen it will restrict output if its prime aim is to maximise profits. Second, while a monopoly may be 'deliberate', there may still be benefits from large-scale economies, etc. Thus while some control of monopoly is usually desirable, it has to be done on the facts of the case, benefits being weighed against the possible economic and social disadvantages – restriction of output, a waste of resources in maintaining the monopoly position (e.g. by advertising), a lack of enterprise through the absence of competition, the exertion of political pressure to secure narrow ends (e.g. by trade unions), and a redistribution of wealth from consumers to the monopolist.

As a result monopolies in the UK are regulated rather than prohibited. Yet any policy is fraught with difficulties. An exact assessment of the public benefits and disadvantages resulting from a monopoly is impossible. Very often, too, the decision as to whether a monopoly is useful or anti-social in character depends on circumstances and therefore varies from one period to another (note the fostering of monopolies in the depression of the 1930s). Moreover, if legislation is proposed, the term 'unfair competition' has to be closely defined in rigid legal terms, though for purposes of control it really requires an elastic interpretation based on economic issues. Last, government policy in another field may affect a possible monopoly situation. Thus tariff protection, by restricting competition from abroad, fosters monopolies in the home market.

Broadly speaking policy can take three main forms:

1 State ownership   When it is important not to destroy the advantages of a monopoly the problem may best be solved by the state taking it over completely; the public then appears to be effectively protected. Freed from the incentive of the profit motive there should be no tendency for state-owned monopolies to make high profits. Should, however, such profits be made they would eventually be passed on to the public in lower prices and reduced taxation.

In practice, however, profits may be masked by inefficiency in operation. Consequently provision must be made for the prices charged to be examined by an independent council and for efficiency checks to be carried out by independent experts.

2 Legislation and administrative machinery to regulate monopolies   This method is usually employed when it is desired to retain monopolies because of their benefits but to leave them under private ownership.

The Monopolies and Restrictive Practices Act, 1948 (since amended) set up a Monopolies Commission to investigate monopoly situations. Upon the Commission's report a Ministerial Order could declare certain arrangements or practices illegal. Subjects investigated include: supply of electric lamps, household detergents, colour film, wallpaper, drugs, breakfast cereals, bricks, duplicating equipment, tendering practices by builders in the Greater London Area, collective discrimination, and restrictive practices in the professions.

3 Breaking up or prohibition of the monopoly   Where the monopoly is on balance detrimental to consumers policy can take the form of breaking it up or prohibiting it by legislation. Thus the state could reduce the period for which patents are granted or it could make their renewal more difficult. Alternatively it can outlaw attempts to eliminate competition, whether by unfair practices, the formation of cartels or restrictive agreements. Total prohibition was the policy at one time followed in the USA.

In the UK an investigation by the Monopolies Commission led to the Restrictive Trade Practices Act, 1956. This: (a) allowed manufacturers and traders to enforce *individual* resale price maintenance through the ordinary civil courts; (b) banned the *collective* enforcement of resale price maintenance through such practices as private courts, stop lists and boycotts; (c) required other restrictive pacts, such as common price and level tendering, to be registered with a new Registrar of Restrictive Trading Agreements, appointed by the Crown; and (d) appointed a new Restrictive Practices Court. The Court sits as three-member tribunals consisting of at least one judge and two lay members, and for a practice to be allowed it must be justified as being 'in the public interest' according to any of seven closely defined 'gateways'. The tribunal's decision is made on a majority basis.

But the 1956 Act still permitted individual suppliers to enforce resale price maintenance for their own products. This was amended by the Resale Prices Act, 1964, which made minimum resale price maintenance illegal, except for goods approved by the Court. To be approved the resulting benefits to consumers must outweigh any detriments.

The Monopolies and Mergers Act, 1965, strengthened and extended the legislation on monopolies. A merger or proposed merger can be referred to the Monopolies Commission where it would lead to a monopoly or would increase the power of an existing monopoly. The Act also increased the government's powers to enforce the findings of the Commission (for example, by giving it powers to prohibit mergers or to dissolve an undesirable monopoly).

The Fair Trading Act, 1973, introduced a new concept with regard to monopoly and consumer protection. Unlike the earlier Monopolies Acts, whose primary concern was whether monopolies might be harmful to economic efficiency and thus not in the 'public interest', the object of this new Act was stated to be to 'strengthen the machinery of *promoting competition*'. The Act:

(a) Created an office of Director General of Fair Trading. Not only did the Director take over the functions of the Registrar of Restrictive Trading Agreements but he also now has the responsibility for discovering probable monopoly situations or uncompetitive practices. Thus the Fair Trading Office provides Ministers with information and advice on consumer protection, monopoly, mergers and restrictive practices.

(b) Empowered the renamed Monopolies and Mergers Commission to investigate local as well as national monopolies, and also nationalised industries and even restrictive labour practices.

(c) Reduced the criterion for a monopoly situation to a one-quarter (minimum) market share.

IV Monopolistic competition

Conditions giving rise to monopolistic competition

Neither perfect competition nor pure monopoly are found frequently in the real world; usually an industry consists of elements of both. A common situation is where there are many firms each making a product which differs only slightly in detail from that of its rivals.

On the demand side each producer tries to differentiate his product by a variety of means, e.g. extensive advertising, free gifts, distinctive wrappers, a brand name. Up to a point 'goodwill' retains customers rather than the actual price charged. Such a producer has some monopoly power, being faced with a demand curve which slopes downwards from left to right. But since there are fairly good substitutes available demand tends to be fairly elastic.

On the supply side, because entry to the industry is possible, the situation is similar to perfect competition. Where one producer can be seen to be making super-normal profits, existing producers tend to copy his product and new competitors start producing a somewhat similar brand.

The equilibrium under monopolistic competition

In the short period each firm is a little 'monopolist', for new firms cannot enter the industry or copy his particular 'gimmick'. He will make super-normal profits, $DABC$ at an output of OM (in Figure 10.13(a)).

Fig. 10.13
Monopolistic
competition

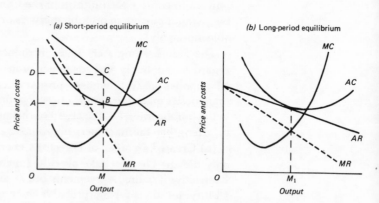

(a) Short-period equilibrium

(b) Long-period equilibrium

In the long period firms are free to enter the industry. They will copy the product of the most successful producer until super-normal profits have disappeared. Moreover, demand for the product of each producer will decrease and become more elastic with the development of better substitutes. The equilibrium output is OM_1 (in Figure 10.13(b)), where price still exceeds MR, with the result that output is less than under perfect competition.

The economic and social effects of monopolistic competition

(1) *Even in the long period firms operate at less than optimum size.* Under perfect competition not only are super-normal profits eliminated but also in the long period each firm is producing where AC is a minimum – the optimum output. At this output factors of production are combined in the correct proportions and the full advantages of large-scale economies are achieved. What happens under monopolistic competition is that firms operate at less than their optimum size, and thus there is some waste in the way in which factors are used.

But we should not assume from the above argument that monopolistic competition is necessarily a 'bad' thing. Not every consumer will want to buy goods which are identical with those bought by other consumers. Different individuals have slightly different tastes. Thus waste in the use of scarce resources can be regarded as the part of the price that has to be paid for variety of choice.

(2) *Costs are incurred in competitive advertising.* In practice, even where there is a high degree of competition, firms marketing a new product have to spend money in bringing its merits to the notice of consumers. Such 'informative' advertising may even allow the advantages of large-scale production to be achieved by expanding demand.

Under monopolistic competition, however, most advertising seeks to persuade people of the superiority of the particular brand. Again this represents a waste of resources; in reality there may be little difference between brands, but factors are used trying to convince the public that it is otherwise.

In practice it is not always easy to draw the line between informative and persuasive advertising. What is 'one man's meat is another man's poison'; and if you adhere to the principle of allowing people to exercise freedom of choice, then you must accept the concomitant – that they are open to be persuaded. What consumers lack is knowledge of goods, and they are thus easy victims to the pressures of advertising. Today there is only a private body, the Consumer's Association (publishing *Which?*), to report on goods to subscribers.

V Oligopoly, and pricing in practice

Pricing where there are few firms

In real life many goods and services are produced by just a few firms, e.g. screws, washing powders, kitchen tiles, lawnmowers, petrol. Here we have 'oligopoly', where pricing policy conforms to no given principles. Sometimes one firm is so dominant that its price is more or less followed by the smaller firms. In other cases firms may be of fairly equal strength but, since their number is small, no one firm can set a price without considering the likely reaction of its competitors. For instance, if it reduces its price, it cannot guarantee a greater share of the market since other firms may retaliate and cut their prices. Occasionally open war between firms may break out; usually they have a tacit understanding that they will not act unilaterally. A change in the price of petrol, for instance, occurs more or less simultaneously for all firms.

Pricing policy in practice

With oligopoly, therefore, firms do not fix a price at an output where MC equals MR. Indeed, in many other cases this principle is not adhered to rigidly. For one thing the optimum output may be unobtainable because of cash-flow difficulties, the result of the capital market not being perfect. For another few markets are so perfectly competitive that individual producers have no control over their price and have such an exact knowledge of the shape of their demand curve that MR can be equated with MC at all outputs.

Pricing policy therefore usually follows more pragmatic methods. Sometimes, for example with government contracts, the firm may follow a 'cost-plus' approach, being allowed what is considered to be a fair percentage addition to basic costs to cover overheads and normal profit; or the firm will, by a process of trial and error, seek to charge 'what the traffic will bear', e.g. the 'black-market' ticket seller.

More usually pricing is on a 'mark-up' basis, the cost of manufacturing alone being calculated accurately with a given and rather arbitrary percentage added for overheads to yield the final selling price. Thus, in selling a book, the publisher calculates the cost of printing and binding, adds a percentage (say 40 per cent) to cover overheads and normal profit, and fixes a final bookshop price which covers these costs plus the author's royalty and the bookseller's margin based on the retail price.

Indeed this may be the only practicable method when firms are producing more than one product, as is usual. A publisher, for instance, could not exist on the sales of one book and, in any case, he would want the extra security of publishing different types of books. Furthermore, in order to survive producers have to pay regard to what is known as 'the product life-cycle', which consists of innovation, growth, maturity, saturation and decline (see Figure 10.14). In the growth period the product shows increasing profitability, for the firm enjoys almost a monopoly position. With time competitors enter; sales increase, but only at the expense of rising advertising costs. Thereafter the market becomes oversupplied or competitors produce improved models, and sales decline. Thus the go-ahead firm will always be planning new products so that one replaces another as each passes through its life-cycle.

Fig. 10.14
The product life-cycle

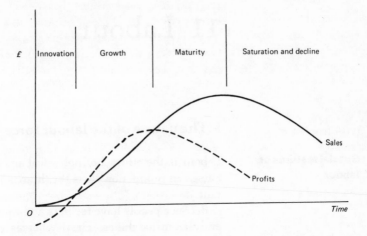

With a many-product firm the exact share of overheads attributable to any one product would be difficult, if not impossible, to ascertain. The mark-up method sidetracks this difficulty. Furthermore, it allows control by the cost accountant, especially as regards maintaining cash flow and assuring profitable production. Where pricing is on the principle of $MC = MR$, there is no certainty that total costs are covered.

11 Labour

I The nature of the labour force

Special features of labour

Labour is the effort, both physical and mental, made by human beings in production. It is the 'human' element which is important.

Because people have feelings and emotion they respond differently from machines. First, whereas a machine which proves profitable can be reproduced fairly easily and quickly, the overall supply of labour does not depend upon its earnings. Other factors are more important in deciding how many children parents have (see pp. 22–3). Second, the effort of labour is not determined solely by the monetary reward offered. The method of payment may affect effort, while raising wages may result in less work being offered. Above all, a contented worker will produce more than an unhappy one; thus job satisfaction or loyalty to a firm, rather than a high rate of pay, may be decisive in inducing an employee to work overtime. Third, labour does not move readily, either occupationally or geographically, in response to the offer of a higher reward. Often such 'immobility' results from strong human contacts. Fourth, workers can combine together in trade unions. Finally, if unemployed for long periods, workers deteriorate physically and mentally.

Both firms and the government must have policies which take account of these special characteristics. Training schemes are essential to improve the skill of workers and thus their productivity. Firms must pay particular attention to psychological and social factors in an effort to secure a contented labour force. Furthermore, they must endeavour to co-operate with the workers' trade-union representatives. Above all, firms have to comply with the constraints imposed by government policy.

The government is vitally concerned with labour. It lays down the conditions of contract, supervises working conditions and prescribes the terms under which a worker may be dismissed. Moreover, it exerts pressure in wage negotiations in order to avoid inflationary wage increases. Above all, it pursues a variety of policies aimed at securing a high and stable level of employment.

Thus employing labour presents particular problems to firms. To what extent must labour be treated differently from other resources? What wages and other conditions will it have to meet? Will sufficient labour with the right kind of skills be available? Does the government stipulate a minimum wage rate? Along what lines shall it bargain with trade unions? To what extent does the government impose special conditions regarding the engagement and dismissal of workers? What are the employer's obligations for what his workers do? What safety precautions must he take? This chapter seeks to provide guidelines to answering such questions.

The supply of labour

The total supply of labour in an economy depends upon:

(1) *The size of population.* The size of the population sets an obvious limit to the total supply of labour. But while it is influenced by economic factors, e.g. through the birth rate and immigration, it is doubtful, especially in more advanced economies, whether economic factors are of paramount importance.

(2) *The proportion of the population which works.* The working population, the proportion of the population which forms the labour force, is determined chiefly by the age distribution, social institutions and customs, the participation rates of married women, the wage offered and, to a lesser extent, by the numbers who can live on unearned incomes.

(3) *The amount of work offered by each individual labourer.* Higher rates of pay usually induce a person to work overtime, the increased reward encouraging him to substitute work for leisure. But this is not always so. A higher wage rate enables the worker to maintain his existing material standard of living with less work, and he may prefer extra leisure to more goods.

Nevertheless, as we shall see, more significant to the firm than the overall supply of labour are the obstacles to mobility which divide up the labour market.

II Determination of the rate of pay

Methods of rewarding labour

Some people are self-employed – window-cleaners, plumbers, solicitors, doctors, etc. As such they are really 'entrepreneurs', securing the rewards when demand is high but accepting the risks of working for a low return. Nevertheless, most workers contract out of risk, accepting a wage which is received whether or not the product of their labour is sold. However, some element of risk-bearing may be incorporated in the wage agreement, e.g.

by commission payments, bonus schemes and profit-sharing arrangements.

In what follows reference will be mainly to the *wage rate* – the sum of money which an employer contracts to pay a worker in return for services rendered. Such a definition includes salaries as well as wages, and makes no distinction between time and piece rates. *Earnings* are what the worker actually receives in his pay packet (his 'take-home' pay) *plus* deductions which have been made for insurance, income tax, superannuation, etc. In practice earnings over a period often exceed the agreed wage rate, additions being received for overtime working, piece rates, or bonus payments.

Where the nature of the work allows workers to be paid on a piece-rate basis as an alternative to time rates, the firm has to consider their respective merits.

1 Time rates   Time rates are more satisfactory than piece rates where:

a   a high quality of work is essential, e.g. computer programming;

b   the work cannot be speeded up, e.g. bus-driving, milking cows;

c   there is no standard type of work, e.g. car repairs;

d   care has to be taken of delicate machinery, e.g. hospital medical tests;

e   output cannot be easily measured, e.g. teaching, nursing;

f   working long hours may undermine health, e.g. laundry work;

g   the labour is by nature a fixed factor which has to be engaged whatever the output, e.g. clerical and selling staff;

h   periods of temporary idleness necessarily occur, e.g. repair work;

On the other hand, time rates have certain disadvantages:

a   lack of incentive for better workers;

b   supervision of workers is usually necessary;

c   agreements can be undermined by working to rule and 'go-slow' tactics.

2 Piece rates   Where output is both measurable and more or less proportionate to the amount of effort expended, piece rates are possible. It is not essential that each invidiual worker's output can be measured exactly. So long as the output of his group can be assessed he can share in the group's earnings.

The advantages of piece rates are:

a   effort is stimulated;

b the more efficient workers obtain a higher reward;

c the need for constant supervision and irksome time-keeping is eliminated;

d interest is added to dull, routine work;

e workers can proceed at their own pace;

f a team spirit is developed where workers operate in a small group;

g workers are encouraged to suggest methods of improving production;

h the employer's costing calculations are simplified;

i output is increased, and the more intensive use of capital equipment spreads overheads.

We see, therefore, that piece rates have advantages for both the employee and employer. Moreover, the lower prices which result benefit the community as a whole. Nevertheless, for the following reasons they are often disliked by trade unions:

a workers may over-exert themselves;

b where piece rates have to be varied according to local conditions or different circumstances, e.g. capital per employee, negotiations for a national wage rate can be made difficult;

c variations in piece rates from one place to another undermine union solidarity;

d the union may lose control over the supply of labour, and this makes it difficult to take strike action or to apportion work in periods of unemployment;

e piece rates are subject to misunderstanding, e.g. an employer who installs a better machine may be accused of cutting the rate if he does not attribute all the increased output to the effort of labour;

f workers may resist being shifted from tasks in which they have acquired dexterity (and which therefore produce high piece-rate earnings) even though the current needs of the factory organisation require such a transfer. Thus employers find that piece rates lead to a loss of control over their employees, and many prefer to pay high time rates to avoid this.

3 Combined wage and piece rates   When deciding the basis of the wage rate both employees and employers want certain guarantees. Workers have a minimum standard of living to maintain, and they desire protection against variations in output which lie outside their control, e.g. weather conditions. On the other hand employers providing expensive equipment must ensure that it is used for a minimum period of time. Thus piece rates are usually incorporated in a wider contract which provides for some basic wage and a stipulated minimum number of hours.

The theoretical
determination of the
wage rate in a free
market

The wage rate is the price of labour and, like other prices, it is determined in a free market by demand and supply.

1 Demand   The demand for labour is made up of the individual demands of all the firms using it. The actual price which a firm is willing to pay for a worker depends upon the addition to receipts which will result. We can give more precision by developing our analysis of the law of diminishing returns. Let us assume that: (a) there is perfect competition in the market where the product is sold; (b) there is perfect competition in buying labour – each firm is so small that it cannot alter the wage rate which it has to pay by varying its demand.

The analysis of the law of diminishing returns above was conducted in terms of physical yields – so many hundredweights of potatoes. But when engaging labour the firm is more interested in what the product sells for. What it asks, therefore, is: 'How much will total receipts increase if an additional worker is employed?' The value of this extra contribution is known as the *marginal revenue product (MRP)*.

The MRP depends not only on the marginal physical product but also on the price at which the product sells. Under perfect competition the producer can sell any quantity at a given price. Hence the *MRP* is equal to the marginal physical product times the price of the product. Thus, by taking the marginal physical products of Table 9.1, and assuming that potatoes sell at £10 per cwt., we can arrive at the *MRP*. For example, when two labourers are employed the total physical product is 8 cwt., which at £10 a cwt. yields a total revenue of £80, and so on.

The farmer in our example will employ an extra worker so long as the *MRP* exceeds the cost, i.e. the wage rate. Thus, if the wage rate were £65 per week, he would engage six workers because the value of the product of the sixth man was £65, and this just covered his wages. If fewer men, say five, were employed, the *MRP* of £75 would exceed the wage rate. On the other hand if seven men were employed, the farmer would be paying the seventh man £5 more than he contributed to receipts.

Of course it might be questioned whether the firm can always estimate the *MRP* of a factor of production. Thus with certain workers such as clerks, teachers, policemen, etc., there is no definite physical product. How then can their marginal physical product, and thus the marginal revenue product, be measured? The answer is simply that it cannot be – but that does not alter the fact that in practice a firm behaving rationally and not 'empire-building' does proceed to engage workers as though it can so estimate.

The *MRP* at different wage rates therefore gives the demand curve of the individual firm for labour (see Figure 11.1). The

Fig. 11.1
The firm's demand
curve for labour

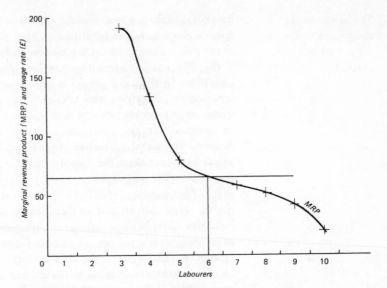

industry's demand curve is the sum of the demands of the individual firms (curve *D* in Figure 11.2). This would be a simple horizontal addition if the price of the product remained unchanged. But it is much more realistic to assume that, as firms engage more labour, the extra output will lead to a fall in its price. The result will be that the industry's demand curve for a factor will fall more steeply than the curve obtained by a straightforward addition of firms' marginal revenue product curves.

Fig. 11.2
The determination of
the price of a factor

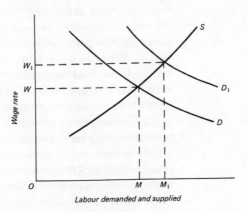

2 Supply The supply of labour will depend upon:

(a) *The response of existing labour to a higher wage rate.* In the short period an industry may find that a wage increase may result in *less* labour being supplied, the higher income enabling workers to enjoy more leisure, as in coal-mining. In the long period,

however, higher wages should attract labour from other industries, occupations or localities so that the long-period supply
curve follows the shape of the S curve in Figure 11.2.

(b) *The cost of attracting workers from alternative uses or
localities.* In the long period a higher wage will attract labour
from other industries and occupations. The extent to which a
given wage increase attracts workers depends upon the elasticity
of demand for the products in these alternative sources. If
demand is inelastic, higher wages can be offered to hold on
to labour, and thus the supply of labour will expand little in
response to the wage rise.

(c) *The mobility of labour.* In the theoretical long period a
higher wage rate should attract labour from alternative uses or
localities. But, because labour experiences particular difficulties
in moving, the 'long period' is delayed indefinitely. Instead the
labour market tends to be divided into a number of separate
smaller markets according to occupation or locality. This can be
explained as follows. A worker may be required: (i) to shift his
job from one industry to another; (ii) to change his occupation;
(iii) to move his home to a different district. Often conditions
dictate that all three types of change take place at the same time,
but this is not necessarily so. Each presents its own obstacles to
changing jobs, and gives rise to the 'immobility of labour'.

(i) *Obstacles between industries.* Provided that it does not
involve a change of occupation or district, a worker can usually
move his job from one industry to another fairly easily. Clerks,
typists, storemen, lorry drivers and porters, for example, are
found in most industries. But middle-aged and older workers
may experience difficulty. Prejudice or tradition in certain industries may also prove to be obstacles. Women, for instance, would
find it difficult to become taxi-drivers in London. Moreover,
loyalty to his firm may prevent a worker from looking elsewhere
even though he has suffered a cut in wages, though obviously this
does not apply if he is unemployed.

(ii) *Obstacles to a change of occupation.* In changing occupations there may be obstacles to entering a new one: a high natural
ability is required in certain occupations; training is costly and
takes time; stringent conditions are prescribed by trade unions or
professional associations; the new job is repugnant, or alternatively some occupations, e.g. the Church, the arts, acting, are so
pleasant that workers are not drawn into another occupation by
the offer of a higher wage rate; workers may be too old to learn a
new job; workers may prefer to remain unemployed in alternative
occupations rather than accept a wage below a recognised
minimum; in spite of prohibiting legislation, there is discrimination on account of sex, colour, social class, or religion; workers
are ignorant of wage rates and opportunities in other occupations.

Of the above the greatest obstacle to occupational mobility is natural ability. In this respect it should be noted that there can be more mobility between occupations, e.g. storeman and clerk, requiring the same level of innate ability than between doctors and dockers, where there are marked differences in the natural ability and training required. The first is sometimes termed 'horizontal' occupational mobility; the second, where there are non-competing groups of workers, is called 'vertical' mobility.

(iii) *Obstacles to a change of district.* When it comes to moving from one part of the country to another workers have to overcome both physical and psychological obstacles. These include: the costs of moving; the difficulty of securing accommodation elsewhere on comparable terms, particularly for council and rent-controlled tenants; social ties of friends, clubs, Church, etc.; family ties, such as the children's education; imperfect knowledge of vacancies or wages paid in other localities; prejudice against certain parts of the country, people at present generally preferring to live in the south-east of the country rather than in the industrial north.

Such immobility of labour means that wage rates can often be more easily explained by supply conditions rather than by demand. Even if there is competition between employers, differences in supply produce differences in the wage rates between occupations, and between localities even for the same occupation. Thus solicitors earn more than their clerks because: (a) on the demand side the services of solicitors are valued more highly; (b) on the supply side the supply of solicitors is small compared with clerks, for more natural ability and longer training are required.

Immobility is also one of the major causes of unemployment, and in Chapter 17 we consider some of the ways in which the government tries to reduce occupational and geographical immobility.

Demand, supply and the wage rate

The reward of a factor, in this case the wage rate, is determined by the interaction of demand and supply. Thus in Figure 11.2, with demand curve D and supply curve S, the wage rate is OW.

The wage rate can rise through an increase in the MRP or a decrease in the supply of labour to the market. MRP can rise through an increase in physical productivity or through a higher selling price of the product. Both would lead to a shift in the demand curve to the right, say from D to D_1. As a result the wage rate rises to OW_1 and the number of men employed increases from OM to OM_1. Higher labour productivity leads to higher employment, other things being equal. Similarly, a decrease in the supply of labour to a particular industry, e.g. because of the attraction of other industries, would have the effect of raising the wage rate but with fewer employed.

Engaging labour   Because of immobility the market for most labour tends to be local. Moreover, with many occupations a firm's knowledge of the going wage rate is often imperfect. Thus, even when there is a nationally agreed wage rate, the actual wage paid may vary from one firm to another since it will be affected by local agreements, bonuses and 'fringe benefits', negotiated separately with individual firms.   This imperfection is reflected by the variety of methods of recruiting labour. Thus we have:

1 Government agencies   Employers notify their requirements, mostly of unskilled and semi-skilled labour, to the employment exchanges and Jobcentres of the Employment Service Agency (ESA). Vacancies are displayed without the name of the firm. If a worker is interested in the job, arrangements are made for an interview with the firm. No fee is charged.

Any employer wishing to recruit staff at managerial, professional, scientific and technical level can do so through Professional and Executive Recruitment, a separately managed organisation within the ESA. Through experienced consultants selection, interviewing and advertising services are offered free to employees, but employers are charged a fee.

For school-leavers local authorities provide careers advice, and the Youth Employment Service arranges job placements according to vacancies notified by employers.

2 Advertising   Few firms rely entirely on government agencies for filling vacancies. For unskilled workers vacancies are advertised outside the works building and in local newspapers. For professional staff and skilled workers national newspapers and, above all, trade journals are used for advertising, though it must be remembered that many such vacancies are filled by internal training and promotion.

3 Employment agencies   Private employment agencies are confined mainly to certain occupations, e.g. secretarial (Alfred Marks) and managerial staff (Brook Street Executive Resources Limited).

The determination of the conditions of employment in the real world   While demand and supply are the underlying determinants of an occupation's basic wage rate, the actual wage and the conditions of employment are strongly influenced by imperfect competition in the labour market, trade-union activity and government intervention.

Imperfection in the labour market arises where one firm is the major employer in a locality. But mainly it is due to trade unions, which (through the closed shop) can establish what is virtually a monopoly in the supply of a given type of labour. We therefore

analyse, in the next section, the economic background to trade-
union activity with reference to its strength in negotiating wage
increases.

The government, too, influences the wage rate through: (a) its
minimum-wage regulations (see p. 186); (b) the legal protection
it affords to workers regarding the conditions of work; and (c) the
over-all guidelines for wage settlements which it lays down from
time to time in its efforts to combat inflation. The first two will be
examined later in this chapter; the third is discussed in Chapter
18 in the context of inflation.

III Trade unions and collective bargaining

**Objectives of trade-
union activity**

Trade unions have many functions, the most important of which
are: (a) providing educational, social and legal benefits for
members; (b) improving standards of work, (c) obtaining pay
increases; and (d) co-operating with the government of the day in
order to secure a workable economic policy and to improve
working and living conditions generally. We are concerned mainly with the last two.

**The process of
collective bargaining**

Collective bargaining is the method of settling the conditions of
employment by employers negotiating with the workers' trade
unions. For its smooth working certain conditions should be
fulfilled. First, it must be pursued with good sense on both sides.
This is enhanced where the industry already has a tradition of
good labour relations and if there is some accepted objective
measure to which wage rates can be linked (e.g. the Index of
Retail Prices, wage rates paid in similar trades, the level of profits
in the industry). Second, both sides should be represented by
strong organisations. Where all employers are linked in an
association there is no fear of outsiders stealing a march by
negotiating independent wage bargains, while if the union can
speak for all its members employers know an agreement will be
honoured. Unofficial stoppages damage the union's reputation
and, to avoid them, there must be regular contact between
employer and union and prompt investigation of grievances on
the shop floor. Third, there must be an understood procedure for
settling disputes. While this must not be so prolonged as to fray
patience, it should exhaust all possibilities of reaching agreement
before a strike or lock-out is called.

In short the procedure of collective bargaining covers (1)
negotiation, and (2) the settlement of disputes.

1 Negotiation   Broadly speaking the machinery for negotiation falls into three groups:

(a) *Voluntary negotiation.* Generally the government has left it to the unions and employers' organisations to work out their own procedures, and today voluntary machinery covers 60 per cent of the insured workers of Great Britain. Because union organisation varies the recognised procedure differs between industries and trades. Indeed it may contain no provision for arbitration when a wage claim is rejected, as in the engineering and shipbuilding industries.

(b) *Joint Industrial Councils.* Most industries have some national joint council or committee which, without outside assistance, thrashes out agreements. Usually it follows the system of Joint Industrial Councils, composed of representatives of employers and workers in the industry. These consider regularly such matters as the better use of the practical knowledge and experience of the work-people, general principles governing the conditions of employment, means of ensuring workers the greatest possible security of earnings and employment, methods of fixing and adjusting earnings (piece rates, etc.), technical education and training, industrial research, improvement of processes and proposed legislation affecting the industry. Although Joint Industrial Councils are sponsored by the government, they are not forced upon any industry, and some important industries, such as iron and steel, engineering, shipbuilding and cotton, which had already developed their own procedure for negotiation, have not formed Joint Industrial Councils. Nevertheless, in 1979 there were some 400 Joint Industrial Councils or bodies of similar character.

(c) *Wages Councils.* In some industries and trades where the organisation of workers or employers is either non-existent or ineffective the government has had to intervene. This started in 1909 when Trade Boards were set up to fix minimum time and piece rates for the 'sweated' trades, such as bespoke tailoring, where home-workers were being paid exceptionally low wages. Subsequently these Boards were increased and in 1945 were renamed Wages Councils and given extended powers. In 1979 there were forty-three such Wages Councils covering the clothing, textile, food and drink, and metalware industries, together with distribution, catering, road haulage and other services. The Councils are appointed by the Secretary of State for Employment and are composed of equal numbers of employers' and workers' representatives together with not more than three independent members. Their task is to fix minimum remuneration and conditions regarding holidays and a minimum week, which, if the Minister approves, become the subject of a Wage Regulation Order, enforceable by law. In addition they may advise the

Minister regarding problems affecting labour in the industry. In agriculture wages are fixed by machinery similar to the Wages Council system. Thus about 15 per cent of insured workers are covered by schemes of statutory wage regulation, as opposed to the 60 per cent where negotiation is on a voluntary basis.

2 Settlement of disputes   Where the negotiating machinery fails to produce an agreement, it is advantageous if agreed procedures exist for ending the deadlock. Three methods can be employed: conciliation, arbitration or special inquiry.

(a) *Conciliation*. In 1974 the Secretary of State for Employment set up an *independent* Advisory, Conciliation and Arbitration Service (ACAS) controlled by a Council whose members are experienced in industrial relations. When efforts to obtain settlement of a dispute through normal procedures have failed, ACAS can provide conciliation if the parties concerned agree.

(b) *Arbitration*. ACAS can, at the joint request of the parties to a dispute, appoint single arbitrators or boards of arbitration chosen from a register of people experienced in industrial relations to determine differences on the basis of agreed terms of reference.

Alternatively the Terms and Conditions of Employment Act, 1959, allows claims that a particular employer is not observing the terms or conditions of employment established for the industry to be referred compulsorily to an Industrial Court for a legally binding award.

(c) *Inquiry and investigation*. The Secretary of State for Employment has legal power to inquire into the causes and circumstances of any trade dispute and, if he thinks fit, to appoint a Court of Inquiry with power to call for evidence. Such action, however, is chiefly a means of informing Parliament and the public of the facts and causes of a major dispute and is taken only when no agreed settlement seems possible.

The Minister's power of inquiry also allows for less formal action in the setting up of Committees of Investigation when the public interest is not so wide and general.

Neither a Court of Inquiry nor a Committee of Investigation is a conciliation or arbitration body, but both may make recommendations upon which a reasonable settlement of the dispute can be based.

The extent to which trade unions can secure wage increases   This brings us to the questions of how and to what extent unions can secure increases in their respective wage rates in conditions of free collective bargaining. We shall assume that the trade union is a 'closed shop' with 100 per cent membership, making it virtually a monopolist in selling that particular type of labour.

Broadly speaking there are three ways in which a trade union can secure a wage increase:

(1) *It can support measures which will increase the demand for labour.* An increase in the demand for labour will come about if the *MRP* curve rises, either through an improvement in the physical productivity of the workers, or by an increase in the price of the product. Thus the National Union of Mineworkers not only supports the National Coal Board's exhortation to miners to improve output per manshift but backs the campaign advertising the advantages of solid fuel for central heating.

The situation is illustrated in Figure 11.3. As marginal revenue productivity rises from *MRP* to MRP_1 wages of existing workers, *ON,* rise from *OW* to OW_1. Alternatively, if there were unemployment, extra men, NN_1, could be employed at the previous wage rate.

Fig. 11.3
The effect of a change in marginal revenue productivity on the wage rate

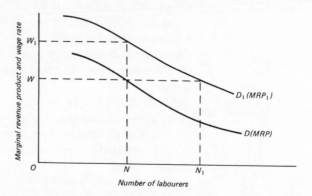

(2) *It can restrict the supply of labour, allowing members to compete freely in fixing remuneration with employers.* Where a trade union or professional association can limit entry it may also stipulate a minimum wage rate or scale of charges. But it need not do so. The supply of plumbers and electricians, for instance, is restricted by apprenticeship regulations, but many work on their own account and *negotiate* their own rewards. Similarly, solicitors, doctors, surgeons, accountants and surveyors are restricted by the necessary professional qualifications, but suggested scale fees are not rigidly enforced.

We can therefore analyse this method of securing a wage increase by the simple demand and supply approach (see Figure 11.4). If the trade union reduces the supply of workers in an occupation from *S* to S_1, the wage rate rises from *OW* to OW_1.

(3) *It can fix a minimum wage rate.* Where wages are raised by restricting entry the trade union does not have to worry about unemployed members. It works simply on the principle that, assuming demand remains unchanged, greater scarcity leads to a higher reward.

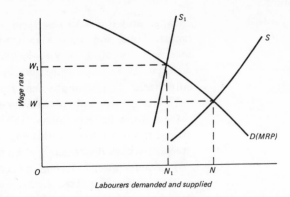

Fig. 11.4
The effect on the wage rate of trade-union restriction of the supply of labour

Labourers demanded and supplied

Most trade unions, however, are faced with a more difficult problem. While they may secure a higher wage rate for their members, their success may be double-edged if many members are sacked as a result. Herein is the rub. What we really have to ask, therefore, is: *under what conditions can a trade union obtain higher wages for its members without decreasing the numbers employed?*

Once again we have to consider conditions of competition.

(a) *Perfect competition in both selling the product and buying labour.* In the short period, even if there is perfect competition, a firm may be making super-normal profits. Here a strong trade union could, by threatening to withhold all its labour, force the employer to increase wages to the point where his super-normal profits disappear.

But this could not be permanent. The long-period equilibrium position is one in which there are no super-normal profits and the wage rate is equal to the *MRP*. A higher wage will represent a rise in costs. Some employers will now be forced out of business (see p. 159) and remaining firms will have to reduce their demand for labour until once again the wage rate is equal to the *MRP*. Thus in Figure 11.4 we will assume that *OW* is the original wage rate fixed by competition and *ON* the number of men employed – the trade-union membership. Suppose the trade union stipulates a minimum wage of OW_1. In the long period employment will then be reduced to ON_1. Given a downward-sloping *MRP* curve this will always be true. Where there is perfect competition both in selling the product and in buying labour, a trade union can successfully negotiate an increase in wages only if there has been increased productivity; an increase without this will merely lead to members becoming unemployed.

The amount of unemployment resulting from such a rise in wages depends upon the elasticity of demand for labour. This will vary with:

(i) *The physical possibility of substituting alternative factors.* As the price of one factor rises other factors become relatively cheaper and the tendency is to substitute them for the dearer factor. Thus, if wages rise, firms try to install labour-saving machinery: that is, they replace labour by capital. But because different factors are imperfect substitutes for each other such substitution is limited physically.

The degree of substitutability is shown by the slope of the marginal productivity curve. Where labour is added to another factor, but is a poor substitute for it, marginal productivity falls steeply; where it is a fairly good substitute, marginal productivity falls more gently. Thus in Figure 11.5 (a) labour is not a good substitute for the fixed factor, capital, and marginal revenue productivity falls steeply. Demand for labour is therefore inelastic, and a wage rise of WW_1 leads to only NN_1 men becoming unemployed. Compare this with Figure 11.5 (b) where labour and capital are better substitutes. Here the same wage fall leads to much more unemployment.

Fig. 11.5
Substitutability
between labour and
capital

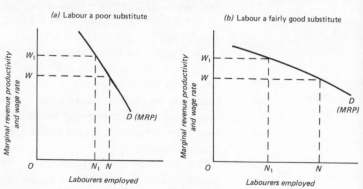

It should be noted that since the possibility of substitution increases overtime the longer the period under consideration, the greater will be the change in the labour force.

(ii) *The elasticity of supply of alternative factors.* Under conditions of perfect competition the cost of a factor to an individual firm will not rise as the firm's demand for that factor increases (see p. 160). But when we are analysing a rise in the wage rate of the workers of an *industry* we must recognise that the whole industry will now be demanding the alternative factors in order to substitute them for labour. This increased demand will raise the price of the alternative factors, again limiting the extent to which substitution is carried out. Thus if the supply of the alternative factor is perfectly elastic, only the physical considerations referred to above will affect the demand for it; if, on the other hand, supply is inelastic, then it is likely that the quick rise in its price will soon make it uneconomic to substitute it for labour.

(iii) *The proportion of labour costs to total costs.* The proportion of labour costs to total costs has two effects. First, if labour costs form only a small percentage of total costs, demand for labour will tend to be inelastic, for there is less urgency in seeking substitutes (see p. 120). Second, if labour costs form a small percentage of total costs, as in steel production, a rise in wages will produce only a small movement to the left of the supply curve of the product. The opposite applies in each case.

(iv) *The elasticity of demand for the final product.* A rise in the wage rate shifts the supply curve of the product to the left. Hence the market price of the good rises. We have to ask, therefore: 'How much will demand for the good contract as a result?' The answer depends upon the elasticity of demand.

If demand is elastic (D_{el}), the quantity of the good demanded will contract considerably, from OM to OM_1 in Figure 11.6. This will mean a large reduction in the numbers employed. On the other hand, if demand is inelastic (D_{inel}), there will be no great contraction – only to OM_2. Here people are willing to pay a higher price for the good (OP_2) and this will cover the increase in wages.

Fig. 11.6
The extent to which demand for the product contracts as a result of a wage increase

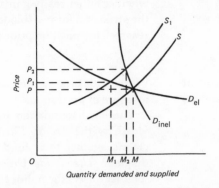

Quantity demanded and supplied

Elasticity of demand depends mainly on the availability of substitutes. Thus demand in export markets is usually more elastic than in the home market, for with the former there are often many competing alternative sources of supply from foreign firms. Consequently, if an industry sells a high percentage of its output abroad, e.g. scientific instruments and machine-tools, the trade union is limited in its ability to secure wage increases.

(b) *Imperfect competition.* If there is imperfect competition in selling the product or in hiring labour, the firm is likely to be making super-normal profits. Here it may be possible for the trade union to wring increased wages from the employer without loss of employment. Since it is a monopolist in the supply of labour, the union can insist that the firm shall employ *all* or none of its members at the new wage rate. Thus the firm may be forced to employ workers beyond the point where $MRP = MC$. The difference would come from super-normal profits, with the firm working on the principle that 'half a loaf is better than none'.

In these circumstances there is a whole range of possible wage rates between the minimum which workers will accept and the maximum which employers are prepared to give rather than lose all their labour. The success of the trade union will therefore depend upon: (i) the extent to which it can maintain its monopoly position by preventing employers from engaging blacklegs, non-union workers or other substitute labour; and (ii) the bargaining ability of its leaders relative to that of the employers. On the one side the union leaders have to estimate how high they can push the wage rate without employers allowing a strike to take place; on the other the employers must judge the lowest rate acceptable without a strike. As each is by no means certain of the other's strength, bluff will play a large part in the negotiations. Such factors as a large order book for the firm's products, costly capital equipment standing idle, or a wealthy strike fund will obviously strengthen the union's hands. Should a strike actually take place, it is usually because of misjudgement by one side; it is doubtful whether either really gains in the long run by strike action. Thus the strike is a form of 'blood-letting', allowing one or both sides to reassess the position prior to further negotiations.

Legal framework of trade-union activity

While trade unions must act within the law, they do enjoy a large measure of protection.

The legal foundation for trade-union development was provided by the *Trades Disputes Act, 1906*, which removed civil claims against their funds for losses incurred through a trade dispute. *The Trade Union Act, 1913*, legalised the use of a 'political levy' for political activities, though members who objected could 'contract out'.

Recent legislation, however, has increased unions' powers. Governments recognise that trade-union co-operation in economic policy is now a necessity. Thus, through the National Economic Development Council, permanent arrangements exist for consultation at the national level between the government, the Confederation of British Industry and the TUC. Of more immediate concern is the agreement of trade unions to a national wages policy in order to control inflation. To this end the 1974 Labour government entered into a social contract with the trade unions which covered reform of the law relating to labour.

The *Employment Protection Act, 1975*, obliges employers to disclose information regarding their firms required by trade unions for purposes of collective bargaining. The Act also protects employees against dismissal for joining a union (though an employee who is dismissed for not joining where there is a 'closed-shop' agreement is given no protection). Moreover, where an employer refuses to recognise the union as the official bargaining agent or to agree to a closed-shop agreement, it can apply to ACAS for an official recommendation.

However, in practice the *Trade Union and Labour Relations Act, 1974*, has had the major effect. Section 13 grants trade unions immunity from tort actions where, in furtherance of a trade dispute, others are induced to break a contract of employment. This has lead to what is known as 'secondary picketing', whereby workers on strike can blockade other companies *whether or not* they are involved in the dispute. Thus in January 1979, lorry drivers were able to blockade ICI and United Biscuits, among other firms.

IV Worker protection

Most firms recognise that the productivity of their workers is dependent upon job satisfaction. In essence such satisfaction means that employees feel that they are treated fairly as regards both the wage rate and the general conditions of employment. Thus many firms provide training schemes, incentives for acquiring skill, medical services, sick pay, canteens, sports facilities, pension schemes and other 'fringe' benefits. Large firms usually have a personnel officer responsible for staff matters, including work-study schemes to combat boredom. By such means employers foster loyalty and good labour relations.

Until the middle of the twentieth century, however, the government confined its role largely to regulating for special conditions, e.g. employment in the mines, minimum wages in the sweated industries, insurance against sickness and unemployment, and generally taking measures to secure full employment.

In recent years trade-union co-operation with the government has produced detailed legislation covering the engagement of labour, working conditions and security of employment.

(1) Engaging labour

(a) Contracts of employment A contract of employment exists as soon as an employee starts work and the same rules apply as to any other contract (see Chapter 6). The contract can be oral or written, except that a contract of apprenticeship must be in writing. Today the contract of employment has ceased to be on a personal basis of employer and employee, being largely governed both by collective agreements between the trade union and employer, and by recent legislation (see below).

The *Contract of Employment Act, 1972*, recognises the inferior bargaining position of a worker and provides that: (i) Employers must, within thirteen weeks, provide employees with a written statement of the main terms and conditions of employment – title of job, pay, hours of work, holiday and sick-pay entitlement, pension scheme, length of notice required and the procedure for dealing with grievances over disciplinary decisions. Many of these points may be covered by referring employees to a particular document, such as a collective agreement or nationally agreed salary scales. (ii) After four weeks employment the employee is entitled to, and must give, a minimum period of notice depending on his length of service, e.g. one week for less than two years employment, but twelve weeks for twelve years or more.

Apart from the above requirements, employers and employees have common-law responsibilities. The *duties of the employer* are to pay wages (providing an itemised pay statement showing the reasons for deductions), take reasonable care of his employees' safety, provide work where this is necessary for earnings, e.g. commission (including guaranteed payments of £6·60 for up to five days per quarter where work is not provided as expected, e.g. because of reduced demand), and meet necessary expenses.

For his part the *employee* must obey the lawful orders of his employer, perform his duties responsibly and act in good faith, e.g. by not revealing business secrets or poaching his employer's customers.

(b) Equal pay   The *Equal Pay Act, 1970*, requires employers to treat men and women equally as regards pay and other conditions of employment for like work or work rated as equivalent. Any difference in their contracts has to be justified by the employer on grounds other than sex, such as qualifications or length of service.

(c) Sex and race discrimination   Under the *Sex Discrimination Act, 1975*, it is unlawful for employers to discriminate on grounds of sex or against married persons, though firms with fewer than six employees are excepted.

In order to promote better race relations the *Race Relations Act*, 1976, outlaws discrimination on racial grounds.

Both Acts cover discrimination in recruitment, training, promotion, etc. Individual complaints go to Industrial Tribunals – the Equal Opportunities Commission and the Commission for Racial Equality. Both conduct formal investigations and issue *Codes of Practice* with a view to eliminating discrimination and promoting equality of opportunity.

(d) Past convictions   To enable a person who has been convicted of a crime to make a fresh start the *Rehabilitation of Offenders Act, 1974*, provided for a 'spent conviction'. This means that when five years have elapsed after a non-prison sentence for a conviction, or ten years after a prison sentence of up to thirty months, the conviction becomes 'spent'. The Act provides that a person need not disclose a spent conviction to a prospective employer, nor shall such a conviction be proper grounds for dismissing or excluding him from any office, profession, occupation or employment.

(2) Working conditions

(a) Health and safety The common law has always held a master to be under obligation to take *reasonable care* for his servant's safety by employing 'a competent staff of men, adequate materials, and a proper system and effective supervision'. Today, however, the firm's obligations are largely specified by statute. Thus the *Factories Act, 1961*, and the *Offices, Shops and Railway Premises Act, 1963*, deal with safety arrangements and the amenities which have to be provided at places of work.

Eventually, however, all provisions for safety at work premises will be covered by the *Health and Safety at Work Act, 1974*. This seeks to:

(i) secure the health, safety and welfare of persons at work;

(ii) protect the public against risks to health and safety arising out of, or in connection with, the activities of persons at work;

(iii) control the storage and use of explosives and highly inflammable or other dangerous substances; and

(iv) control the emission of noxious or offensive substances into the atmosphere.

The Act operates through the Health and Safety Commission and the Health and Safety Executive. The Commission provides information and advice, and proposes regulations regarding training and research, and the Executive is mainly concerned with enforcing the legislation. Employers are responsible for maintaining safe premises and plant, providing instruction and training of employees and ensuring safe entrances and exits. These duties are criminally enforceable. Employees also have to act with reasonable care for safety and to co-operate with the employer in observing the Act's provisions.

(b) Industrial injuries The *Social Security Act, 1975*, now provides for compensation to employees injured at work or who contract a disease as a result of the nature of their employment. An accident covers any unexpected mishap, even if caused by another employee's misconduct. Entitlement to benefit is not based on fault on the part of the employer.

(3) Security of employment

(a) Termination of employment and unfair dismissal A contract of employment ends automatically if it is entered into for a fixed period; otherwise it may be terminated by either party giving reasonable notice (see above).

But the *Employment Protection Act, 1975,* provides against *unfair dismissal.* An employer has to justify dismissal on grounds of an employee's capability, conduct, redundancy or other substantial reason. An employee who thinks he has been unfairly dismissed can complain to an Industrial Tribunal within three months of dismissal provided he has twenty-six weeks' continuous employment or has not reached the normal retiring age. If the complaint that the employer has acted unfairly or unreasonably is upheld, the Tribunal can order reinstatement, or, if this is not practicable, award compensation against the employer. A code of practice has been drawn up by ACAS, and employers are expected to follow the procedure recommended by it.

Employers have complained that Tribunals tend to favour the employee, resulting in a growing number of claims for unfair dismissal.

(b) Redundancy payments   In a dynamic economy it is inevitable that people will have to seek new jobs as their industry declines. However, to help the employee financially and to encourage movement to another industry, the *Redundancy Payments Act,* 1965, requires the employer to make a lump-sum compensation payment for employees who have completed two years' continuous employment. The exact amount depends upon the employee's age, length of service and weekly pay. Employers are able to claim 41 per cent of the cost from a Redundancy Fund into which a part of National Insurance contributions are paid.

12 Occupying Premises

I The location of the business

In deciding where to produce a firm has to weigh the advantages of producing in a particular locality against the level of rent there compared with elsewhere.

Location advantages

The advantages of producing in a particular locality can be classified as: (a) natural, (b) acquired, (c) government-sponsored.

(a) Natural advantages Costs are incurred both in assembling raw materials and in distributing the finished product. With some goods the weight of the raw materials is far greater than that of the finished product. This is particularly true where coal is used for heat and power, e.g. in iron and steel production (see Figure 12.1). Here transport costs are saved by producing where raw materials are found (e.g. on coal and iron-ore fields), or where they are easily accessible (e.g. near a port).

Fig. 12.1
Production of pig iron

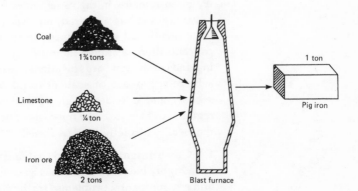

On the other hand with some industries the costs of transporting the finished product are greater than those of assembling the raw materials, e.g. ice-cream, mineral waters, beer, furniture, metal cans and glass containers. With these it is cheaper for a firm to produce near the market for its goods. Thus while the British

Steel Corporation has one main plant for producing steel tubes at Corby, Northants, where the iron ore is mined, Walls has ice-cream factories close to most large concentrations of population, and Metal Box manufactures its containers in over forty factories throughout Britain.

Suitability of climate may also affect location. Thus Lancashire's humid atmosphere helped the cotton spinning and weaving processes. Indeed in agriculture climate is usually decisive, given satisfactory soil conditions.

Under 'natural advantages' we can also include an abundant supply of cheap labour. This may be important in attracting certain industries, e.g. shipbuilding to Malta.

(b) Acquired advantages   Improved methods of production, the development of transport, inventions and new sources of power may alter the relative importance of natural advantages and so change an industry's location. Thus as high-grade iron-ore fields have become exhausted and improved techniques have reduced coal consumption, it is now cheaper to transport coal than the iron ore to produce pig iron, and so the industry has shifted from the coalfields to the low-grade iron-ore fields of the East Midlands. Similarly improved transport may upset the relative pulls. By transporting coal and iron ore to Dagenham, the Ford Motor Company can produce pig iron on a *consumption* centre. Finally, new inventions, such as humidifiers and water-softeners, make an industry less dependent upon a particular locality.

Yet we must not overstress the importance of the above changes. Even when natural factors have disappeared, an industry often remains in the same region because of the 'man-made' advantages it has acquired, e.g. steel, cotton. Such advantages were mentioned earlier when we studied external economies of concentration: a skilled labour force, communications, marketing and commercial organisations, nearby ancillary industries (to achieve economies of scale or to market by-products), training schools and a widespread reputation for the products of the region. All help to lower the costs of production, thereby making the locality attractive to new firms.

(c) Government-sponsored advantages   Unemployment in such highly localised industries as coal, cotton and shipbuilding, and environmental problems (traffic congestion, pollution, housing, etc.) in regions attracting new and expanding industries has led the government to offer firms financial inducements to set up plants in Development Areas (see p. 292).

The level of rents in different areas

Location advantages have to be weighed against the cost of land (or, where it is hired, rent). This cost varies from one locality to another and is determined by the market mechanism. Since other firms, possibly from other industries, may be looking for the same site advantages, competition will fix the price of land at the highest which the keenest firm is prepared to pay. This will be the firm which puts the greatest value on the land's advantages compared with land elsewhere. Thus early in its history it seemed that the cotton industry might settle on Clydeside, for this had all the natural advantages of South-east Lancashire. But it also had deep water – and shipbuilding firms were prepared to pay extra for this advantage. For cotton manufacturers this extra cost exceeded any disadvantage of being in Lancashire. Thus shipbuilding firms settled along the Clyde, and cotton firms settled in Lancashire.

In the final analysis, therefore, it is not the absolute advantages of a district which decide where a firm locates but the advantages relative to those of other districts. Thus an industry whose outlay on unskilled labour forms a high proportion of its production costs would, other things being equal, be able to bid more for land in an area of cheap labour than one whose spending on such labour was minimal. And in town centres we see the same principle at work – shops oust other businesses, and houses are converted into offices.

Other influences on location

A firm will normally choose a site where the advantages are greatest compared with its cost. But even for a comparatively new industry where natural advantages are important we cannot assume that they will be decisive. Thus historical accident largely accounts for the British Leyland plant at Cowley on the outskirts of Oxford, for the old school of William Morris came up for sale

Fig. 12.2 Factors influencing the siting of a business

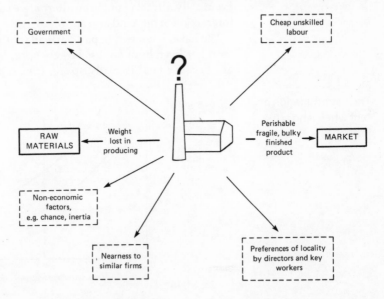

just as he was expanding his production of cars from his original cycle works.

Moreover, electricity has now practically eliminated dependence on a coalfield site. Yet firms may still go to the original areas because of the advantages acquired over time. Others may choose to be nearer their markets. Some 'footloose' firms have even located in certain districts particularly south-east England, largely because the managing directors (or their wives) have preferred living there!

The various factors influencing location are summarised in Figure 12.2 on page 199.

II Determination of the cost of land

The market mechanism

While the type of building erected on the site will affect the rent which has to be paid for premises, the major influence is the special characteristics of the site, and we shall concentrate on this 'land' element. We use the 'price of land' and 'rent' interchangeably since the former is simply the capitalised value of the latter. Thus if the current yield on a factory investment is 10 per cent, a factory whose annual net rent is £100,000 will have a capital value of £1 million.

The rent of land is determined, like that of other factor services, by demand and supply. The demand for land depends upon its productivity – its marginal revenue product. The supply of land for a particular use expands as the price rises, for the higher price eventually attracts land from alternative uses. Price is fixed by the interaction of demand and supply.

We have, however, to pay particular attention to supply. Once land has been built on it is largely specific to a given use. Above all, because land is really space, it is impossible to increase the

Fig. 12.3
The determination of
rent when land is fixed
in supply

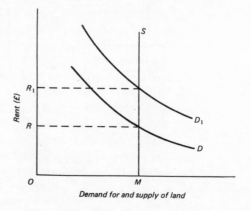

Demand for and supply of land

area of certain sites, e.g. Oxford Street and the City of London, except by building upwards. Such fixity of supply means that rent is largely determined by current demand. Thus in Figure 12.3 it is assumed that the supply of land is fixed at OM. This means that the rent is determined by demand. When this increases from D to D_1, the rent rises from OR to OR_1. Thus rents in Oxford Street depend upon the demand for shops there (which in its turn depends upon people's spending) and rents in the City of London depend upon the demand for offices there (which in turn depends upon the level of trade).

A note on 'economic rent'

It should be observed that the reward of any factor fixed in supply is determined by demand. This applies to the services provided by, say, Kevin Keegan and Sophia Loren for their ability is unique to themselves. Most of their earnings are in the nature of 'economic rent', the term used by economists to describe that part of the reward factor which results from some fixity of supply.

Much capital equipment, too, is for a time fixed in supply. Thus once a factory is purchased and equipped to produce cars it will take time to adjust its capacity fully; in the meantime how much the factory earns will be largely dependent upon the demand for cars. In time, however, the factory's capacity can be altered, and the economic-rent element disappears. To allow for this the economic rent of fixed factors is sometimes described as 'quasi-rent'.

Buying premises

Once the most advantageous location for the business has been decided the firm can obtain premises, either buying or renting. Established firms with capital reserves can buy outright. Since the cost is incurred once and for all it gives a hedge against future inflation.

Premises may be bought either freehold or leasehold. Without going into the legal technical details, *freehold* means that the rights to both the buildings and land are purchased outright. Nevertheless the deeds may include *covenants* restricting their use, or *easements* which allow other users certain rights over the land, e.g. of access or to lay a water-pipe. *Leasehold* means that the land is leased on a long term, usually ninety-nine to 999 years, for erecting the buildings, a fairly small freehold ground rent being paid each year to the lessor, the owner of the freehold. When the lease expires the land reverts to the freeholder together with the buildings on it; thus the shorter the lease remaining, the smaller is the hedge against inflation and the lower the price at which the leasehold can be sold. Leaseholds are common where the owner of the land wishes an estate, such as an industrial estate, to be developed as a whole, for the lease can impose conditions, e.g. concerning the use of the premises and the upkeep of roads and services, to secure maximum advantage for the occupiers of the estate as a whole.

Renting premises

Shortage of capital or the possibility of employing available funds in the development of the business means that most firms rent their premises. This has been true of government departments and local authorities, as extra accommodation has been required for expanding functions in recent years. Premises are taken on a lease, which today is usually about twenty-one years. The rent paid varies with the locality and the particular site, and also with the use, construction and condition of the building. Thus rents of large, air-conditioned office blocks in the City of London are in the region of £25 per square foot, whereas similar offices in Birmingham are only £2 per square foot. There is less variation in the rents of factories since location is of less importance. Thus with cheaper land and lower costs of construction their rents may only be a little over £1 per square foot. Because of inflation leases are now subject to rent reviews at intervals of three, five or seven years. Usually the tenant is responsible for keeping the premises fully repaired and insured, and there may be provisions regarding sub-letting or the assignment of the lease, etc. Landlords, who are often institutions, must allow the tenant to use the premises without hindrance for the purposes agreed.

Tenant protection

Just as the private tenant of a dwelling is protected from eviction or large rent increases by the *Rent Act, 1977*, a business tenant enjoys a similar measure of protection by the *Landlord and Tenant Act, 1954*.

The business tenant will normally have taken his premises on a lease and, since this is a contract, the landlord has no cause for action against him so long as the terms of the lease are observed. Moreover, subject to any restrictions contained in the lease, the tenant can usually assign his lease with the consent of the landlord and such consent cannot be withheld unreasonably even though the tenant may be receiving payment for the lease.

Difficulties are most likely to arise when rents come up for periodic review or when the lease runs out. Normally rent increases are agreed mutually or through an independent valuer acting as arbitrator. If there is a deadlock, the new rent will be fixed by the County Court. At the end of the lease it is important for the business to continue trading at the same premises, for any change may mean a substantial loss of goodwill. Thus the *Landlord and Tenant Act, 1954*, provides for the tenancy to continue irrespective of whether the term granted has come to an end or a normal notice to quit has been served. Persons renting agricultural holdings are protected by the *Agriculture Holdings Act, 1948*, while the tenant may still be unprotected in the case of

a mining lease, premises licensed for the consumption of intoxi-
cating liquor except where the accommodation or restaurant
business is a substantial proportion, or premises occupied by an
office-holder or employee of the landlord. Moreover, tenancies
created for less than six months are not protected unless provision
is made for renewing the tenancy or if it has continued for over
twelve months.

Although the landlord cannot regain possession except on
grounds mentioned below, it is possible for him to obtain a new
lease on improved terms provided the detailed procedure of the
Act is followed. In most cases the terms of the new lease can be
settled by agreement. If this is impossible, the tenant can apply
for a new tenancy, either to the County Court or to the High Court
according to the rateable value of the premises, and the respective
court will resolve the issues in dispute. The rent has to be the
open-market rent for the property, but in fixing this any goodwill
or improvements made by the tenant over the past twenty-one
years have to be disregarded.

The possible grounds for the landlord claiming possession are:
(a) if the tenant has broken his obligations to repair and maintain,
or has been persistently late in paying his rent, or has been guilty
of other substantial breaches of his obligations; (b) if the landlord
provides equivalent alternative accommodation for the tenant; (c)
where the premises are in separate sub-lettings and the landlord
can show that the total of these is less than the rent which could be
obtained from letting the property as a whole; (d) where the
landlord wishes to redevelop the property; and (e) where he
wishes to occupy the property himself either for business or
residential purposes (but not if he has owned the property for less
than five years). In the last two cases the tenant can obtain
compensation for disturbance.

Somewhat similar protection is afforded to tenants of agricultural holdings under the *Agriculture Holdings Act, 1948*, except
for grazing land, provided the agreement is for less than one year.
Moreover, by the *Agriculture (Miscellaneous Provisions) Act,
1976*, if a near relative has worked on the farm for five out of the
past seven years when the tenant dies, the relative can claim the
tenancy; but the tenancy cannot pass in this way more than
twice.

III Obligations of the occupiers of premises

**Restrictions on the use
of premises**

Before buildings can be erected or altered planning consent must
be obtained from the local planning authority, usually the district
council. A structure plan is prepared by the county authority

zoning land into agricultural, industrial, commercial or residential use, and the proposed premises must be within the appropriate zone. Even then it must satisfy the planning authority as regards its position, size, shape and materials. Nor can the use of premises be changed outside its purposes class, e.g. from a supermarket to car showroom or from a house to offices, without the consent of the planning authority. Usually, in order to save costs, the applicant has prior discussions with the local planning office, and proposals will be modified accordingly. In order to save expense outline planning permission is applied for; if this is granted, the applicant can proceed with preparing detailed plans. If planning permission is refused, there is a right of appeal to the Secretary of State for the Environment, whose decision is based largely on the report of his inspector.

Apart from planning the actual building must conform to strict building regulations mainly to ensure that the structure is sound and safe, particularly as regards fire precautions. Land and premises may be compulsorily acquired, e.g. for building a motorway or school, but the owner has to be compensated at current market values.

Safety requirements

We saw in Chapter 11 that the *Health and Safety at Work Act, 1974,* imposed over-all responsibilities on employers for the safety of workers and visitors to his premises. Additionally the occupier of land or premises is also legally liable for 'nuisance' or 'negligence'.

Nuisance may be public or private. A *public nuisance* is an act not warranted by law or an omission to discharge a legal duty which causes inconvenience to the public at large, e.g. obstructing a highway, polluting rivers, and offences under the Clean Air Acts, Public Health and other Acts dealing with pollution. Control is largely the responsibility of local authorities, in the first place usually by advice, but if necessary the Attorney General can apply for an injunction or institute criminal proceedings.

A *private nuisance* is a tort, giving rise to a civil action. It includes damage to a neighbour's premises by an unauthorised act or omission of the defendant. The basis of the law is that, while a landowner can do as he pleases on his own land, he must not cause harm to another's. Thus a neighbour can complain of the loss of enjoyment of his premises through excessive noise, vibration, smoke, smells, etc.

Three conditions are necessary to create nuisance:

(1) The interference with another's enjoyment of premises is *unreasonable*. But the annoyance must not be a trifling one about which the average reasonable person would not complain. Moreover, regard must be paid to the time, locality and all the circumstances. Thus a person who buys a house near a church

must expect the bells to be rung for services, weddings, funerals and regular practices.

(2) The particular use complained of must be *unauthorised*. There is no remedy for a legal act, e.g. extracting water from one's soil even though it causes damage to a neighbour, or raising river banks even if this leads to flooding of the land of an adjacent owner.

(3) Actual damage must be proved, consisting of: (a) physical injury to person or property, or (b) substantial interference with the plantiff's standard of comfortable living.

Where nuisance exists it is usually the *occupier* who is liable, since he either creates or condones the nuisance. Action can take the form of damages, abatement, or an injunction.

Negligence makes a person liable for harm caused by (a) a wrongful act, or (b) conduct which in the circumstances the law regards as *negligent*, i.e. a failure to exercise the care expected of a prudent and reasonable person. This duty of care applies to the occupier of premises for all persons entering those premises, and is covered mainly by the *Occupiers' Liability Act, 1957,* as amended by the *Defective Premises Act, 1972.*

The Act lays down that an occupier owes all visitors a 'common duty of care' unless that duty has been restricted by agreement. This means that he must take reasonable care for the safety of visitors having regard to the purpose for which they have been invited. Thus extra care would be required for children, but special risks of work, e.g. for a window-cleaner, would not be included.

The *Defective Premises Act, 1972,* concerns the duties of landlords. Where premises are let under a tenancy and the landlord accepts an obligation for maintenance or repair, he must take reasonable care to see that others are safe from personal injury or damage to their property arising from defects in the state of his premises.

As regards trespass, the House of Lords held (*Herrington v. British Railways Board 1971*) that modern ideas of social justice impose upon all occupiers of land a duty to act with 'common humanity' towards trespassers whose presence is reasonably foreseeable. It seems that an occupier's financial resources are relevant to 'common humanity', thus requiring a large company to take more elaborate precautions than a private occupier to safeguard children who trespass on land to play.

It should be noted that strict liability applies to an occupier of land (see p. 8).

13 Capital: Its Sources and Employment

I The firm's need for liquid capital

Cash flow

If a firm is to remain solvent, it must have adequate *cash flow*. This is simply the difference between finance coming in and payments on outgoings. A surplus adds to reserves; a deficit reduces reserves (see Figure 13.1).

**Fig. 13.1
Cash flow**

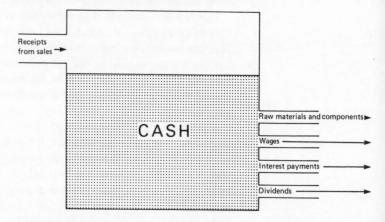

Ultimately all outgoings – production costs and depreciation of buildings, machinery, etc. – must be covered by revenue from sales. Initially, however, spending exceeds revenue; the cash flow has to be maintained by borrowing.

But creditors will not forgo repayment indefinitely, especially if it appears that the fortunes of the firm are unlikely to improve in the foreseeable future. They may then foreclose on their collateral, possibly forcing the firm into liquidation. Many small businesses, e.g. builders, fail because commitments are stretched beyond their capacity to generate income from sales, e.g. through late payments by customers.

In passing it should be noted that the cash-flow problem is not unique to firms in the private sector. The central government, local authorities and nationalised industries have similarly to watch their financial position since revenue tends to lag behind expenditure. This gives rise to the Public Sector Borrowing Requirement (see Chapter 18).

Types of capital required

Capital requirements can be classified broadly as working capital and fixed capital.

Working capital is for purchasing 'single-use' factors – labour, raw materials, petrol, stationery, fertilisers, etc. – more or less the variable factors referred to in Chapter 9. The principal sources of working capital are banks, which mainly lend to bridge the time gap between expenditure on labour and raw materials and receipts from the sale of the finished product. Other sources are trade credit, finance companies, factor houses, tax reserves, inter-company finance, and advance deposits from customers.

Fixed capital covers factors which are used many times – factories, machines, land, lorries, etc. Finance to purchase such factors has to be raised since their revenue-earning capacity stretches well into the future. Nevertheless to some extent it may be possible to convert fixed capital by renting buildings, hiring plant and vehicles or buying on deferred payments through a finance company. Normally, however, fixed-capital requirements are larger than for working capital. Moreover, lenders recognise that they part with their money for a longer period and accept a greater risk. Thus finance for fixed capital tends to be more difficult to raise than for working capital.

Markets for the provision of liquid capital

The liquid capital required by firms comes from that part of the community which lends savings. The market is the institution which brings borrowers and lenders together, making funds available to firms at a price – the rate of interest. Saving represents refraining from spending on consumer goods, thereby setting free resources for the production of *producer* or *capital goods* required by firms. As we saw in Chapter 1, such goods increase our productive capacity. Thus financial markets fulfil an essential function in the market economy.

But because finance is required for different purposes, by different types of firms, by the government and the nationalised industries, and for different periods of time, there is a great variety in the institutions providing or arranging such loans as well as in the type of loan. Our immediate task, therefore, is to examine these markets in order to appreciate why firms finance their operations in certain ways. We concentrate on the money markets (dealing in short-term loans) and the capital market (where medium and long-term capital is raised). The joint-stock banks (the major source of working capital) and the Bank of England (which exercises over-all control over the availability of finance) are discussed in Chapter 18.

None of the money markets nor the capital market are formal organisations in that buyers and sellers meet regularly in a particular building to conduct business. Instead they are merely a collection of institutions which are connected, in the case of the money markets, by dealings in bills of exchange and short-term loans and, more loosely in the case of the capital market, through channelling medium and long-term finance to those requiring it. As we shall see later, within each market there is a high degree of specialisation.

Moreover, because it is such a large borrower, the government's requirements tend to dominate these markets, affecting the rates which have to be paid on short and long-term loans. Above all, as we will see in Chapter 18, it actively controls the cost and availability of funds. The complete structure is shown in simplified form in Figure 13.2.

Fig. 13.2
The provision of
finance in the UK

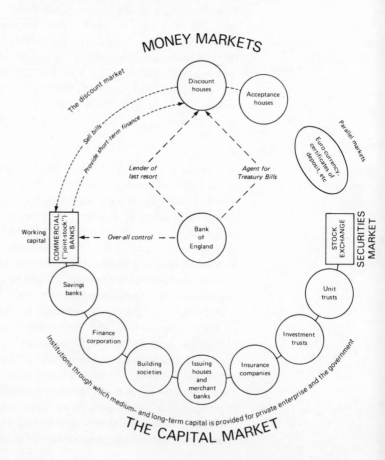

II Money Markets

The Discount Market

Bills of exchange are an important source of short-term finance – the commercial bill for firms, the Treasury Bill for the government. The Discount Market comprises the institutions linked by dealings in bills – discount houses, merchant banks acting as acceptance houses, commercial banks, and the Bank of England.

It is customary in foreign trade for an importer to be allowed a period of grace, usually three months to pay for goods. This is arranged through a *commercial bill of exchange.*

Suppose *A* in London is exporting cars worth £10,000 to *B* in New York. When he is ready to ship the cars he draws up a bill of exchange, as shown in Figure 13.3. This is sent to *B* together with copies of the shipping documents to prove that the cars are on the ship. *B* 'accepts' the bill by writing 'Accepted' and his signature across the face of the bill, and then returns it to *A*. This acceptance of the bill by *B* is necessary before the original *bill of lading,* the documentary title to the cars, is handed over.

Fig. 13.3
A commercial bill of exchange

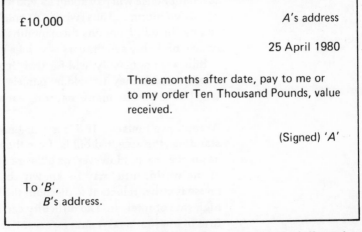

£10,000   *A*'s address

                                                        25 April 1980

                            Three months after date, pay to me or
                            to my order Ten Thousand Pounds, value
                            received.

                                                        (Signed) '*A*'

To '*B*',
    B's address.

A can now do one of three things: (a) hold the bill until it matures; (b) endorse the bill and then get a merchant to whom he is indebted to take it in settlement; (c) sell the bill, usually to a discount house. (Now see Figure 13.4 overleaf.)

Discount houses   Probably *A* will choose the latter of course. So, after endorsing it, he takes it to one of the eleven *London discount houses.* The exact amount paid for the bill will depend on the length of time to maturity, the prevailing short-term rate of interest, and the opinion of the discount house as to *B*'s financial standing. If the bill has still three months to run and that the prevailing rate of interest on that class of bill is 12 per cent, the

Fig. 13.4
Operations of the
Discount Market

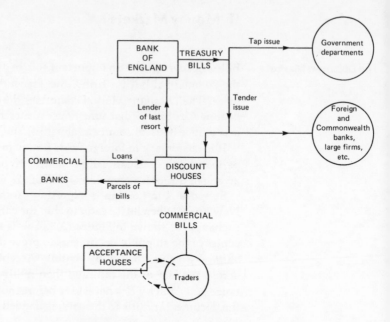

discount house will pay about £9,700 for it. This process is known as 'discounting'. Thus while *A* quickly regains liquidity by selling the bill, *B* obtains three months' credit, during which time he will probably sell the cars which he has imported.

Bills are not usually held for their full currency. Instead, after about a month they are sold in 'parcels' to the commercial banks, who like to have so many maturing each day.

Acceptance houses   If *B* is a well-known firm of high financial standing, the accepted bill is, from the risk point of view, almost as good as cash. However, as bills are drawn on firms in all parts of the world, little may be known about *B*. Thus the discount house is either reluctant to discount the bill or will only do so at a high rate of interest. The difficulty can be overcome by getting a firm of international repute to 'accept' responsibility for payment should *B* default. It is obvious that any firm accepting such a bill must have adequate knowledge of the creditworthiness of the trader upon whom the bill is drawn. Such knowledge is possessed by the merchant banks, such as Lazards, Barings and Rothschilds, who commenced as traders but later specialised in financing trade in particular parts of the world. In their capacity of accepting bills such merchant banks are known as *acceptance houses*. For the service they charge a small commission of about ¾ per cent, which is willingly paid because the rate of discount on a 'bank bill', i.e. one bearing the name of an acceptance house, is lower than on a 'trade bill' (a bill accepted only by a trader) or on a 'fine trade bill' (where the merchant is of good standing).

In recent years the business of accepting has declined. This has been due to: (a) the diminished use of the commercial bill in international trade; (b) the decline of London as the world centre for financing foreign trade; and (c) the increased competition of the commercial banks in accepting bills, largely through the development of the 'reimbursement credit'. With this, B, the importer, induces his own bank in New York to secure an acceptance credit for him in London, which means that he can instruct A to draw the bill on the London branch of his own bank or on a London bank or acceptance house. The New York bank makes itself responsible for the payment of the bill, and so all the London bank or acceptance house has to do is to satisfy itself as to the financial standing of the New York bank. This simpler procedure means that reimbursement credits can be granted at very low rates of interest.

The decline in the use of the commercial bill coincided with a large increase in government borrowing through *Treasury Bills.* A Treasury Bill is really a bill of exchange drawn by the Treasury on itself, usually for a period of three months (ninety-one days), though occasionally two-month (sixty-three-day) bills are issued. Since such bills are only a short-term loan, they represent the government's cheapest method of borrowing – just over 12 per cent. Treasury Bills are issued in denominations of £5000 upwards, and since the minimum sale is £50,000 they are primarily for institutional investors.

The commercial banks   The commercial banks fulfil two main functions in the Discount Market – providing the discount houses with funds, and holding bills to maturity.

The discount houses do not themselves have sufficient finance to buy all the bills, commercial and Treasury, offered them. They overcome this difficulty, however, by borrowing money from the commercial banks at a comparatively low rate of interest. Then, by discounting at a slightly higher rate, they make a small profit. The banks are willing to lend at a low rate because the loans are of short duration, often for only a day, and need not be renewed if there is a heavy demand for cash from their ordinary customers.

The commercial banks can earn a higher rate of interest by themselves holding bills for a part of their currency. However, by convention they do not bid for them directly but buy from the discount houses when they still have about two months to run.

The Bank of England   The Bank of England enters the Discount Market as follows:

First, it is the agency by which the government issues Treasury Bills. This issue is achieved by two methods, 'tap' and 'tender'. Government departments, the National Savings Bank, the

Exchange Equalisation Account, the National Insurance Fund, and the Bank of England Issue Department, all of whom have funds to invest for a short period, can buy what bills they want at a fixed price, i.e. 'on tap'. This price is not published.

The discount houses and other purchasers (such as Commonwealth and foreign banks) can obtain their issue by 'tender'. Every Friday, the Treasury, acting through the Bank of England, invites tenders for a specified amount of bills, usually between £200 and £300 million.

Second, the Bank of England is the 'lender of last resort'. When the discount houses are pressed for money because the commercial banks will not renew their 'call money', the Bank of England will lend to them at the declared 'minimum lending rate' (see p. 317).

Parallel money markets

As a result of restrictions placed on bank lending new markets in short-term loans developed to meet the specific requirements of particular borrowers and lenders. Indeed the existence of such markets has encouraged funds to be lent short term, for they have made it easier for lenders to regain liquidity.

The following are the most important of these comparatively new markets:

(a) *Inter-bank deposits.* This is a market bringing together all banks, including merchant banks, British overseas banks and foreign banks, so that those having funds surplus to their immediate requirements can lend to those having outlets for short-term loans.

(b) *Local authority deposits.* Local authorities borrow on the open market and are willing to make use of very short-term money. Brokers now exist for placing with them short-term funds of banks, industrial and commercial companies, charitable funds, etc. Such brokers also deal in longer-term local authority bonds.

(c) *Negotiable certificates of deposit.* Certificates of deposit enable the banks to borrow for periods from three months to five years. They are similar to a bill of exchange drawn on the bank by itself. For the bank they are for a longer period than an ordinary time deposit, thus facilitating medium-term lending. For the lender they offer a higher rate of interest, while the market in them means that they can be sold whenever cash is required.

(d) *Euro-currency balances.* Euro-currency deposits are simply funds which are deposited with banks outside the country of origin but which continue to be designated in terms of the original currency. The most important Euro-currency is the dollar. As a result of the USA's continuing adverse balance of payments, branches of European banks have built up dollar balances as customers were paid for exports. These balances are offered to brokers in London (where interest rates have been higher than in New York), and are placed mainly with companies or banks (e.g. Japanese) operating on an international scale to finance foreign trade or investment. While the dollar still dominates the market, other European currencies are now dealt in, chiefly the Deutschmark and the Swiss franc.

(e) *Other markets.* Smaller specialist markets have developed in *Finance house deposits* and *inter-company deposits.* Thus finance houses have obtained funds by issuing bills which are accepted by banks and discount houses. Similarly, in periods of tight credit firms which are short of finance turn towards other companies which temporarily have funds to spare.

III The capital market

While the money markets developed to supply short-term finance to trade and the government, industry obtains most of its 'working' capital from the commercial banks (see Chapter 18). But long-term capital for both the public and private sectors is obtained through the capital market. As can be seen from Figure 13.5, this consists, on the one hand, of the suppliers of long-term

Fig. 13.5
The capital market

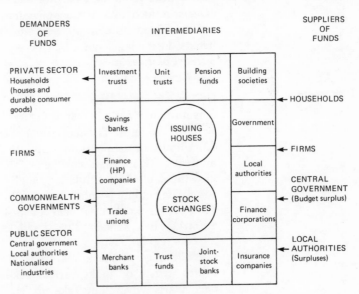

Notes:
(1) Arrows merely indicate direction, not particular intermediaries.
(2) Intermediaries collect relatively small amounts of capital which are channelled to where they are wanted.
(3) Some intermediaries are mainly concerned with old issues.
(4) Issuing houses assist the movement of funds; stock exchanges provide a market in old securities and thus encourage the provision of new funds.

capital and, on the other, of those requiring such capital, the two being connected by a number of intermediaries, usually of a specialist nature. Some of these intermediaries have already been described; here we look briefly at the others.

Insurance companies

Insurance companies receive premiums for insuring against various risks. Some of these premiums, such as those received for insuring ships and property, are held only for relatively short periods, having, apart from the profit made, to be paid out against claims. But with life insurance, endowments, annuities, etc., premiums are usually held for a long time before payments are made. Hence insurance companies have large sums of money to invest in long-term securities. These investments are spread over government and other public stocks, the shares and debentures of companies, property, and mortgages. Today 'institutional investors', of which insurance companies are the most important, supply the bulk of savings required for new issues.

Investment trusts

Investors usually try to avoid 'putting all their eggs in one basket' by buying securities in different types of enterprise. However, this requires knowledge of investment possibilities and, above all, sufficient resources. The small investor can overcome these difficulties by buying shares in an investment trust. This invests over a wide range of securities and, after paying management expenses, the net yields from these investments are distributed as a dividend on its own shares. Thus investment trusts are not 'trusts' in the legal sense but merely companies formed for the purpose of investment.

Unit trusts

Unit trusts are a development of the investment trust idea, but they differ in two main respects. First, they are trusts in the legal sense of the term. Trustees are appointed, while the trust deed often limits investments to a specified range of securities, e.g. minerals, financial securities, property, energy, European growth, capital accumulation, high income, etc. Second, the aggregate holding is split into many 'units' of low nominal value. Thus even a small investment covers a range of securities. Many unit trusts have schemes linked with assurance, savers subscribing on a regular basis.

While most of the funds are used to purchase existing securities, trusts do make capital available for new investment, particularly when they take up 'rights' issues of shares they already hold.

Savings banks

The National Savings Bank and Trustee Savings Bank provide savings facilities mainly for small depositors, since holdings are limited to £10,000 per person. Deposits are invested in securities, mostly government and similar securities, prescribed for the trustees.

Trust, pension and trade-union funds

All these accumulate income which is reinvested in government securities, shares, property, etc.

Building societies

These have a specialised function – the supply of long-term loans on the security of private dwelling-houses purchased for owner-occupation. Their funds are derived chiefly from money invested in them by the general public, but their shares are not dealt in on the Stock Exchange, being cashable upon notice. Their liquid reserves are usually invested in government stock and local authority bonds.

Finance companies

These borrow savings from the public and obtain loans from banks in order to finance the hire purchase of both consumer goods and machinery. The rates at which they borrow are comparatively high because of the greater lending risks involved, and for a similar reason the rates at which they lend are high. Many joint-stock banks now engage in hire-purchase finance through their own subsidiary finance companies.

IV The Stock Exchange

Its function

A stock exchange is really an organised market for exchanging 'securities', i.e. claims to loans or shares. Although there are 'stock exchanges' in most of the larger cities of the UK, the London exchange is by far the most important and henceforth will be referred to as 'the Stock Exchange'. A glance at the financial pages of any daily newspaper will reveal the nature of the securities dealt in – British funds (government stock and the stock of the nationalised industries), Commonwealth and foreign government stock, corporation stock (issued by local authorities such as the Greater London Council, or by public utility under-takings such as the Thames Water Authority), and the stocks and shares of all types of industrial and commercial companies.

The Stock Exchange is privately owned, and the 'proprietors' are the members who between them hold the shares which provided the capital for its buildings. Its affairs are controlled by an elected Council of thirty-six members.

Members and their work

Members are either 'brokers' or 'jobbers', but they are not allowed to act in both capacities.

A stockbroker acts as the agent for his clients, executing business on their instructions and giving them investment advice. He earns commission on the business he transacts, but he is not allowed to advertise. In effect he acts as the link between the investing public, who wish to buy and sell securities, and the *jobber,* the actual dealer who buys and carries a stock of securities in order to resell them later. The difference between broker and jobber is best shown by an example.

Mr. *A* wishes to buy 800 25p ordinary shares in Unilever Ltd. He therefore telephones his broker or bank manager (who will contact the broker who acts for the bank), giving him the necessary instructions. He will either name the maximum price at which he will buy or instruct the broker to buy at the lowest price possible. On the floor of the Stock Exchange the broker goes to that part which specialises in the leading industrial ordinary shares. He approaches a jobber and enquires the price of 25p Unilever Ordinaries but he does not say whether he wishes to buy or sell. Suppose the jobber replies: 'Four-sixty to four sixty-six.' This indicates that he is prepared to buy at the lower and sell at the higher price. The difference between the two prices is known as the 'jobber's turn' and is the normal source of the jobber's profit, the size of spread depending on the jobber's estimate of the risk involved in dealing in that particular security. The broker can accept the price, try to get the jobber to lower his price, or else move on to other jobbers in the hope of doing better. Let us suppose that he considers 466p satisfactory. He then informs the jobber that he wishes to buy 500 shares, the bargain is struck, and both broker and jobber make notes in their dealing books. The broker, having arranged the deal, sends to Mr *A*, or to the bank acting for him, a contract note (see Figure 13.6).

The transfer stamp represents revenue charged on all transfer deeds (except British government stock). It is charged only on purchases. All bargains have to be settled on the next 'Account Day', which usually falls fortnightly on a Tuesday, though government and municipal stock is 'for cash', meaning that settlement is immediate.

Economic functions

Critics of the Stock Exchange tend to ignore its real functions and to concentrate on its speculative aspects. It is true that the facilities offered by the Stock Exchange do provide openings for speculation. The fortnightly account allows a speculator to buy securities at the beginning and sell at a profit (or loss) within fourteen days without ever having to put up any money. A speculator who buys securities because he thinks the price will rise is said to be a 'bull'. He is thus an optimist, buying shares, not because he wants to keep them, but because he hopes to sell them at a profit. On the other hand a speculator who is a pessimist

Fig. 13.6
A contract note

INVOICE NO.   1475

To. Mr A.N. Other
Client No. 436485

BARGAIN DATE
AND TAX POINT
7th November 1979

WE THANK YOU FOR YOUR INSTRUCTIONS AND ADVISE HAVING **BOUGHT** FOR YOUR
ACCOUNT SUBJECT TO THE RULES AND REGULATIONS OF THE STOCK EXCHANGE

AMOUNT	STOCK OR SHARES	PRICE	CONSIDERATION		
800	Unilever Limited Ordinary 25p Shares	466p	3728	00	N
	TRANSFER STAMP		75	00	N
	CONTRACT STAMP			60	N
	COMMISSION 1½% on money		55	92	T
	TOTAL VAT @ 15%		8	38	
	FOR SETTLEMENT 19 November 1979	£	3867.90		

SPENCER THORNTON & CO.
MEMBERS OF THE STOCK EXCHANGE

CONTRACT NOTE AND TAX INVOICE
FOR SERVICES RENDERED

WE RECOMMEND THAT THIS DOCUMENT
BE RETAINED FOR FUTURE REFERENCE

is known as a 'bear', and he sells securities he does not possess because he expects the price to fall before they have to be delivered. Sometimes, if a person's credit stands high with his broker or if he can put up security, he may be permitted to 'carry over' his commitments from one Stock Exchange account to the next. Such a transaction is known as a 'contango'.

The difficulty concerning speculation is that both optimism and pessimism are contagious and the market becomes extremely susceptible both to panic and over-confidence. Indeed expectations are 'self-fulfilling': persons who expect the price of securities to rise bid for them, *thereby* sending up their price, and vice versa. The result is that the prices of stocks and shares may be written up and down, not through a change in their earnings prospects, but simply through waves of confidence or mistrust, e.g. the South Sea Bubble (1720) and the Wall Street Crash (1929).

Even so we must not forget that some speculation may be advantageous. Expert professional operators such as the jobbers tend to steady prices through their function of holding stocks (see Chapter 8). This also permits securities to be bought and sold at any time, thereby making them more liquid. The great difficulty occurs in distinguishing harmful speculation from genuine investment, for with all investment there is a certain element of risk. In any case the magnitude of the speculative business must not be over-estimated. Most purchases represent genuine investment conducted on behalf of investment trusts, insurance companies, building societies and private individuals.

The truth is that, for the following reasons, an organised market in securities is an indispensable part of the mechanism of a capitalist economy.

(1) *It facilitates borrowing by the government and industry.* If people are to be encouraged to lend to industry and the government, they must be satisfied that they will be able to sell easily such investments should the need arise. Such an assurance is afforded to any holder of a security quoted on the Stock Exchange, for it provides a permanent market bringing together sellers and buyers. Indirectly, therefore, the Stock Exchange encourages savers to lend to the government or to invest in industry.

(2) *Through the jobbers it helps to even out short-run price fluctuations in securities.* While the jobber himself may often speculate, in the short run he acts as a buffer to speculation by outsiders. This is because he does not merely 'match' a buyer with a seller but acts like a wholesaler, holding stocks of securities. Since he specialises in dealing in certain securities, he obtains an intimate knowledge of them. Thus when the public is pessimistic and selling, he may be more optimistic in his outlook and consider that the drop in price is not likely to continue. He therefore takes these securities on to his book. Similarly, when the public is rushing to buy, he will, when he considers the price has reached its topmost height, sell from his stocks. The effect in both cases is to even out the fluctuations in price, for in the first case he increases his demand as supply increases, and in the second he increases supply as the demand increases.

(3) *It advertises security prices.* The publication of current Stock Exchange prices enables the public to follow the fortunes of their investments and to channel their savings into profitable enterprises.

(4) *It protects the public against fraud.* The *Official List* of securities is a guarantee that securities listed are reputable. Permission to deal is not given to members unless the Council is satisfied on this score, and it may be withdrawn if any doubts arise about the conduct of a company's affairs. Moreover, the Council insists on a high standard of professional conduct from its members. Should any member default the investor is indemnified out of the Stock Exchange Compensation Fund.

(5) *It reflects the country's economic prospects.* The movement of the market acts as a barometer which points to the economic prospects of the country as 'set fair' – or otherwise.

V Methods of financing a company

Sources of finance for the sole trader and partnership were reviewed in Chapter 1. Here we consider how a new company raises its long-term capital by: (1) selling shares; and (2) borrowing.

(1) Shares   A 'share' is exactly what the name implies – a participation in the provision of the capital. Shares may be issued in various units, usually from 5p upwards, purchasers deciding how many they want. Such an investment, however, involves two main risks. First, profits may be disappointing, and the price of the share may fall. Second, share prices in general may be falling just when the owner wishes to sell. To minimise these risks investors usually buy shares in different companies, together with debentures and government bonds having a fixed rate of interest.

(a) *Ordinary shares.* The dividend paid to the ordinary shareholder depends mainly upon the profitability of the company. However, the ordinary shareholder's dividend ranks last in order of priority, while should the company be forced into liquidation the ordinary shareholder is repaid only after other creditors have been paid in full. Thus the ordinary share is termed 'risk capital'. In return each ordinary shareholder has a say in the running of the company, voting according to the number of shares held. At a general meeting directors can be appointed or removed, changes made in the company's method of raising capital and conducting business, and auditors appointed. Thus, because they take the major risks and decisions regarding the policy of the company, the ordinary shareholders are the real 'entrepreneurs'. In practice, however, their rights are rarely exercised. Usually few shareholders take the trouble to attend meetings, while unless the company is large the directors may control a high proportion of the shares and so be in a strong position. Indeed this may be achieved by making all new shares non-voting 'A' shares. Thus directors tend to be self-perpetuating.

(b) *Preference shares.* If the investor prefers a slightly reduced risk, he can buy a preference share entitling him to a dividend payment before the ordinary shareholder but one fixed at a given rate. Should the company be forced into liquidation the preference shareholder usually ranks above the ordinary shareholder in the redemption of capital.

Preference shares may be 'cumulative': if the company cannot pay a dividend one year, arrears may be made up in succeeding years before ordinary shareholders receive any dividend.

Since 1965 preference shares have lost popularity through their unfavourable tax treatment (see below).

(2) Borrowing   The long-term loans of a company are usually obtained by issuing 'debentures', redeemable after a specified period. These bear a fixed rate of interest (about 14 per cent) which, being a first charge on the company's profit, means a lower risk to the investor of there being no return. Moreover, should the company fail, debenture-holders are paid out first. In fact 'mortgage debentures' are secured on a definite asset of the company. Should the company be unable to meet its interest charges or to redeem the loan when due, the debenture-holders can force it into liquidation.

The purchaser of a debenture takes less risk should the company fail. But because he is merely lending money he enjoys no ownership rights of voting on management and policy. On the other hand a company whose profits are subject to frequent and violent fluctuations is not well-placed for raising capital through debentures. The method is best suited to a company making a stable profit (adequate to cover the interest payments), and possessing assets, such as land and buildings, showing little depreciation were the company to go into liquidation.

A company which has a large proportion of fixed-interest loans to ordinary shares is said to be 'highly geared'. Such a company will be able to pay high dividends when profits are good, but will be unable to make a distribution when profits are low. Where profits are expected to rise in the future, therefore, a company may prefer to raise capital for expansion by issuing debentures if the cost of doing so is not too high.

But it is the present-day corporation tax which is the main impulse in this direction. Debenture interest (but not preference-share interest) is an accepted cost for the purpose of calculating tax. Thus it reduces taxable profits. On the other hand, if finance is raised by shares, there is no prior interest charge, and profits (which are subject to tax) are that amount higher. This tax advantage has, since the introduction of corporation tax in 1965, led companies to finance capital expansion as far as possible by fixed-interest loans rather than by the sale of shares. Preference shares are now rarely issued.

Financing the expansion of a company

One reason why small companies predominate is the difficulty of financing expansion. If the firm cannot retain sufficient profits or raise finance by mortgaging buildings, the only alternative is to seek additional investors. This usually means converting to a public company. The public can then be asked to subscribe for additional shares or debentures.

But the high cost of a public issue make it uneconomic to raise less than £150,000. This means that the difficult stage in the expansion of a firm occurs when its capital is in the region of £50,000, for it is still too small to contemplate a public issue. The gap may be bridged in three main ways. First, a stockbroker may be able to arrange for a life insurance company or an investment trust to purchase shares or debentures since such institutions are less concerned with the illiquidity of such stock. Second, in the new issue market both issuing houses and merchant bankers arrange or provide medium-term capital to bridge the gap prior to making a public issue. Third, capital may be available through certain specialised finance corporations. Thus for agriculture there is the Agricultural Mortgage Corporation (which lends on the security of land and buildings), and for film making the National Film Finance Corporation. For small firms Charterhouse Development Ltd and Credit for Industry Ltd are among those who will help with long-term finance. More important is the Industrial & Commercial Finance Corporation, a body financed by the joint-stock banks, which provides capital for businesses, not necessarily companies, too small to make a public issue. But in order to obtain a loan the firm has to pass a searching investigation regarding its present financial position and business prospects. Larger loans are provided by the Finance Corporation for Industry. Finally, the National Enterprise Board may finance development of approved projects and provide technical advice.

Where a large amount of capital is required, say above £150,000, it is usual to obtain a Stock Exchange quotation. This is only given by the Stock Exchange Council to a public company which has been subjected to a thorough examination. Once the introduction has been completed the capital required can be raised by a Stock Exchange 'placing', an 'offer for sale', or a 'public issue by prospectus'.

The first is the usual method when only about £150,000 is required, for the costs of underwriting and administration are less. An issuing house, stockbroker or investment company agrees to sell blocks of the shares privately to institutions known to be interested in such issues.

For larger amounts up to £300,000 an offer for sale is a likely method. The shares are sold *en bloc* to an issuing house, which then offers them for sale to the public by advertisement. Although the issuing house makes a modest profit, underwriting costs are avoided.

When more than £300,000 is required, a public issue by prospectus is usual. Here the company's objective is to obtain from the public in a single day the additional capital required. Hence it must advertise well and price its shares a little on the cheap side. The advertisement is in the form of a prospectus which sets out the business, history and prospects of the company together with its financial standing and the security offered.

The sale is usually conducted through an issuing house, which advises the company on the terms of the issue. It will also arrange to have the issue underwritten, by finding institutions such as merchant banks who, in return for a small commission, will take any of the issue left unsold. Nevertheless such underwriters do not have to rely entirely on permanent investors, for speculators known as 'stags' are usually operating, and they buy the shares hoping to resell them quickly at a small profit.

In recent years there has been an increasing tendency to give existing shareholders the first option on new shares through a 'rights issue'. These are offered in proportion to the shares already held, usually at a favourable price. (See Figure 13.7 for a summary of the advantages and disadvantages of various forms of private-sector firms).

VI Investment in fixed capital

Investment by firms

We now turn to the firm's use of liquid funds. Net investment over a given period of time is the net addition to fixed capital after an allowance has been made for depreciation through wearing out or obsolescence. It should also be noted that spending on research and customer relations may be an important form of investment producing 'industrial property', such as patent rights, copyrights, trade marks and goodwill (see later), while training of workers represents investment in the labour force.

As we saw in Chapter 1, the use of capital equipment increases production and is essential for exploiting natural resources or reaping the benefit of new discoveries, e.g. nuclear fission, and inventions, e.g. micro-chips. Firms demand capital, therefore, because of its productivity.

On the other hand capital equipment can only be produced by diverting resources from consumer goods. This means that some people must be willing to postpone consumption. However, since a bird in the hand is worth two in the bush, people who postpone consumption are given a reward, which can be referred to as 'the rate of interest'. Thus the cost to firms of obtaining capital equipment is the rate of interest which has to be paid.

Capital investment and uncertainty

Because the rewards of investment are in the future they are fraught with risk. The original assumptions upon which the estimates were based may be upset by events – a fall in demand for the product, an increase in the price of raw materials, or political upheavals cutting off vital supplies.

Fig. 13.7
Forms of private-
sector firms

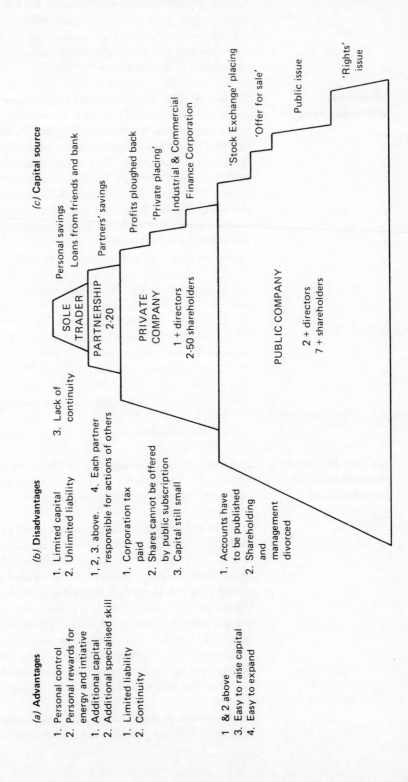

(a) Advantages

1. Personal control
2. Personal rewards for
   energy and intiative

1. Additional capital
2. Additional specialised skill

1. Limited liability
2. Continuity

1 & 2 above
3. Easy to raise capital
4. Easy to expand

(b) Disadvantages

1. Limited capital
2. Unlimited liability
3. Lack of
   continuity

1, 2, 3, above.   4. Each partner
responsible for actions of others

1. Corporation tax
   paid
2. Shares cannot be offered
   by public subscription
3. Capital still small

1. Accounts have
   to be published
2. Shareholding
   and
   management
   divorced

(c) Capital source

Personal savings
Loans from friends and bank

Partners' savings

Profits ploughed back
'Private placing'
Industrial & Commercial
Finance Corporation

'Stock Exchange' placing
'Offer for sale'
Public issue
'Rights'
issue

SOLE
TRADER

PARTNERSHIP
2-20

PRIVATE
COMPANY

1 + directors
2-50 shareholders

PUBLIC COMPANY

2 + directors
7 + shareholders

Such uncertainty means that: (a) the return to investment in capital equipment can be no more definite than a flow of yields (which we will assume are yearly) which the firm reasonably expects; and (b) some allowance must be made for the risk of inaccuracy in the estimates.

Differences in investment projects

But a firm with limited funds has to choose between its investment opportunities. Thus, if it is contemplating producing its own components but is short of capital for expansion it will have to select the most profitable items, continuing to purchase the rest from outside suppliers. This means that it has to compare projects, allowing not only for differences in expected yields (Net Annual Revenue), but also for differences in initial cost and in the timing of yields. Thus in Table 13.1 all four projects differ as regards the size of expected yield, the timing of future yields and estimated life of the project. Yields are assumed to be net of all operating costs and tax, and to accrue at the end of each year.

Table 13.1 Differences in capital projects

Project	Initial capital cost (£000)	Net Annual Revenue (£000) Year 1	Year 2	Year 3
A	100	50	50	50
B	100	100	10	—
C	100	—	50	120
D	100	100	50	—

Methods of evaluating the productivity of capital projects

Projects can be evaluated by different methods which vary in complexity. The simpler ones are, as we shall see, only preferred where special considerations apply.

(1) Cut-off period   This method chooses a period by which the initial cost must be recouped. If in our example this period were two years, all projects except C would be acceptable, preference being given to D on account of its higher total yield. The difficulty is that project C is rejected solely because returns accrue late in its life irrespective of whether it is a desirable project. Nevertheless using a cut-off period to choose D could be justified where: (a) project D hinged on an innovation which could not be protected by patent and was likely to be occupied by other firms within two years; and (b) political uncertainty necessitated recouping the initial cost within two years.

(2) Pay-back period   Here, investment options are ranked according to how long yields take to recoup the initial outlay. In our example both B and D achieve pay-back in year 1. This method can be justified where uncertainty, either as regards future cash returns or obsolescence of equipment, is marked, for then a possible quick exit must be borne in mind. But it fails to take account of: (a) differences in the timing of yields earned before the pay-back date; and (b) yields earned after the pay-back date. On the latter count, for instance, D is obviously superior to B.

(3) Average rate of return   The average rate of return is calculated by totalling the yields, dividing by the years of a project's life, and expressing this average as a percentage of the initial cost. With project D this would be $150/2 \times 100/100 = 75$ per cent.

This method has two main disadvantages. First, it depends upon the number of years chosen. Thus, if in year 3 D had a yield of 20, it would cease to rank above C although its over-all profitability had increased! As a result the method produces a bias in favour of short-term investments having high yields. Second, it ignores the pattern of yields, high earlier yields being treated the same as low later yields.

The major criticism of all the above methods is that they fail to take into account both the number and the timing of yields. Other things being equal the greater the number of yields, the more profitable the investment. Similarly, early yields have the advantage that they can be reinvested profitably or used to reduce borrowing. Both the number and timing of yields are allowed for by the discounted cash flow (DCF) and the internal rate of return (IRR) methods described below.

(4) Discounted cash flow   Here costs and yields are both discounted at a given rate of interest and aggregated in order to obtain their net present value (NPV). Thus, if we take 8 per cent as the discount rate, the DCF of project A is:

Year			(£000)
0	initial cost 100	=	−100·0
1	$\dfrac{50}{1·08}$	=	+ 46·3
2	$\dfrac{50}{(1·08)^2}$	=	+ 42·9
3	$\dfrac{50}{(1·08)^3}$	=	+ 39·7
NPV = total discounted cash flow		=	28·9

It should be noted that the NPV of a particular investment depends upon the rate of discount chosen: the higher the rate of discount, the lower will be the NPV.

5 The internal rate of return (Keynes's marginal efficiency of capital)   Here projects are ranked according to the rate of discount which needs to be applied to costs and future in order to achieve an NPV which equals zero. For example, with project D we have:

$$\frac{100}{(1+r)} + \frac{50}{(1+r)^2} = 0$$

where we have to solve for r, the IRR. Here it is 37 per cent.

The advantages of this method are: (a) it does not require the firm to specify a rate of discount (as with NPV), since r is derived automatically from expected net benefits; (b) it is easier to take account of the risk element than with NPV since the difference between the IRR and the rate of interest at which funds are borrowed will indicate whether there is sufficient margin to cover risks; and (c) it conforms with the more usual business practice of comparing rates in order to assess profitability.

In practice it is likely that only the largest firms use the IRR method of appraising investment projects. Small firms follow the pay-back method, using a three to five-year period.

VII Industrial property

Capital need not have a physical existence; as already noted, the skill of a worker represents capital. A similar form of capital is what is known as 'industrial property' – patents, copyrights, trademarks, registered designs and goodwill. Since all these can be bought and sold, the rights to them are protected by the courts, either by granting an injunction to restrain someone else from using them or by awarding damages for unauthorised use.

Patents

In order to protect an organisation which has devoted time and money to research, e.g. on inventions or the development of new products, the Patents Act, 1977, allows the invention to be patented, giving protection against its use by competitors for twenty years. The invention must be new and unique and capable of some form of industrial application.

Patents are protected by the Comptroller of Patents and the Patents Court of the Chancery Division. Both can award damages, and the Court can grant an injunction against both the offender and anyone who indirectly gains a benefit from an infringement.

Employees can patent an invention if it does not arise from the normal course of their duties. On the other hand, if a job contributed to the new discovery or development, the latter has to be surrendered to the employer. In this case the employee can claim compensation through the Patents Court.

The Patents Act applies only to the UK and wider protection necessitates registration in other countries. However, the European Patent Convention established a European Patent Office and extends national patents to all signatory countries, including some outside the EEC.

Copyright

Copyright protects literary, musical and a variety of printed works, e.g. maps, charts, plans and drawings. Copyright for authors, musicians, etc., lasts from the time of writing to fifty years after the author's death. The works then become public property and can be reproduced without restriction.

Any form of reproduction, e.g. a near imitation, which might be prejudicial to the owner of the copyright is a breach of copyright and constitutes a criminal offence carrying the penalty of a fine or even a prison sentence for subsequent breaches. Usually, however, the owner seeks an injunction and compensation by way of damages. Punitive damages may be awarded for a flagrant infringement.

Goodwill

Goodwill refers to the benefit and advantage derived from the good name and connection of a business resulting largely from the reputation of the owner or the quality of his products.

Anybody who buys the business, therefore, is acquiring an additional asset – the regular customers that are attached to it. To protect its saleable value a covenant is usually contained in the contract preventing the seller from soliciting customers or setting up in competition within a certain distance (though the specified distance must be 'reasonable' for the type of business). The courts will enforce such an agreement provided it is not contrary to the public interest in that it simply produces a monopoly.

VIII The responsibilities of an organisation to those who contribute capital

Companies and the profit objective

Because capital is a scarce resource organisations have a duty to the community at large to ensure that it is used as efficiently as possible. But firms have direct responsibilities to those who actually provide them with funds. In the public sector this responsibility is to all the people who comprise the state, for it is they who, as lenders or taxpayers, make liquid capital available for public works or the nationalised industries. Chapter 14 surveys the methods by which public-sector firms are made accountable for their operations.

Here we are mainly concerned with firms in the private sector. With sole traders and partnerships the capital is mostly subscribed by the owners. Lenders of funds, e.g. banks and finance houses, usually require collateral and, if the conditions of the loan are not fulfilled, the lender may foreclose.

With a company the position is slightly different. Some people, e.g. debenture-holders, banks and insurance companies, make what are virtually straight money loans, often directly charged against specific assets of the company. Provided the interest and capital is paid when due they exercise no rights of control. On the other hand the shareholders are the owners of the company, and the directors are responsible for ensuring that both their legal and economic rights are observed.

Their legal rights are governed by the Companies Acts. The company must: (a) hold an Annual General Meeting, giving the shareholders at least twenty-one days' notice; (b) allow shareholders to speak at the AGM and to vote on resolutions, either directly in person or by proxy; (c) provide shareholders with a copy of the Annual Report and Accounts; and (d) hold a General Meeting of shareholders whenever the financial structure of the company is to be altered.

Only about 1 per cent of shareholders attend AGMs. As noted earlier, they have little say in the running of complex organisations. But they require a satisfactory dividend on their risk capital and security of capital in real terms. To achieve these objectives the directors have the responsibility of making the company as profitable as possible, even though 'profit' tends to be an emotive word and firms which make large profits may be frowned upon. Thus, to put the company's economic responsibility into perspective, it is helpful to analyse profits a little more closely.

The nature of profit
It is through profits, and losses, that the market economy works. But we must be careful to distinguish between three types of profit.

As we saw in Chapter 9, *normal profit* is necessary to induce firms to accept the uncertainty inherent in acquiring fixed factors ahead of actual receipts from the sale of the finished product. Thus normal profit is the cost which has to be met if the firm is to be retained in the industry even in the long period.

But there may be an additional profit – *super-normal profit*.

This arises because, in the short period, certain factors such as machinery and key workers are fixed in supply. In the long period this is not so and, if there is competition between firms, super-normal profit tends to disappear (see Chapter 10). Nevertheless since in a changing economy firms have to make forecasts, there are always likely to be some firms enjoying super-normal profit simply because their managers' forecasts and decisions are more accurate.

Monopoly profit is obtained by excluding competitors; thus it is not competed away even in the long period. While it might stimulate research, such profit does not fulfil the functions mentioned above and is largely an economic rent gained at the expense of consumers.

The role of profits

We can therefore summarise the role of profits in a market economy as follows:

(1) *Normal profit induces firms to accept the uncertainty inherent in a dynamic economy.* The level of normal profit will vary with the industry; thus it will be higher for oil exploration than for selling petrol.

(2) *Abnormal profit indicates which industry should expand and which should contract.* When a firm produces a good which proves to be popular with consumers it probably makes super-normal profit. This indicates that output should be expanded. On the other hand losses show that consumers do not want the good and production should contract.

(3) *Super-normal profit encourages firms to increase production.* Profits not only indicate that consumers want more of a good; they are also the inducement to entrepreneurs to produce those goods. As we saw in Chapter 10, super-normal profits act as the spur for existing firms to enter the industry. On the other hand, when losses are being incurred, firms go out of production and the industry contracts. Thus losses are as important as profits in the operation of the market economy.

(4) *Super-normal profit provides the resources for expansion.* An industry making super-normal profit can secure the factors necessary to expand. First, profits can be ploughed back, while shareholders will respond to requests for further capital, usually through 'rights' issues. New firms can enter the industry because investors will subscribe to a company intending to operate where the level of profits is relatively high. Second, profits allow expanding firms to offer higher rewards to attract factors. In this way resources are moved according to the wishes of consumers.

(5) *Profits ensure that production is carried on by the most efficient firms.* In a competitive industry the firm making the largest profit is the one whose costs are lowest. It will have an incentive to expand production and, if necessary, can afford to

pay more for factors to do so. Less efficient firms must copy its methods to retain factors. In any case the increased output of the more efficient firm will eventually lower the price of the product. As a result inefficient firms make losses – profits become negative.

To sum up, profits and losses are the means by which the process of natural selection occurs in the market economy. Where there is competition it is wrong to regard profits as being somewhat immoral. The exception is monopoly profits, which do not motivate a full distribution of resources according to the wishes of the consumers.

IX Insolvency

The firm must generate sufficient profits to pay interest on loans and repay capital when due. Where it cannot do so it becomes 'insolvent'. If it is a corporation, it is 'liquidated' or 'wound up', and ceases to exist. If it is a sole trader or partnership, it is declared 'bankrupt'.

Liquidation

Liquidation can be:

(a) *Compulsory* – by either the Companies Court (a part of the Chancery Division of the High Court) or a County Court if the company's paid-up share capital does not exceed £120,000. The chief grounds for liquidation are that the company cannot pay its debts, though it can be wound up for failing to deliver the statutory report to the Registrar of Companies.

The company's assets are taken over by the *Official Receiver,* who reports on the company and summons a meeting of creditors to appoint a liquidator and a committee of inspection to supervise its conduct.

The *liquidator* becomes an officer of the court and conducts the winding-up, receiving and managing the company's assets.

(b) *Voluntary* – by resolution of the company. If the company is solvent, members can supervise a winding-up, appointing a liquidator to distribute the company's assets. But where it is insolvent, the winding-up is by the creditors, who appoint a liquidator and committee of inspection.

Winding-up by order of the court or by resolution of the company terminates the powers of directors, the contracts of employment of employees and the transfer of shares or company property.

The duty of the liquidator is to take control of the company's property, carry on the company's business, collect its assets and discharge its debts and liabilities. When the winding-up is complete, the usual method in the case of compulsory winding-up is for the liquidator to apply to the Registrar of Companies for the name of the company to be struck from the Register. In a voluntary winding-up the liquidator will lay an account of the winding-up before final meetings of creditors, and submit a return on these meetings to the Registrar. Three months after registration the company is deemed to be dissolved.

Bankruptcy

The aims of proceedings in bankruptcy are: (a) to ensure that a debtor's assets are insufficient to meet his liabilities; (b) to see that there is a fair distribution of assets to the creditors; and (c) to allow the debtor to start anew, relieved of the burden of his debts.

For bankruptcy proceedings to be commenced a person must have committed an 'act of bankruptcy'. This may occur in a number of ways, the most usual being where the debtors gives notice to any of his creditors that he has suspended, or is about to suspend, payment of his debts.

Within three months of the act of bankruptcy the debtor or creditors may, provided the sum concerned is at least £200, present a *bankruptcy petition* to the court. At the hearing of the petition the debt must be proved, when the court will make a *receiving order* (advertised in the *London Gazette* and a local paper) whereby the Official Receiver is appointed by the Department of Trade.

The debtor places a detailed statement of affairs with the Official Receiver. At the first meeting of creditors which follows, they must decide whether to accept any arrangements the debtor may have proposed or whether to seek to have him made bankrupt. There follows the *public examination,* in which the debtor is questioned on oath in open court. If the debtor's arrangements are not accepted, the court will adjudge him bankrupt, notice of the adjudication is then vested in his *trustee in bankruptcy*, whose function is to realise the debtor's assets and distribute the proceeds among the creditors.

At any time after the adjudication order the bankrupt may apply to the court for an order of *discharge*. The Insolvency Act, 1976, provides for an automatic discharge after five years, unless one has been granted already. An undischarged bankrupt commits an offence if he obtains more than £50 credit without informing his creditors that he is an undischarged bankrupt. Nor can he be a company director or an MP within five years of his bankruptcy.

Part IV

The Public Sector

14 The Allocation of Resources through the Public Sector

I Introduction

The basic weaknesses of the market economy in allocating resources

The market economy allocates resources because supply responds to price signals. Its main strengths are that, through demand, individual preferences affect the price of a good, and through the profit motive, resources are used efficiently in supplying goods. Part III of this book has explained how both are achieved, and how some inefficiencies, e.g. through monopoly power, may be corrected by government action.

In certain circumstances, however, such market intervention is inadequate. First, 'community goods', such as defence and street lighting, cannot be supplied through the price system since it is impossible to exclude 'free-riders'. Second, 'public goods', e.g. parks, where additional use involves no marginal cost, are not fully used when charges have to be levied. Third, either through ignorance or miscalculation of future benefits, people, even if they had sufficient income, may devote an insufficient proportion of that income to purchasing 'merit' goods such as housing and education. Fourth, the project may be so large that only the government can provide the capital required, particularly where there is some doubt if revenue will cover total costs, e.g. atomic energy, coal-mine modernisation. Fifth, external costs and benefits may be so widespread that only the government can take full account of them, e.g. New Town development, airport construction.

Forms of public-sector organisation

Where any of the above conditions hold it is necessary or likely that the good or service will be provided by the state. The actual form of organisation will vary between:

(1) the government department;
(2) a local authority;
(3) a nationalised industry;
(4) other quasi-government bodies.

Each has different strengths and weaknesses according to the functions which have to be performed and the methods available for covering costs.

'Needs' in the public sector

Whereas goods and services are supplied in the private sector in response to effective demand, the government departments and local authorities provide goods and services according to 'needs', a social rather than an economic concept. For example, owner-occupied houses are only built if there is an effective demand for them. In contrast, the public sector regards good housing as one of its social obligations. The authorities therefore decide arbitrarily on the standard of an adequate housing unit, and housing policy consists of making good the deficiency between the number of such units available and the number of households to be accommodated.

II The government department

The need for 'public accountability'

When the state provides goods and services consideration has to be given to two fundamental principles, each pulling in opposite directions.

The first, 'public accountability', arises because British democracy requires that where the state is granted powers it shall be answerable, in some form or another, for the way in which those powers are exercised. The citizen requires some assurance that powers granted to the state to produce goods and services are not abused by authoritarianism, inefficiency or monopolistic exploitation.

The second principle is 'economic efficiency'. The difficulty is that, by insisting on strict public accountability, we may so tie the hands of those running the state services that they cannot operate efficiently.

Accountability through the government department

The most efficient form of accountability is achieved when a government department produces the goods or services, for at its head is a Minister who accepts full responsibility for its work. He is subject to examination in Parliament, having to explain general policy in debate and to answer questions on even minor details of administration. In finance, too, there is also strict control: the Treasury ascertains that money is spent economically and within the limit authorised by Parliament, and further checks are carried out by the Expenditure Committee and the Public Accounts Committee (see p. 57).

But this form of accountability has certain inherent snags. First, Parliament is basically a forum for discussing major political issues rather than for dealing with administrative details. In any case, MPs are laymen without the necessary technical knowledge to exercise proper control. Second, Parliament would be overworked if it tried to exercise detailed control. Third, frequent questions in Parliament on the decisions of civil servants can lead to their taking a 'play-for-safety' attitude or the line of least resistance. The Opposition probes mainly with political ends in view. Civil servants are therefore hardly likely to follow a bold, imaginative policy which, should it fail, could excite considerable criticism when, by taking an alternative middle-of-the-road line, they can settle for a less troubled life. Fourth, Treasury control over finance is restrictive in character. Whereas private enterprise only requires proposed expenditure to be justified by over-all profits, the Treasury insists that each individual item of service is provided at the lowest possible cost.

To sum up, accountability clashes with economic efficiency. Thus the government department form of organisation is most appropriate for dealing with community and public goods which are basically non-commercial, in that (because charges cannot be levied) their cost is covered by taxation; or in providing 'merit' goods where only nominal charges are levied; or where functions are basically supervisory or control, e.g. foreign affairs, tax collection.

The economics of government decision-making

Government responsibility for defence, education, roads, airports, parks, health services, etc., means that it accepts responsibility for making decisions regarding the allocation of resources. In particular all involve investment decisions, but, since capital is limited, it has to be apportioned so as to obtain the greatest possible satisfaction. The type of question which has to be answered continually is: Should we build a new aircraft-carrier or develop a new all-purpose aeroplane for the RAF? How much should be spent on university education? Is investment in a new motorway justified? What is the best site for a new airport? Should land be purchased for the National Trust or should the money be spent on a rare work of art? How much can we afford to devote to kidney machines in view of the claims of cancer research? Should housing be provided by rebuilding or improving existing houses?

The difficulty is that, since community, public and merit goods are provided free or considerably below market price, indications of the desirability of investment which the price system provides are almost non-existent. Some allowance, too, has to be made for external costs and benefits. For instance, the usual cost–revenue criterion may be inappropriate when there is unemployment, for a road scheme which gives work to unemployed men reduces the real cost. Finally, the government can pay more attention to the wishes of unborn generations, allowing these to sway a decision in purchasing land for the National Trust or buying a painting for an art gallery.

Government decisions often depend upon subjective political considerations. For example, education is free partly as a means of redistributing income, and comprehensive education is required largely for egalitarian and social reasons. But deciding investment solely at the political level has serious defects now that the government has increased its involvement in the economy. First, the number and complexity of the decisions which have to be made at government level makes some decentralisation of decision-making (something which is achieved automatically by the price system) desirable. Second, the one-man, one-vote method of electing the government does not weight votes according to the intensity of satisfaction gained or lost by a given investment. For instance, the simple majority decision would allow two voters marginally in favour of a new motorway to outvote one voter who would suffer considerably by it. Third, political decisions are essentially subjective, whereas economic efficiency in resource allocation requires that objective criteria be used as far as possible.

The role of cost–benefit analysis (CBA)

Thus, for much government decision-making, a new technique, known as cost–benefit analysis, has been evolved. This works by identifying all the relevant benefits and costs of a particular scheme and then measuring them in money terms. This allows all the benefits and costs to be aggregated, as it were, in the form of a balance-sheet upon which the ultimate decision can be made.

For example, the benefits resulting from a new motorway would obviously include: the time saved in travel, fuel economies, the reduction of congestion in towns through which motor-traffic formerly passed, the reduction in road accidents, and the extra motorists who could now make day trips. Against this, however, would have to be set the cost of constructing the motorway, the additional noise suffered by nearby residents, the congestion on the feeder roads, the toll of animal life, and so on. It is obvious, however, that giving a monetary value to such benefits and costs can run up against serious theoretical and practical difficulties. Where market prices are available, the benefits and costs are fairly definite, e.g. the cost of building the motorway. But if no charges are made for the use of the motorway, how do we know the possible value of the benefits received? The number of motorists likely to use the road can be estimated, but how do we value the journey each makes since some are travelling on business and others on leisure? Similarly, with accidents avoided, we can estimate the saving to the hospital service, police time, etc., but how do we value the physical suffering which does not take place? And the motorway may result in fewer deaths: what price do we put on the saving of human life? Similar problems arise in valuing such intangibles as noise, traffic congestion and the toll of animal life. It may be possible to give a price by analogy, e.g. the fall in the value of houses resulting from the noise or the life-span earning power of people dying in accidents, but none can be completely satisfactory.

At best, therefore, all CBA can do is to lay bare the issues, emphasising the possible margin of error in any figures given, so that some definite magnitudes of the various items which have to be considered are made available to the decision-makers.

Even so, CBA cannot be used where political decisions dominate. For instance, how much is spent by Britain on defence will depend upon subjective views as to how far the Soviet Union's expansionary aims are a threat to Britain and to what extent such expenditure can be trimmed in order to expand the social services. Similarly, comprehensive education is often advocated as a means of promoting a more integrated society, while local authority housing may be provided in areas of high land values, e.g. Hampstead, in order to achieve a 'social mix'. While social factors can be identified, it is almost impossible to measure them satisfactorily.

Moreover, it may be difficult to apply CBA to certain decisions. Consider, for instance, a local authority which is spending £1 million on swimming facilities. The decision rests between: (a) one swimming-bath of Olympic standards which, while it could be used for local people, would also bring prestige to the town; (b) three smaller swimming-baths, each capable of providing training facilities and holding galas; and (c) six very small baths specifically designed to teach children to swim. The advantages of each are largely immeasurable by CBA since they embrace so many intangibles. As a result councillors would decide subjectively (perhaps on political lines) at a council meeting.

Nor can a firm CBA decision be applied where a project involves irreversible decisions, such as the survival of a species of animal or plant, since it is impossible to estimate the current cost of a decision which would deny future generations the opportunity to choose.

Finally, there is always the problem of deciding on the cut-off point as to the benefits and costs to be included and the time horizon. The viability of a project could rest on this, and there is always the temptation for interested parties to extend the cut-off point in order to justify particular preferences.

Such problems, together with the practical difficulties of measuring intangibles, mean that CBA cannot be fully objective.

Thus its role is limited to presenting systematically all the information relevant to a decision and to indicate the weight which can be placed on the accuracy of the calculations submitted. By doing so it ensures that the claims of rival pressure groups are assessed and all the relevant issues fully debated before the ultimate political decision is taken.

III Local authorities

The advantages of local authority provision

While some local authorities may provide trading services, e.g. municipally owned transport, their activities are mostly concerned with community, public and merit goods, e.g. environmental services, roads, parks, education, housing. Making local authorities responsible has certain advantages:

(1) *Those who run local services are local people responsive to local needs and attitudes.* In contrast administration from Whitehall makes for uniformity throughout the country.

(2) *It allows close contact between the governed and those who govern.* When administration is at the local level people can get in touch directly with the persons who make decisions and the officials who carry them out. This tends to eliminate the frustrations and delay associated with bureaucracy.

(3) *It facilitates continuity of policy.* While councils are usually run on party lines, most decisions are of an administrative character, so that only on few issues, e.g. comprehensive schools, is there a political division. Generally, therefore, all councillors can work together to decide the best long-term policies for the community, something which might be hampered if services were administered by a central government subject to swings of the political pendulum.

(4) *It provides for a division of power between Whitehall and Town Hall.* Thus a local protest, e.g. on a proposed airport or motorway, serves to remind central government that its decisions must respect local feelings and loyalties.

(5) *Local authorities lighten the burden of administration –* which would otherwise put a severe strain on Westminister and Whitehall.

The structure of local government in England and Wales

The local government structure of England and Wales is almost identical but, although broadly parallel, Scotland and Northern Ireland have some differences. The general scheme is two-tier (see Figure 14.1).

Outside the conurbations England and Wales are divided into 'counties', which in turn are divided into 'county districts', and

Fig. 14.1
The structure of local
government in
England and Wales

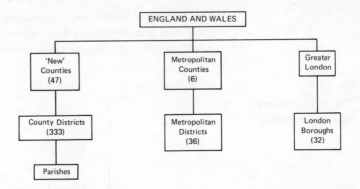

below these may be parishes (which provide minor local amenities such as sports facilities and village halls, and may monitor planning applications being considered by the district council).

In six conurbations – complexes of towns centred on Liverpool ('Merseyside'), Manchester, Birmingham ('West Midlands'), Leeds–Bradford ('West Yorkshire'), Sheffield ('South Yorkshire') and Newcastle–Sunderland ('Tyne and Wear') – there is a special Metropolitan system whereby the districts have greater powers than elsewhere. In London, the other main conurbation, a similar structure operates through the Greater London Council and the thirty-two London Boroughs.

Functions of local authorities

Local councils provide their services on the authority of Parliament. Most of their functions are *obligatory* and action can be taken against them if they are neglected. Others, such as libraries and trading services, are *permissive*, the authority undertaking them at its discretion.

The work of local authorities can be classified into five main groups:

(1) *protection*, e.g. the police and fire services;

(2) *regulation and control*, e.g. the licensing of cinemas, the inspection of weights and measures and of food and drugs, and consumer protection;

(3) *personal*: services for individuals directly, e.g. education, housing, the care of children and old people;

(4) *environmental*: to maintain and improve people's surroundings by providing public health and sanitary services (e.g. refuse disposal), roads, street lighting, parks, museums, libraries, community centres;

(5) *trading*: services provided on a commercial basis, e.g. passenger transport, entertainments.

Figure 14.2 sets out the major services and how they are allocated between the different authorities. As a general rule the *counties* provide those services which are best administered over a wide area or which are most economically provided on a large scale and therefore for a large population, e.g. education. The *county districts* are basically sanitation and housing authorities.

Fig. 14.2
The main services of
local government

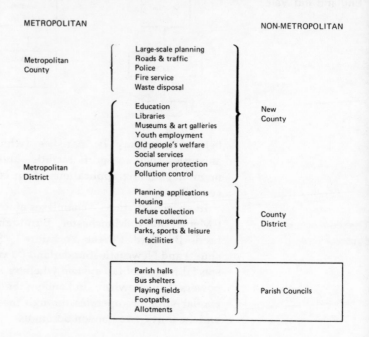

As already noted, the *metropolitan districts* perform many of the county functions. *London* broadly follows this 'metropolitan' pattern.

The local authority as a
form of business
organisation

Responsibility for carrying out the functions of the particular local authority rests with the *council,* the elected body.

Any person above 21 years of age is qualified to be a councillor if he or she is a British subject and a local government elector for the area. The usual disqualifications regarding crime and illegal practices apply, but no deposit is required from a candidate. Voting is on the basis of the ordinary residence qualification, and procedure is similar to that for parliamentary elections, except that usually more than one candidate has to be chosen.

Councillors hold office for four years. In the districts one-third of the councillors retire in each of the first three years of a four-year cycle. In the counties elections for *all* the county council seats are held in the fourth year. The system is illustrated in Figure 14.3

To preside over council meetings authorities which have been granted 'borough' or 'city' status elect a Mayor, while others elect a Chairman. While council elections are usually fought on party lines, the Mayor or Chairman usually stands above politics

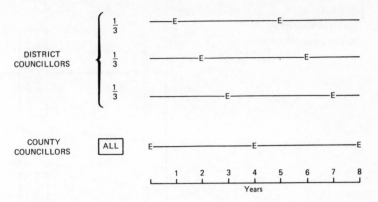

**Fig. 14.3
Local government
elections**

during his or her term of office. Most of his or her time is occupied on civic duties, and he or she is therefore usually paid a salary and an expense allowance.

**The committee
system**

Apart from meeting infrequently councils are normally too large to consider business in detail. Nor are any councillors the equivalent of the full-time Ministers at Whitehall who take charge of departmental policy. In local government this function is performed by *committees* (see Figure 14.4). Certain committees are required by law to be appointed, e.g. finance, social services and education; the rest are decided by the council. Committees are usually given executive as well as advisory functions. Indeed the council may delegate to the committees all its powers, except those for levying a rate or raising a loan.

The key figure in a committee is the Chairman: not only is he in close and regular contact with the corresponding chief officer, but he instigates much of the committee's work, the nearest equivalent to the Chairman or Managing Director of a company.

The policies decided upon by the council and its committees are put into effect by paid *permanent officers*. Since the only compulsory appointments are Education Officer and Director of Social Services, councils have great flexibility in planning their management structure. In practice most appoint a Chief Executive, Treasurer, Engineer, Surveyor, Housing Manager and Parks Superintendent, according to the services operated.

Since they are composed mainly of laymen having limited time for council work, the committees are very dependent upon the professional advice of their permanent officials on current policy and future development. This produces a delicate situation. On the one hand a strong-minded official is in a position to dominate the elected representatives who, in a democracy, should have the ultimate control. On the other hand an enthusiastic official should not feel frustrated. The task of the committee is to harness his professional skills to the service of the community but without

**Fig. 14.4
The structure of a
district council**

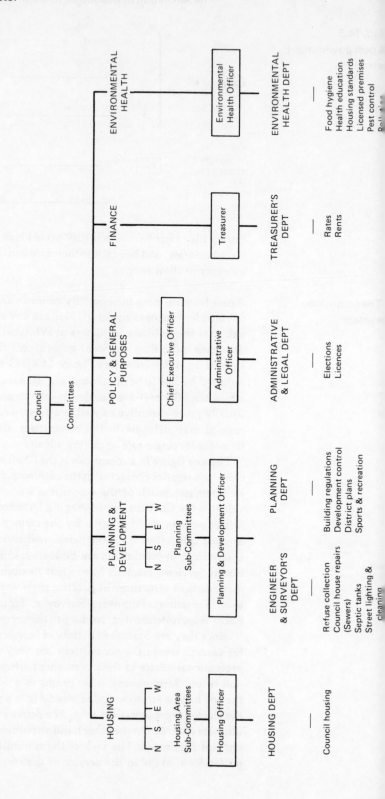

relinquishing control. Here the committee chairman can be a major force; apart from being in touch with the chief officer between committee meetings, it is he who largely decides whether policies suggested by the official are to be encouraged or restrained.

Particular attention has to be paid to the *co-ordination of committees* if one of the advantages of local government – bringing a wide range of interdependent services within one system – is not to be reduced.

Although there is of course no Prime Minister as in central government, in some large authorities the leader of the majority party plays an important role. There is often, too, something akin to an Inner Cabinet, for the Policy Committee (which often consists of the chairmen of the other committees) guides general policy and decides on priorities.

Councils achieve a measure of co-ordination through interlocking membership, whereby councillors each join more than one committee so that usually every committee has at least one member of every other committee. Moreover, at the administrative level, the practice now tends towards appointing a Chief Executive Officer having management expertise, and he deploys a unified management team of departmental officers.

Paying for local services

Every year the Treasurer of each council submits an estimate of expenditure for the coming year to the Finance Committee. This committee, which usually consists of the Chairmen of the other committees, considers these estimates and decides how the money is to be raised. By far the largest single item of spending is education (see Figure 14.5). Other major items are highways, police and social services.

Spending is of two kinds, capital expenditure and current expenditure.

Capital expenditure is incurred on such items as new houses, schools, roads, etc. The benefits from these projects extend far into the future and it would be unfair to throw their full cost on the ratepayers of one particular year. Such expenditure is therefore covered by long-term loans which, together with the interest on them, are repaid over a number of years. Councils borrow mainly on the open market but, where they find this difficult, they can obtain funds from the Public Works Loans Board, which is financed by central government funds.

Current expenditure refers to the everyday spending necessary to run services (e.g. housing administration and repairs, teachers' salaries, student grants) and to pay interest charges. Obviously if a council is to pay its way, it must balance current expenditure with current income from charges, government grants and rates.

**Fig. 14.5
Local authority
revenue and
expenditure, 1973–4**

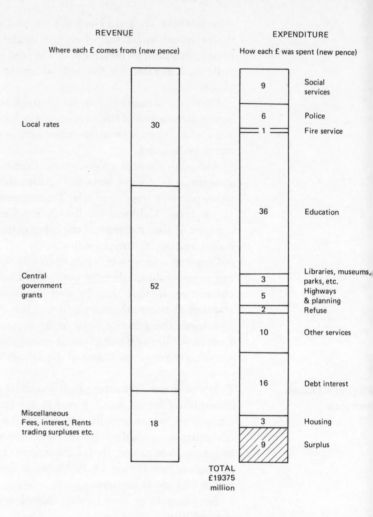

REVENUE
Where each £ comes from (new pence)

Local rates	30
Central government grants	52
Miscellaneous Fees, interest, Rents trading surpluses etc.	18

EXPENDITURE
How each £ was spent (new pence)

9	Social services
6	Police
1	Fire service
36	Education
3	Libraries, museums, parks, etc.
5	Highways & planning
2	Refuse
10	Other services
16	Debt interest
3	Housing
9	Surplus

TOTAL
£19375
million

Charges have the advantage that those who benefit from the service pay at least a part of its cost, as with rents for housing, admission fees to swimming-baths, and fines on overdue library books. But while some trading services make a profit (especially lotteries), most local government activity is concerned with providing community, public and merit goods whose cost has to be covered mainly from taxation, either central or local.

Government grants, which now provide 52 per cent of the revenue of local authorities, are made for the following purposes:

(a) to offset the defects of the rating system by transferring more of the burden to general taxation;

(b) to assist local authorities with services of national concern, e.g. roads, police, education, and so on;

(c) to ensure a minimum standard in the provision of such services;

(d) to help the poorer authorities;

(e) to encourage local authorities to provide services above the minimum required; and

(f) to assist in special emergencies, e.g. floods.

The basis upon which grants are made must achieve the above objectives without destroying local control or initiative, or committing the government to expenditure beyond the ceiling it feels it can afford. Thus while grants based on a *percentage* of the service's cost or of so much per *unit* encourage local authorities to spend more than the bare minimum, they make it difficult for the government to control its own spending. The *general or block* grant – a single, annual lump sum to be used at the local authority's discretion – avoids this but only at the risk of discouraging those authorities which are keen to improve and develop services. Their extra revenue has to be found from local sources.

The result is that today there are two main types of grant:

(1) *Grants in aid of specific services.* Calculating the grant on a percentage basis, e.g. police (50 per cent), highways (50–75 per cent according to the class of road), encourages high standards. On the other hand it necessitates careful central audit to ensure that spending is not wasteful. Thus a grant of so much per unit, irrespective of whether standards above the minimum are provided (e.g. in housing), is easier to administer.

(2) *The rate support grant.* This is a block grant to assist with other services and to help the poorer authorities. It is calculated on a formula which includes in it a number of factors such as the rate resources of the authority, the density of population, and the number of young and old people in the area.

In addition some help is given by the Exchequer to reduce the 'domestic rate', i.e. the rate on dwellings, as opposed to commercial and industrial property.

Rates are levied to cover the amount by which spending exceeds revenue from charges and government grants. They are calculated as follows. All buildings and land within the authority's area are given a 'net rateable value' by valuation officers of the Board of Inland Revenue. The figure is the amount at which the property might reasonably be expected to be rented, less the cost of upkeep.

The rates which have to be paid by the occupiers of this property are calculated according to the total amount which has to be raised and the rateable value of the area. Suppose a district has a rateable value of £10 million, and that it has to raise £5 million towards its own spending, and £1 million to cover the 'precept' from the county council. This total of £6 million would be obtained by levying a 60p rate. This means that the occupier of a house rated at £300 would have to pay annual rates of £180, usually by two payments in advance each October and April or by a monthly scheme.

The rating system has certain advantages for financing local government services:

(a) because it is a tax reserved for local authorities, it strengthens their independence by providing an income free from the control of Whitehall;

(b) the rate yield can be predicted accurately;

(c) evasion is difficult;

(d) it is simple and cheap to administer; and

(e) most households make a contribution to local services, thereby encouraging responsibility.

On the other hand a system originating some 400 years ago is bound to have weaknesses for providing finance on today's scale. The most important criticisms are:

(1) Until the introduction of the system of rate rebates in 1967 rates tended to bear more heavily on poorer families. People may live in a large house because they have a large family. In any case we consider that taxes should be progressive (taking a higher proportion of the rich person's income) and should make allowances for family responsibilities.

(2) Unlike most other taxes the yield does not automatically increase with inflation or greater prosperity. Instead the rate poundage has to be increased, and the unpopularity of this deters councils from improving services by spending more on them. The deterrent effect is heightened by the fact that elections tend to be held soon after the rate is fixed each year.

(3) Property improvement is discouraged because it increases the rateable value, and thus the rate payments.

(4) The poorer districts have a lower rateable value, yet these are likely to require higher spending on local services.

(5) The derating of agricultural land since 1929 is now an anomaly which adds to the rate burden of rural areas.

(6) Assessments of rateable value cannot be completely objective, and the shortage of skilled valuers tends to delay periodic reassessment.

The defects of the rating system have resulted in: (a) a demand for other local taxes, e.g. a local income tax, sales tax, or the retention of licence revenue, e.g. from motor-vehicles; (b) increased help by way of government grants; (c) the introduction of rate rebates (90 per cent covered by government grants) for persons with small incomes; and (d) certain local councils running lotteries.

The control of local authorities

While authorities must enjoy a large measure of independence if they are to excite local interest, they cannot have complete autonomy. Some central control may be necessary:

(a) to ensure minimum standards, particularly of those services which are of national importance, e.g. education and highways;

(b) to control local spending (about 10 per cent of national expenditure) in the interests of national economic policy;

(c) to require that the central government's own principles apply, e.g. comprehensive education and council-house sales;

(d) to improve efficiency; and

(e) to protect local citizens against wasteful expenditure, undue pressure from vested interests, or even from corruption, as in the notorious Poulson case.

Control over local authorities is exercised by: (1) Parliament, which authorises powers; (2) the courts, which define and enforce powers; and (3) the appropriate government department, which supervises the use of powers.

1 Parliament The existence, constitution and powers of local authorities depend upon Parliament, the sovereign body. Acts of Parliament require local authorities to perform certain functions, and permit others. Making certain duties obligatory protects the individual from parsimonious and slack authorities; defining them safeguards him from the over-ambitious and autocratic.

Permissive powers serve to encourage the more progressive authorities to act in the interests of the community. Where an authority requires still wider powers it can promote a private bill or, in certain circumstances, proceed through Provisional or Special Procedure Orders (see p. 55).

Parliament is mainly concerned with the general scope of local functions. The government in power, however, may require that they are fulfilled in a particular way. Should local authorities not respond quickly or adequately to directives and other methods of central control, the government may use its majority in Parliament to enforce its wishes. Thus in 1976 the Labour government introduced an Education Act to compel local authorities to reorganise schools on comprehensive lines.

2 The courts The courts decide whether powers have been exercised according to statute. On the one hand they can compel negligent authorities to fulfil their statutory obligations; on the other they can prevent them from exceeding the powers authorised. Plaintiffs can seek a prerogative order of *mandamus* or an *injunction* to compel the authority to fulfil its legal obligation, an order of *prohibition* or an injunction to prevent the authority from acting illegally, or a declaration of the court that the authority's action is *ultra vires*, i.e. outside its legal powers.

3 Ministerial control While judicial control remains an important safeguard for the individual, it requires only that local authorities fulfil their bare legal responsibilities. Statutes, too, are principally concerned with the broad scope of functions. How these functions are performed rests largely with the relevant government department.

The Act dealing with the local authorities' powers usually imposes responsibilities on the appropriate Minister. He can exercise various forms of control, which include:

(a) *advice*, by way of consultation, circulars, leaflets, etc.;

(b) *directives*;

(c) *action in default*, if the council continues to neglect its duties; for example, in 1973 the government appointed its own housing administrator because the Clay Cross Council refused to raise council-house rents in accordance with the Housing Finance Act, 1972;

(d) *grant withdrawal*;

(e) *loan sanction refusal*;

(f) *audit* (a thorough financial examination), and *surcharge* (an order for councillors to reimburse mis-spent funds);

(g) *inspection*;

(h) *approval* of certain schemes;

(i) *judicial decisions* when appeal is to the Minister, e.g. on refusal of planning permission;

(j) *approval for the appointment or dismissal of certain officers*, e.g. Chief Constables;

(k) *confirmation of bye-laws* and sanction for Provisional and Special Procedure Orders;

(l) *conditions laid down by rules, orders and regulations* made by the Minister under the authority of the parent Act.

This is a formidable list of controls, but seldom do the more negative forms have to be used. Generally local authorities work in harmony with the appropriate department, consulting with it and accepting advice in the true spirit of improving their services to the community. Above all the department tries to give the local authority as free a rein as possible, for this is the whole reason for, and spirit of, local government.

IV The nationalised industries

Reasons for nationalisation

In addition to providing community, public and merit goods the state has in recent years taken over the production of certain goods and services from the private sector, nationalising such industries as coal, gas and electricity supply, iron and steel, shipbuilding, aerospace.

Nationalisation, however, does not automatically solve the problem of allocating resources; it simply means that the ultimate economic decisions are taken by the government. But in making those decisions the government can allow for external benefits and costs (e.g. keeping the shipyards working at a loss because the men would otherwise be idle), overcome the temptation of a monopoly industry to maximise profits by restricting output (e.g. producing up to the point where price equals marginal cost) and redistribute income through its pricing policy (e.g. low-priced transport for senior citizens).

While the precise arguments for nationalisation depend upon the particular industry, the following are those most generally advanced:

(1) *Single control over all firms in the industry enables the full advantages of large-scale production to be achieved.* Competition between firms may result in their working at less than optimum size. Uncertainty as regards rivals' plans may inhibit investment because of fear of over-investment by the industry as a whole. It may also lead to duplication of research and unnecessary design differences in both the capital equipment and the final product. The National Coal Board, for instance, has developed a standard pattern of miners' safety helmet.

Similarly nationalisation secures commercial and financial economies. Competititve advertising between firms (but not industries) is eliminated, while, in borrowing, a state-owned industry can usually obtain finance more cheaply than a private firm.

(2) *State ownership is essential for the necessary capital investment.* Private owners may not have the resources or may be n willing to commit themselves to long-term capital outlays. Thus, for security and technical reasons, atomic energy has been developed by the state, while the railway modernisation programme would have been too risky for private enterprise. Moreover, losses may possibly be justified by external benefits, e.g. relief of unemployment, less congestion on the roads.

(3) *State ownership is a means of controlling monopoly.* As we have seen, 'natural' monopolies are to a large extent inevitable. It is argued that controlling such monopolies, especially the public utilities, by state ownership ensures that they will work in the public interest and not merely for high profits.

(4) *A pricing policy can be adopted which allows a highly capitalised industry to 'break even' on all costs.* Where initial fixed costs are very high, e.g. railways, electricity gas and airways, no single price can produce sufficient total revenue to cover total costs.

However if a firm in a monopoly position is allowed to discriminate between different customers by charging them the amount which each is willing to pay, it can increase total revenue. Such price discrimination is used by British Rail (e.g. cheap day trippers and students are charged lower fares than commuters), while Electricity Boards have a standing charge to help towards their fixed costs and charge different rates according to the level and time of consumption. However, since these are essential public utilities, it is held that such monopolies should be state-owned.

(5) *The efficiency of key industries must be guaranteed.* There are certain industries, e.g. iron and steel, and power, upon which most other production depends. Others, e.g. atomic research, are vital for defence. Such industries, it is argued, should not be regarded merely as a source of private profit (with their expansion or contraction depending upon this) but be run by the state in the wider interests of the nation, especially as regards full employment and defence.

(6) *Productivity will increase through improved attitudes of employees.* It is argued that not only will workers enjoy better working conditions but the fact that the state is the employer and not a firm striving for shareholders' profits will have a psychological benefit resulting in increased worker productivity.

The public corporation as a form of business organisation

When the government embarked on its nationalisation programme in 1945 the disadvantages of the government department form of organisation discussed above were highlighted. The industries being transferred from the private sector were concerned with economic functions, not the administration of particular policies. As such they served the everyday needs of the whole community, and so their contact with people was much greater than occurs in traditional fields of government. This meant that the House of Commons, as a supervisory body, would have been overworked by parliamentary questions. Moreover, accountability through Parliament would have made it difficult to pursue long-term objectives because the Minister in charge could change with a reorganisation of government. Finally, civil servants are not chosen to provide the dynamic and imaginative management required for large commercial undertakings.

The answer to these defects was to make the nationalised industries the responsibility of public corporations. The objective was to get the best of both worlds: on the one hand the world of energetic industrial enterprise found in the market economy; on the other the world of accountability to the public, to whom it belongs and whom it serves (see Figure 14.6).

Organisation of the nationalised industries

The organisation of the nationalised industries, based on the principles outlined above, presents some common features.

(1) The Boards are 'bodies corporate'. This means that they

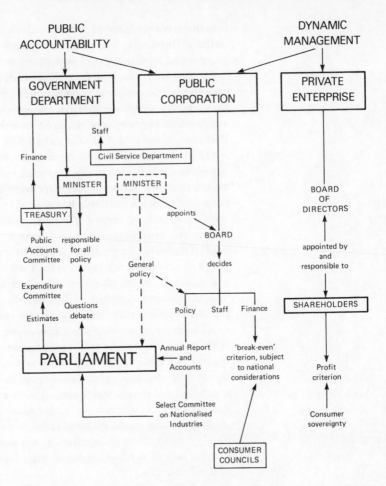

Fig. 14.6
Organisations for
providing goods and
services

have a legal identity and therefore, like a company, have a life of their own, can own property, and sue and be sued in the courts.

(2) Assets of the industry are vested in the Board, and the nationalising Act usually gives the Board instructions as to its general responsibilities. Thus the National Coal Board is charged with:

(a) working and getting coal in Great Britain;

(b) securing the efficient development of the industry; and

(c) making supplies of coal available, in quality, size, quantity and price as may seem to be best calculated to further the public interest in all respects.

(3) A Minister is given over-all control. He exercises, as it were, the shareholders' rights in a company, the 'shareholders' being the community. It is the Minister, therefore, who appoints the Board's members, though the nationalising Act usually specifies their general qualifications. In addition the Minister may give the Board general directions as to how it is to perform its

functions with regard to matters which appear to him to affect national interests, e.g. by authorising capital development, supervising borrowing and appointing auditors.

In this way the Boards enjoy freedom in their day-to-day operations but possible subordination in general policy. While they are not subject to parliamentary questioning on details of administration, they are required to submit annual reports to Parliament, which are usually debated for a day.

(4) In financial and staffing matters the Boards are free from Treasury control. Originally they were expected to pay their way, taking one year with another, free from state subsidy, but with some, e.g. British Rail, this has proved impossible. They engage their own staff, arranging pay and conditions of service through employees' organisations.

(5) To provide some direct representation for consumers, *consumers' councils* have been established for the coal, electricity, gas and transport industries. They consist of twenty to thirty unpaid members appointed by the Minister. Nominations for membership are from bodies he selects as being representative of consumers, e.g. women's organisations, professional associations, trade unions and trade associations. While the coal industry has two national councils, one for industrial and the other for domestic users, the 'consultative councils' of other industries are organised on a regional basis. These councils: (a) deal with complaints and suggestions from consumers; and (b) advise both the Boards and the Minister of the views of consumers. Unfortunately, either through ignorance, remoteness of the offices, or general lack of confidence, consumers have so far made little use of these councils.

To sum up, public corporations are made accountable through:

(a) the responsibility of the Minister for appointing Board members and ensuring that the Boards' policies harmonise with the government's over-all economic strategy;

(b) Parliament, which examines how the Minister exercises his responsibilities, probes through its Select Committee on the Nationalised Industries, and debates the Boards' annual reports;

(c) consumers' councils.

The detailed organisation of Boards has varied; we can illustrate from the coal and electricity industries.

The Coal Industry Nationalisation Act, 1946, set up the *National* Coal Board, and this determines the rest of the organisation of the coal industry. In practice there has been reorganisation from time to time. At present there are 289 collieries, with all but three grouped in seventeen areas, each controlled by a Director responsible to the NCB. The remaining three collieries (in Kent) are controlled by a general manager responsible to the NCB. The day-to-day working of the collieries is under the direction of colliery managers.

It seems, however, that originally the problem of size was underestimated, for later nationalising Acts have tended towards decentralisation. Thus the Electricity Council, established in 1948, is really only a central representative body for the industry as a whole, and is composed mainly of the chairmen of the twelve Area Boards, with an independent chairman or vice-chairman appointed by the Minister. The Area Boards were themselves set up by the nationalising Act, and the assets of the industry were vested in them. They were also given the *statutory* responsibility for the distribution of electricity. Each Board adopted its own pattern of organisation and arrangements for fulfilling its statutory obligations.

Circumstances, however, may change, requiring a new organisation. For instance the discovery of natural gas meant that distribution had to be organised centrally. Thus in 1973 the original twelve Area Boards (similar to electricity) were replaced by a single British Gas Corporation, which took over the assets of the Area Gas Boards (see Figure 14.7).

Fig. 14.7
The organisation of a
nationalised industry

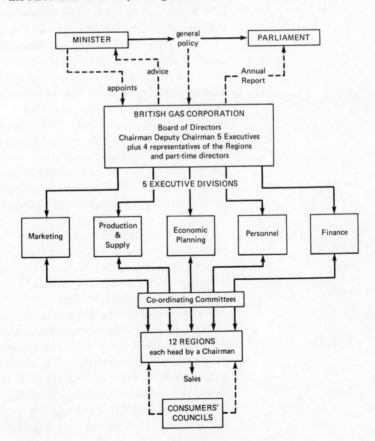

Economic problems of nationalisation and of efficiency in the public sector

Apart from the constitutional problems – internal organisation, the Minister's exact responsibilities, the extent and opportunities for parliamentary review – many economic problems still remain to be resolved.

First, problems arise because often nationalised industries are monopolies. On the demand side there is some loss of consumer sovereignty. For instance, a person can choose initially between gas, electricity, coal and oil for central heating, but thereafter is more or less committed. Should he resent subsequent price rises, the ultimate sanction – taking his custom elsewhere – is hardly available. On the supply side, too, there are grounds for concern. Prices are fixed with the object of covering costs, but what guarantee is there that costs are kept to a minimum by efficient operation? It is often felt that periodic independent efficiency investigations should be made or some form of private competition allowed, e.g. in postal services.

Second, problems of co-ordination arise in managing these vast industries, and already there has been some movement towards greater decentralisation, e.g. in electricity supply, postal services and telecommunications. However, these same problems exist in the private sector, and there seems little reason why state industry should be inferior in its ability to solve them.

Third, some economists have criticised investment decisions in many of the nationalised industries, arguing that there has been over-investment in the coal industry and possibly in the railways. Scarce capital could have been better employed elsewhere, e.g. in the construction of motorways. While some error is bound to occur in a dymamic economy (the discovery of natural gas, for instance, upset the NCB's projections of future demand for coal), there is a feeling that initially the nationalised industries were favoured in the allocation of capital because the government had a vested interest in their success. The present criterion is that any investment project should show a minimum ten per cent return on capital.

Fourth, the nationalised industries have not yet really discovered how and when to award wage increases, especially when losses are being made! Threats of strikes in these basic industries, e.g. coal and railways, have led to government intervention, and an aggravation of the wage–cost inflationary spiral.

Finally, although the industries were required to pay their way taking one year with another, some have failed to do so. Partly this has resulted from a miscalculation of demand and costs; partly it has been due to the government's use of the nationalised industries to further wider aims such as price stability (e.g. by restricting increases in the price of gas, coal, electricity, fares, etc.),income redistribution (e.g. by encouraging free travel for senior citizens), social policy (e.g. by retaining loss-making rural railway lines), and full employment and regional balance (e.g. by supporting shipbuilding on Clydeside and the North-east coast).

As a result the government has had to write off accumulated deficits (e.g. coal, railways) or subsidise heavily (e.g. shipbuilding). More than that these wider policy objectives have prevented some nationalised industries from following pricing policies which would have enabled them to break even. The difficulty with many nationalised industries, as we saw above, is that fixed costs are so high that no *single* price can generate sufficient revenue to cover total costs. While the electricity-supply industry has used price discrimination and a two-part tariff to enable it to break even, other industries, notably the railways, have been allowed to operate price discrimination only in a downward direction, fares being reduced where demand is elastic (e.g. students and senior citizens) but not raised where demand is inelastic (e.g. commuters and rural passengers). Generally speaking those who use the services should bear the cost; this is fair and also makes for economy in consumption. Only where there are identifiable external benefits are subsidies to cover deficits justified.

V Other quasi-government bodies

Although the public corporation form of organisation was highlighted by the post-1945 nationalisation programme, the practice of setting up semi-independent government bodies subject to some public control has a much longer history. Even in Tudor times the Commissioners of Sewers had supervisory duties regarding the disposal of sewage, and in the eighteenth century the turnpike trusts were responsible for providing and maintaining certain roads.

During the twentieth century, however, such semi-independent bodies have increased considerably, e.g. the National Trust, the University Grants Committee, the National Film Finance Corporation, the Milk Marketing Board and the British Council. All are concerned with the allocation of resources, and all are subject to some degree of public control even though in some cases e.g. the Church Commissioners, this only means submitting an annual report to Parliament.

Recent expansion of these quasi-autonomous national government organisations (Quangos) has provoked criticism. Such growth has arisen mainly because the state has increasingly intervened in the provision of goods and services. The objective has been to allow these bodies to operate with the minimum of ministerial control so that they can formulate their own policies, cover the particular needs of the regions for which they are responsible and, in certain cases, accept the risks inherent in running a commercial enterprise. Such quangos cover Regional Water Authorities, Regional Health Authorities, the Equal Opportunities Commission, the Manpower Services Commission, the Commission for Racial Equality, the Health and Safety Commission, the Development Corporations of New Towns and, most controversial of all, the National Enterprise Board.

Part V

Government Stabilisation Policy

15 Government Direction of the Economy

I Introduction

Objectives of government economic policy

In Chapter 3 we drew together the various reasons for government interference in the market economy under three broad objectives: allocation of resources, stabilisation of the economy, and redistribution of income. The first objective has already been discussed in the context of both the market economy and the public sector. In the following four chapters we consider the second objective, stabilisation of the economy.

Once again, however, it must be emphasised that rarely are these three objectives mutually exclusive. For instance, monetary measures to stabilise the economy also affect the allocation of resources and the distribution of wealth and income. Thus not only does a rise in the rate of interest hit in particular those firms needing large amounts of capital, but it reduces the value of wealth held by persons and institutions who have invested mainly in long-term government stock (see p. 306).

Government stabilisation policy

Government stabilisation policy is concerned with:
(a) full employment;
(b) a balanced regional development;
(c) a stable level of prices;
(d) growth of national income; and
(e) a healthy overseas trading position.
In considering these it is not sufficient to concentrate simply on an examination of particular markets. Instead we have to look at the economy as a whole in order to explain how expansion and contraction of national income can occur.

II Measuring the national income

The principle of national income calculations

Once we know how fluctuations in national income arise the government can act to promote stability. It must, however, be able to assess the impact of its measures. This necessitates having quantitative information of the national income. Although the collection of statistics proceeds continuously, the principal figures are published each year in the *National Income and Expenditure* (Blue Book).

The principle of calculating national income is as follows. Income is a flow of goods and services over time: if our income rises, we can enjoy more goods and services. But, to enjoy goods, they must first be produced. A nation's income, then, is basically the same as its output over a period. Thus national income is the total money value of all goods and services produced by the country during the year. The question is: 'How can we measure this money value?'

We can approach the problem by studying the different ways in which we can arrive at the value of a table. Figure 15.1 shows that the value of the table can be obtained by taking the value of the final product (£10) or by totalling the value added by each firm in the different stages of production. Thus the output of the tree-grower is what he receives for the tree (£3), which, we will assume, cost £2 in wages to produce, leaving £1 profit. The output of the saw-miller is what he receives for the timber (£5) less what he paid for the tree. Again, this output (£2) is made up of wages and profit. And so on. The total of these added values equals the value of the final table. Thus we could obtain the value of the table by adding the *net outputs* of the tree-grower (forestry), the saw-miller and table manufacturer (manufacturing) and the retailer (distribution).

**Fig. 15.1
The value of the total product equals the sum of values added by each firm**

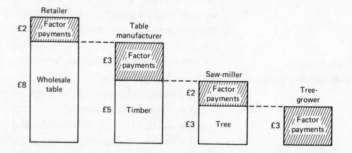

Alternatively, instead of putting these individual outputs in industry categories, we could have added them according to the type of factor payment – wages, salaries, rent or profit. This gives us the *income* method of measuring output.

Thus, if we assume (a) no government taxation or spending, and (b) no economic connections with the outside world, we can obtain the national income either by totalling the value of final output during the year (i.e. the total of the value added to the goods and services by each firm) or by totalling the various factor payments during the year – wages, rent, profit.

There is, however, a third method of calculating the national income. The value of the table in Figure 15.1 is what was spent on it. If the table had sold for only £9, that would have been the value of the final output, with the final factor payment – profit to the retailer – being reduced to £1. Thus we can obtain the national income by totalling *expenditure* on final products over the year.

It must be emphasised that the money values of output, income and expenditure are *identical by definition*. They simply *measure* the national income in different ways. This was shown by the fact that factor payments were automatically reduced by £1 when the table sold for £9 instead of £10.

To summarise, the national income is the national output – the total value of all goods and services produced by the country during the year. We can regard it as:

(1) the cost of the national output expressed as the earnings (wages, rent, profit) of all the factors of production combining to produce it;

(2) the total amount spent on final goods and services for consumption and investment purposes during the year;

(3) the total of the values of the goods and services produced by the various industries, public authorities, etc., during the year.

Before we proceed to examine in more detail the actual process of measuring these three identities, it is convenient if we first consider some of the inherent difficulties.

Difficulties in calculating national income

Complications arise through:

1 Arbitrary definitions (a) *Production.* In calculating the national income only those goods and services which are paid for are normally included. Because calculations have to be made in money terms, the inclusion of other goods and services would involve imputing a value to them. But where would you draw the line? If you give a value to jobs which a person does for himself – growing vegetables in the garden or cleaning the car – then why not include shaving himself or driving to work, and so on? On the other hand excluding such jobs distorts national income figures, for, as an economy becomes more dependent on exchanges, the income figure increases although there has been no addition to real output! (see also p. 269).

An imputed money value *is* included for certain payments in kind which are recognised as a regular part of a person's income earnings, e.g. goods produced and consumed by a farmer.

(b) *The value of the services rendered by consumer durable goods.* A TV set, dish-washer, car, etc., render services for many years. But where would we stop if we imputed a value to such services? A toothbrush, and pots and pans, for example, all render services over their life. All consumer durable goods are therefore included at their price when bought, subsequent services being ignored.

The one exception is <u>owner-occupied houses</u>. These are given a notional rent to keep them in line with property owned for letting, where rents are included, either directly or as profits of property companies. This also prevents national income falling as more people become owner-occupiers!

(c) *Government services*. Education and health services, although provided by the state, are no different from similar services for which some persons pay. Consequently they are included in national income at cost. But what of certain other government services? A policeman, for instance, when helping children to cross the road is providing a consumer service. But at night his chief task may be guarding banks and factories, and in doing so he is really furthering the productive process. To avoid double-counting this part ought to be excluded from output calculations. In practice, however, it would be impossible to differentiate between the two activities, and so all the policeman's services – indeed all government services (including defence) – are included at cost in calculating national output (see also p. 269).

2 Inadequate information   The sources from which data are obtained were not specifically designed for national income calculations. For instance, the Census of Production and the Census of Distribution are only taken at approximately five-year intervals. As a result many figures are estimates based on samples.

Information, too, may be incomplete. Thus not only do income-tax returns fail to cover the small-income groups, but they err on the side of under-statement.

But it is 'depreciation' which presents the major problem, for what firms show in their profit and loss accounts is affected by tax regulations. Since there is no accurate assessment of real depreciation, it is now usual to refer to Gross National Product (GNP) rather than to National Income (see p. 267).

3 The danger of double-counting   Care must be taken to exclude transfer incomes when adding up national income (see p. 265), the contribution to production of intermediary firms when calculating national output (see p. 267) and indirect taxes when measuring national expenditure (see p. 267).

A fourth way in which a form of double-counting can occur is through 'stock appreciation'. Inflation increases the value of stocks but, although this adds to firms' profits, represents no increase in real income. Such gains must therefore be deducted from the income and output figures.

4 Relationship with other countries (a) *Trade.* British people spend on foreign goods, while foreigners buy British goods. In calculating national *expenditure,* therefore, we have to deduct the value of goods and services imported (since they have not been produced by Britain) and add the value of goods and services exported (where income has been earned in Britain).

(b) *International indebtedness.* If a father increases his son's pocket-money, it does not increase the family income. Instead it merely effects a redistribution, the father having less and the son more. But if the boy's aunt makes him a regular allowance, the family income is increased. The same applies to the nation: while transfer incomes, e.g. retirement pensions and student grants, do not increase national income, payments by foreigners do. These payments arise chiefly as interest and dividends from loans and investments made abroad. In the same way foreigners receive payments for investments in Britain. Net income from abroad (receipts less payments) must therefore be added to both domestic expenditure and output.

Government calculations of the national income

Figures for GNP are calculated for income, expenditure and output. Because information is incomplete results are not identical. In practice the expenditure figure is taken as the datum, income and output differences being treated as a residual error.

1 National income *National income* is the total money value of all incomes received by persons and enterprises in the country during the year. Such incomes may be in the form of wages, salaries, rent, or profit.

In practice income figures are obtained mostly from income-tax returns, but estimates are necessary for small incomes. Two major adjustments have to be made:

(a) *Transfer incomes.* Sometimes an income is received although there has been no corresponding contribution to the output of goods and services, e.g. unemployment-insurance benefit and interest on the National Debt. Such incomes are really only a redistribution of income within the nation – chiefly from taxpayers to the recipients. Transfer incomes must therefore be deducted from the total of all incomes.

(b) *Income from government activities.* Personal incomes and the profits of companies are obtained from tax returns. But the government also receives income from its property and may make a profit from such sources as the public corporations. Similarly local authorities may show a surplus on their trading activities – water supply, housing, transport, etc. Such income earned by public authorities must be added in.

2 National expenditure National expenditure is the total

Table 15.1 *Calculations of the national income of the UK, 1978 (£m.)*

INCOME

	£mn.
Income from employment	98,156
Income from self-employment	13,245
Profits of private companies and public enterprises	22,651
Rent	11,125
Total domestic income	145,177
less Stock appreciation	−4,249
Residual error	1,071
Net property income from abroad	836
Gross National Product	142,835
less capital consumption	−18,310
National Income	124,525

EXPENDITURE

	£mn.
Consumers' expenditure	96,086
Central government final consumption	32,693
Gross capital formation (investment) at home, including increase in stocks	30,746
Total domestic expenditure at market prices	159,525
plus Exports of goods and services	47,636
less Imports of goods and services	−45,522
Net property income from abroad	836
less taxes on expenditure	−23,238
plus subsidies	3,598
Gross National Product at Factor Cost	142,835
less capital consumption	−18,310
National Income	124,525

OUTPUT (see Table 1.1)

Source: *National Income and Expenditure* (Blue Book), London, HMSO, 1979.

amount spent on consumer goods and services and on net additions to capital goods and stocks in the course of the year.

Figures for calculating national expenditure are obtained from a variety of sources. The Census of Distribution records the value of shop sales, while the Census of Production gives the value of investment goods produced and additions to stocks. But these censuses are not taken every year, and gaps are filled by estimates from data provided by the *National Food Survey* and the *Family Expenditure Survey*.

Market prices are swollen by indirect taxes, e.g. VAT, or reduced by subsidies, e.g. on welfare milk, council housing. What we are trying to measure is the value of the national expenditure which corresponds to the cost of the factors of production (including profits) used in producing the national product. This is known as 'national expenditure at factor cost' and is obtained by deducting indirect taxes from and adding subsidies to national expenditure at market prices.

Adjustments necessary for exports and imports have already been referred to (see p. 265). (Now see Table 15.1 for national income and expenditure calculations for 1978.)

3 National output   National output is the total of consumer goods and services and investment goods (including additions to stocks) produced by the country during the year. It can be measured by totalling either the value of the *final* goods and services produced or the value added to the goods and services by each firm, including the government. (Now see Figure 15.2 for a summary of the three ways of measuring 'national income'.)

Gross national product and national income

In the course of production machinery wears out and stocks are used up. This represents depreciation of capital. If we make no allowance for this but simply add in the value of new investment goods produced, we have *gross national product*. But to be accurate the calculation of total output should include only net investment, i.e. the value of new investment goods and stocks less depreciation on existing capital and stocks used up. This gives the net national product, which is the true national income for the year (see Figure 15.3).

The uses of national income calculations

1 To indicate the over-all standard of living   Welfare is not identical with wealth (see p. 4), but wealth bears the closest single relationship to it. Income, the flow of wealth, is therefore the nearest indication of welfare.

Nevertheless the national income figure cannot be accepted solely on its face-value. Thus although the national income of the UK was £32,000 million in 1967 and £124,525 million in 1978, it does not automatically follow that everybody had quadrupled his

**Fig. 15.2
Summary of gross
national product
calculations**

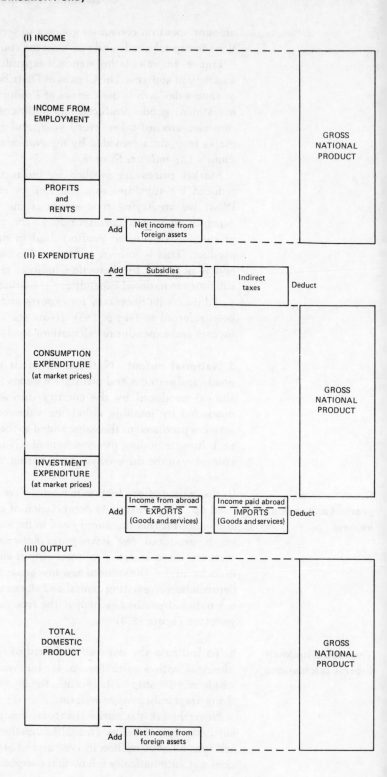

Fig. 15.3
Gross national product
and national income

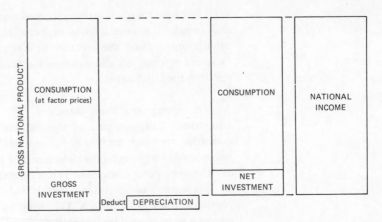

standard of living over that period. The following qualifications
have to be made:

(a) Some of the increase may be due to inflation.

(b) The national income figure must be related to the size of
population; thus average income per head is a better indication of
well-being.

(c) The standard of living of a person depends upon the
quantity of consumer goods and services he enjoys. But the
increase in national income may have come about mainly through
an increase in the production of producer goods. While these
goods enable a higher standard of living to be enjoyed in the
future, they do not increase *present* welfare.

(d) The increase in national income may have come about
through a surplus of exports over imports. This represents investment overseas, and thus (c) above applies.

(e) The average income per head figure is merely a statistical
average. It does not indicate how any increase in national income
is distributed; it may go mostly to a few rich persons (as in the oil
sheikdoms of the Middle East), leaving the others little better off.

(f) National income figures do not reflect the quality of life. An
increase in national income may be the result of longer working
hours, inferior working conditions, longer journeys to work, or
more housewives at work (with less comfort in the home).

(g) All government spending is included at cost in national
income calculations, no distinction being made between expenditure on consumer services and expenditure on defence. As a
result, if spending on the social services were cut to pay for
rearmament, national income would be unchanged!

(h) The national income figure is swollen when people pay for
services which they previously performed themselves. Thus a
married woman who returns to teaching but pays a woman to do
her housework adds to the national income twice – although the
only net addition is her teaching services.

(i) Because national income figures are based on private costs and benefits, external costs or benefits do not enter into the calculations. Thus the erection of electricity pylons would be included at cost, no allowance being made for the social cost of spoiling the landscape.

2 To compare the standard of living of different countries Comparisons of the national incomes of different countries are often necessary for practical purposes. How much help should be given by the rich countries to the very poor? Which are the very poor countries? What contribution should be made by a country to an international body, such as the United Nations, the EEC and NATO? What is the war potential of a country as indicated by its GNP per head?

But when used to compare countries' standards of living national income figures must be subjected to qualifications additional to those mentioned in (1) above:

(a) Because figures are expressed in different currencies they have to be converted into a common denominator. Using the exchange rate for this purpose is not entirely satisfactory, for the rate is determined by factors, e.g. capital movements, apart from the respective internal purchasing power of currencies.

(b) Different people have differenct needs. The Englishman has to spend more on heating than the Indian. Obviously the Englishman is no better off in this respect – though the national income figures, by valuing goods at cost, would indicate that he is.

(c) The proportion of national income spent by different countries on defence varies. Countries which spend less can enjoy consumer goods instead, but average national income does not indicate the difference.

(d) Countries vary as regards the length of the average working week, the proportion of women who work, the number of jobs which people do for themselves, the degree to which goods are exchanged for money, and the accuracy of tax returns. Some allowance must be made for all of these factors.

3 To calculate the rate at which a nation's income is growing Is the national income growing? Is it growing as fast as it should? Are the incomes of other countries growing faster? Is there sufficient investment to maintain future living standards? The answers to these and similar questions can be found by comparing national income figures, though for the reasons given above some caution must be observed.

4 To establish relationships which arise between various parts of the economy If, for example, national income figures revealed a relationship between the level of investment and growth, or between education expenditure and growth, or between profits and the level of investment, such information would be useful in planning the economy.

The figures might also indicate trends, e.g. changes in the output of different industries, which are helpful to firms in planning production, though more use is likely to be made of specific government statistics (see Chapter 8).

5 To assist the government in managing the economy   Some central government planning is now regarded as essential for achieving full employment, a stable currency and a satisfactory rate of growth. But this requires having figures for the various components of the national income, such as consumption spending, investment, exports, imports, etc. How these can be used is explained in the chapters which follow.

16 Cyclical Fluctuations in Income and Employment

I The nature of unemployment

What do we mean by 'full employment'?

Although today 6 per cent of the working population are unemployed, this compares favourably with pre-war Britain, where, in the worst year of 1932, the national unemployment rate was 22.1 per cent. Unemployment results in machines, land and buildings standing idle; as a result the standard of living is lower than it need be. But the real curse is the human misery that results. Many persons, without work for years, lose hope of ever finding a job; in any case skills deteriorate as the period of unemployment lengthens. Thus unemployment is usually discussed in terms of labour.

We say that unemployment exists where people capable of and willing to work are unable to find suitable paid employment. But where an economy is constantly adapting to changing conditions, there will always be some persons unemployed as they switch jobs or as seasonal or casual work comes to an end. Some 2 to 3 per cent unemployment must be allowed for this.

The causes of unemployment

Unemployment may occur for many different reasons, and these must be distinguished if the appropriate remedies are to be applied.

1 Normal or transitional There will always be some people changing jobs. In certain occupations, e.g. unskilled labour in the construction industry, workers are not employed regularly by any one employer; when a particular contract is completed labour is made redundant. Occasionally, too, workers are discharged when a factory is being reorganised.

Unemployed workers usually register at the local employment exchange, forming a pool of labour from which employers can fill vacancies. But how large should this reservoir of labour be? If it is too large, workers remain unemployed for long periods, if it is too small, production is dislocated through bottlenecks in filling vacancies, employers holding on to labour not currently needed, job-switching just for the sake of change and, above all, through strikes in support of claims for higher wages.

2 Seasonal   Employment in some industries, e.g. building, fruit-picking and holiday catering, is seasonal in character. The difficulty is that the skills required by different seasonal jobs are not substitutable. To what extent, for example, can hotel workers become shop assistants at Christmas? Seasonal employment is not completely avoidable. But it can be reduced if a small regular labour force will work overtime during the 'season' and admit such persons as students and housewives during the busy period. The price system may sometimes help. Thus, by offering off-season rates, hotels at holiday resorts can attract autumn conferences.

3 Frictional   Frictional unemployment occurs where there are unemployed workers of a particular occupation in one part of the country but a shortage of the same type of work in other parts. Thus today there is a surplus of unskilled and manual labourers in the north of England, whereas firms in the London area have vacancies unfilled.

Two main reasons can be suggested for this type of unemployment – ignorance of available opportunities, and immobility of labour.

4 International   Because the UK is so dependent on international trade, she is particularly vulnerable to unemployment brought about by a fall in the demand for her exports. Such a fall may occur because:

(a) *The prices of UK goods are too high to be competitive in world markets.* If home price rise, for example because of wage increases, the export market is likely to be hit severely. The demand for exports is usually highly elastic, since substitutes are often available from competing countries. The effect on employment is shown in Figure 16.1. The wage increase moves the supply curve from S to S_1. Because demand is elastic there is a considerable fall in the demand for the good, from OM to OM_1. The industry, and therefore employment, contracts.

(b) *Incomes of major importing countries may be reduced by a recession or a deterioration in the terms of trade* (see p. 15). If incomes of importing countries fall, their demand for UK goods, especially those having a high income elasticity of demand, will be likely to decrease. This is what happened following the increase in the price of oil in 1973 (see p. 18).

Fig. 16.1
The effect on employment of a wage increase in an export industry

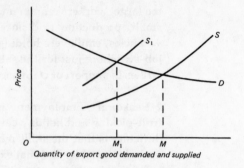

Quantity of export good demanded and supplied

5 Structural   Structural unemployment, like the frictional variety, results largely from the immobility of labour; but in this case it is brought about by long-term changes in the conditions of demand and supply. It is associated, therefore, with major changes in the economy, particularly in the export industries.

On the demand side there may be a change in any of the factors influencing the conditions of demand. The price of substitutes may fall (Dundee jute products have largely been replaced by plastics), or foreign buyers may switch to competitors' goods (British shipyards have been hit by Japanese competition). On the supply side new techniques or the exhaustion of mineral deposits may make labour redundant. Automation has reduced ICI's demand for workers at Stockton; exhaustion of the better coal seams has led to a closure of pits in South Wales and Mid-Scotland.

Where an industry has been highly localised in a particular area, the resulting unemployment may be well above the national average.

6 Cyclical   Cyclical unemployment refers to the alternative booms and slumps in the level of industrial activity which have occurred over the last 100 years. It was the major cause of the high unemployment of the 1930s.

In comparison with the 1930s, however, depressions since 1945 have been fairly mild, and are termed 'recessions'. For this we are largely indebted to J. M. Keynes, who showed that cyclical unemployment occurred because total demand was insufficient to keep the economy fully employed. His analysis, and the policies which follow from it, are so important that they form the subject-matter of the rest of this chapter.

The other types of unemployment are largely the result of frictions – the immobility of labour – which make the price system work imperfectly. Here an approach based on demand and supply in a *particular* labour market can provide an explanation (see Chapter 11).

II The link between spending and production

The circular flow of
income

When unemployment is *general* throughout the economy, we have to consider the demand for goods as a whole.

We will begin by repeating in simplified form the identity which exists between income and expenditure. Take a simple example. A teacher buys a table from a carpenter. With the money he receives the carpenter pays the timber merchant for the wood, who in turn pays the man who cut the wood. But where did the teacher obtain the original money to buy the table? Simply from the carpenter, the timber merchant, and the tree-feller, who each use part of their receipts to pay fees to the teacher for instructing their children. So with the other goods the teacher buys. Thus there is a circular flow of income – one person's spending becomes another person's income. Spending is therefore necessary for earnings.

The same applies to the economy as a whole; at any one time spending equals income. Suppose, for instance, that in the economy, all production is in the hands of a giant firm which owns all the land and raw materials and employs all the labour. The firm's income consists of the receipts from the sale of its product. Since it owns all the raw materials and land, these receipts must equal what it pays out in wages and what it has left in profits. This was the principle upon which we measured national income.

Since spending on goods, determines the receipts and thus the profits of firms, it is of vital importance in deciding the level of their output and thus of the aggregate level of activity. To explain more fully, we use Figure 16.2 which shows the money flows which correspond to the movement of factors and goods in the outer ring of Figure 3.2 – payments by firms for factors and expenditure of households on goods. The first represents income of households; the second represents receipts of firms.

If spending on goods and services is maintained, factor payments can be maintained; in other words the profitability of production is unchanged and thus firms have no cause to vary output. If, however, for some reason or another spending should fall, some of the goods produced by firms will not be sold, and stocks will accumulate. On the other hand, if spending on goods and services increases, stocks will be run down. Production has become more profitable and, as a result, output is expanded.

Three important points emerge from our discussion so far:

(1) There is no impetus towards a contraction or expansion of production if spending on goods and services equals spending (including normal profits) by firms on factors of production.

(2) The level of production, and therefore of employment, is closely related to the level of spending.

Fig. 16.2
The circular flow of
income

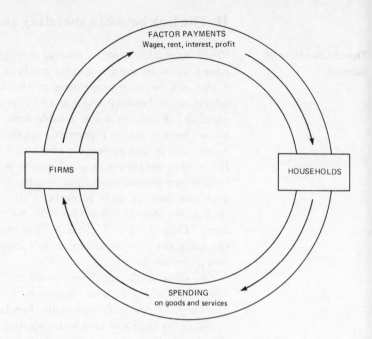

FACTOR PAYMENTS
Wages, rent, interest, profit

FIRMS

HOUSEHOLDS

SPENDING
on goods and services

(3) There is nothing to guarantee that spending will be sufficient to ensure a level of production where all factors are fully
employed.

Definitions and
assumptions

Before we show how changes in spending occur, we must make
some simplifying assumptions.

We define net profit as gross profit less retentions for depreciation. We assume:

(1) *All retentions for depreciation are actually spent* on replacement investment. Thus when in future we speak of 'investment' it
refers solely to net additions to fixed capital and stocks, i.e. net
investment.

(2) *All net profit is distributed to the owners of the risk capital.*
This means that there is no 'saving' by firms.

(3) *There is no government taxation or spending.*

(4) *There are no economic connections with the outside world;
it is a 'closed' economy.*

From the above assumptions it follows that: (a) the sum of the
factor payments is equal to national income (equals national
output) as defined in Chapter 15; and (b) income equals disposable income.

(5) *There are no changes in the price level.* Thus any changes in
the money value of national income reflect changes in real output.

(6) *The level of employment is directly proportionate to the
level of output.* In practice this may not be strictly true: existing
machinery, for example, may be able to produce extra output

without additional labour. But the simplification does allow the level of employment to be linked directly with the level of national income.

III Reasons for changes in aggregate demand

Aggregate demand

Our task, therefore, is to discover why changes occur in the national income (hereafter symbolised by Y). Now, as we have just shown, Y depends upon the level of spending, which we shall refer to as aggregate demand (abbreviated to AD). Thus we can find out why Y changes by discovering why AD changes.

Changes in *AD*

Let us return to our example of the teacher. Suppose he earns £4000 in a given year. Most of it will be spent on consumer goods and services – but not all. Some will probably be put aside for a 'rainy day'. That part of income which is not spent we can say is 'saved'. What happens to it? The money could be hidden under the mattress: in this case it is 'hoarded', and is obviously lost to the circular flow of income. But the teacher is more likely to put it in a bank, where it is safer and earns interest. Is it still lost to the circular flow of income?

So far we have looked only at spending on consumer goods. But spending can also be on capital goods and stocks, i.e. on investment. Firms go to their banks (and other institutions) to borrow money to purchase capital goods. Thus the sum deposited by the teacher stands a good chance of being returned to the circular flow of income by being 'invested', i.e. spent on additional capital goods or stocks. And if exactly the same amount of money saved by the public is spent by firms on investment, the level of AD is maintained (see Figure 16.3) and Y is unchanged.

But suppose that the amount saved does not coincide with what firms wish to invest. This can come about by either a change in the amount invested or by a change in the amount spent by consumers.

Let us first assume that consumers' spending remains constant. If now firms reduce the amount they borrow for investment, AD is smaller. On the other hand, if firms increase their investment, AD will be larger.

Alternatively the amount of income spent on consumer goods may alter. Investment, we will now assume, remains unchanged. Here, if more is spent out of a given income, AD will increase; if less, AD decreases.

What it is important to recognise is that in an economy where people are free to dispose of their incomes as they please, and

Fig. 16.3
The level of income maintained through investment

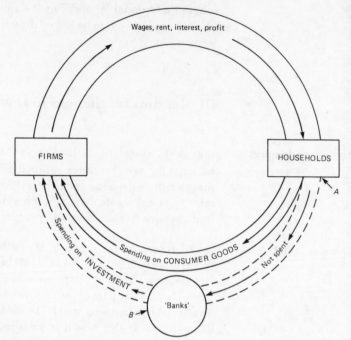

where firms are largely left to make their own investment decisions, a difference can easily exist between the amount of income 'saved' (i.e. that which people do not wish to spend) and the amount which firms wish to invest. This is because, in their spending, households and firms act for different reasons and mostly independently of one another. Two questions have therefore to be asked: (1) What determines spending on consumer goods and therefore saving (at position A in Figure 16.3)? (2) What determines investment spending (at position B)?

In our analysis consumption, i.e. spending on goods and services, will be given the symbol C; saving, i.e. income not spent on consumption, S; investment, i.e. spending on net additions to capital goods and stocks, I.

IV Consumption and saving

(1) Consumption and saving by households: 'personal saving'

Income is received as wages or salaries, rent, interest and profits. With it households buy the consumer goods they need. That part of income which is not spent has been defined as 'saving'. Hence $Y = C + S$, $C = Y - S$, and $S = Y - C$.

C and S, therefore, are merely two sides of the same coin. Thus, whenever we consider C or S, we must examine the factors which influence both spending and thrift.

Spending decisions are more important in the short run, for a person's first concern is to maintain his standard of living. They are influenced by:

(a) *Size of income.* A small income leaves no margin for saving. Only when a man has satisfied what he considers are his basic needs will he save a part of his income. Indeed, if current income falls below this level, he may spend some of his past savings or borrow in order to maintain the standard of life he is accustomed to.

But we can go further. As income increases, the proportion spent tends to decrease; or, as it is often put, there is a *diminishing marginal propensity to consume.*

The above conclusions are illustrated diagrammatically in Figure 16.4, where the curve *C* shows how consumption changes with income. Below an income of *OD* there is dissaving. At *OD* all income is consumed. At higher incomes the proportion spent falls and saving occurs.

**Fig. 16.4
The relationship
between consumption
and income**

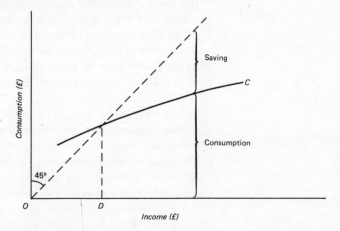

(b) *The time lag in adjusting spending habits.* It takes time for a person to adjust his standard of living as his income increases. In the short period, therefore, saving increases.

The above two factors explain the *shape* of the consumption curve – how spending changes as income changes. But we still have to account for the position of the curve – what determines the proportion of any given income which is spent. This amount can vary (i.e. the position of the *C* curve may change) as a result of:

(c) *Changes in disposable income.* We have assumed that firms have distributed all net profits and that there is no government taxation or transfers. In practice both profit distribution and government taxation will affect the size of income available for spending. Increased direct taxation, for instance, by reducing disposable income, would lower the *C* curve.

(d) *Government policy.* By its fiscal policy the government can influence the proportion of income consumed. Thus the replacement of indirect taxes by a more progressive income tax or a higher corporation tax would tend to take more from savers and less from spenders and so have the effect of increasing consumption.

(e) *The distribution of wealth in the community.* Because the proportion of income saved usually increases with income, greater equality of incomes is likely to reduce the aggregate amount saved out of a given national income. Redistributive taxation therefore tends to increase total consumption.

(f) *The invention of new consumer goods.* In recent years family cars, TV sets, hi-fi equipment, central heating and dishwashers have all induced spending, especially when backed by intensive advertising.

(g) *Hire purchase and other credit facilities.* A decrease in the initial deposit or an extension of the period of repayment encourages spending. Easier bank credit also encourages spending.

(h) *Anticipated changes in the value of money.* If people consider that the prices of goods are likely to rise, they bring forward their spending rather than save for the future.

(i) *The age distribution of the population.* Since most saving is done by people over 35 years of age, an ageing population will tend to reduce the propensity to consume of the community as a whole.

In the long period people have some concern for their future standard of living, and *thrift* exercises a greater influence on the disposal of income.

The main *factors determining thrift* are:

(a) *Size of income.* As already shown, saving increases as income increases and at an increasing rate.

(b) *Psychological attitudes.* Some communities are by nature more thrifty than others, providing against sickness, unemployment, old age, and for the education of dependants. On the other hand ostentation – the desire to 'keep up with the Joneses' – may provide a motive for a high rate of spending.

(c) *Social environment.* Apart from influencing the general attitude to saving, environment can be a major factor in other ways. Such institutions as savings banks, building societies, insurance companies, unit trusts, etc., encourage regular thrift – so that much saving out of income is contractual. Political conditions, too, influence saving habits. Countries continually threatened by war or revolution do not provide the stable background necessary to encourage thrift.

(d) *Government policy.* The government can influence people's attitude to saving in a variety of ways. In the UK it tries to stimulate personal saving through the rate of interest offered, income-tax concessions (e.g. on National Savings Bank interest) and special devices (e.g. Savings Certificates, Premium Bonds and index-linked SAYE). On the other hand a comprehensive state social-insurance and pension scheme may reduce personal saving.   At one time it was thought that people could only be induced to postpone consumption, i.e. to save, by offering interest as compensation. This view, however, is now largely rejected, chiefly because much saving is contractual e.g. insurance and mortgage payments. Above all the dominant factor is the ability to save, i.e. the level of income.

Apart from households, saving can be achieved through retentions by businesses and the government (see Figure 16.5).

Fig. 16.5
Saving in the UK, 1978
(£ million)

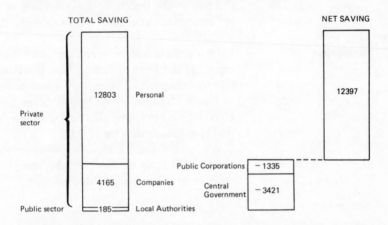

(2) Business saving

Saving by businesses (which in volume remains fairly stable) is achieved by not distributing to shareholders all the profits made in a year. Some profits are usually retained, either to be 'ploughed back' for the expansion of the business or to be held as liquid reserves in order to meet tax liabilities or maintain dividends when profits fluctuate. The chief factors affecting this type of saving are:

(a) *Profits*. Transfers to reserves are dependent upon and stimulated by the level of current profits.

(b) *Subjective factors*. Profits are likely to be retained when directors are expansion-minded or financially prudent.

(c) *Government policy*. An increased tax on *distributed* profits or a 'dividend freeze' would be likely to increase company saving.

(3) Government saving

Central government saving is achieved chiefly through a 'budget surplus', revenue exceeding current government expenditure. The surplus may be necessary: (a) to provide for the government's own investment and loans; and (b) to ensure that, with personal and business saving, total saving will so cover total investment that aggregate demand will be sufficient to produce full employment without inflation (see p. 286).

Recently, central government expenditure has been so high that the difference has had to be covered by borrowing. A Public Sector Borrowing Requirement (see p. 305) means that there is dissaving.

Public corporations are similar in many ways to ordinary businesses. But as their operations are more directly under government control, and their capital requirements are largely covered by the Treasury, their saving and investment are included under the public sector.

Local authorities, too, may have a budget surplus, but in practice they account for only 6 per cent of total saving.

Thus in the public sector spending is determined chiefly by government policy, both economic and political.

Conclusion

In the private sector spending (and therefore saving) depend upon (a) the level of income, i.e. the size of AD, and (b) other factors influencing the amount spent out of income. In comparison with changes in AD these other factors are fairly stable. Hence the main factor affecting short-term changes in consumption spending is the size of AD!

We have therefore to look elsewhere for the reason why AD changes. It is to be found in the comparative instability of the other form of spending – investment.

V Investment spending

Investment for purposes of national income calculations is spending over a given period of time on the production of capital goods (houses, factories, machinery, etc.) or on net additions to stocks (raw materials, consumer goods in shops, etc.). It takes place in both the private and public sectors of the economy.

Investment in the private sector

A firm will only invest if it thinks that it will eventually prove profitable. There are, therefore, two main considerations to bear in mind: (a) the expected yield from the investment; (b) its cost. More precisely, marginal revenue productivity of an addition to investment must at least equal marginal cost.

The yield on the investment will depend largely on the demand for the consumer good the firm produces. Hence the firm is chiefly concerned with estimating future demand for these consumer goods. In forming an opinion, the firm is most likely to commence from a position regarding which it does have some definite knowledge, i.e. the present demand for those goods. If that demand is buoyant and has remained so for a fairly long period, the firm will probably view the future optimistically. On the other hand if present demand is low and has shown itself resistant to attempts to increase it, the future, to say the least, will appear somewhat gloomy. But since the current demand for goods, i.e. the level of consumption, depends chiefly on the level of income, we can say that investment is likely to be greater, the higher is AD.

Technical developments, like the internal combustion engine, atomic energy, automation and North Sea gas and oil, give an added impetus to investment.

Furthermore, the effect of government policy has to be considered. Changes in policy add to uncertainty. Is corporation tax likely to be increased? Will inflation compel the government to carry out restrictive policies? In contrast the government may stimulate private investment by subsidies or generous tax allowances, and revive optimism by increasing its own investment.

This brings us to the *cost* of investment. This is represented by the cost of borrowing money to finance it – the rate of interest (chiefly that on debentures). A low rate tends to stimulate investment. If the rate rises, marginal projects cease to be profitable, and so the level of investment falls.

However, whether the rate of interest has a major influence on investment is doubtful. For one thing, investment decisions, especially for large firms, are the result of long-term planning. Any alteration of plans through a change in the rate of interest might throw the whole programme out of phase. For another, firms allow a considerable safety margin when deciding on investment, probably expecting to recover its cost within five years. This margin is thus sufficient to absorb a relatively small rise in the rate of interest. Even the holding of stocks may not be affected by the rate of interest. Convenience is more likely to decide the minimum held. In any case the rate of interest may be only a small part of the cost of holding stocks – warehousing, etc., being relatively far more important. Above all, compared with firms' expectations, the rate of interest is of secondary importance. Thus, especially when it comes to reviving investment, a fall in the rate of interest tends to have little effect.

Investment in the public sector

Capital expenditure is incurred by the central government, nationalised industries and local authorities.

Much of central government investment is fairly stable, depending chiefly on policy commitments. To a large extent, too, the same is true of the capital expenditure of the nationalised industries, for in deciding whether or not to expand their capacity they will be guided by their social obligations as well as by their financial position. Thus in periods of unemployment they might increase their investment.

Local authority investment tends however to react to changes in the rate of interest, especially spending on new houses. If, after applying government grants, the cost of borrowing is not covered by the rents charged, increased rates have to be levied. Because this may be disastrous politically, local authority house-building may be reduced to mere slum clearance.

The real importance of public investment is that it is subject to direct government control. Thus, should private investment be deficient, the government can increase its spending on its own capital projects. (Figure 16.6 summarises the investment situation in the UK in 1978.)

Fig. 16.6
Investment in the UK 1978 (£ million) (Net fixed capital formation at home and value of physical increase in stocks and work in progress)
Source: *National Income and Expenditure* (Blue Book), London, HMSO, 1979.

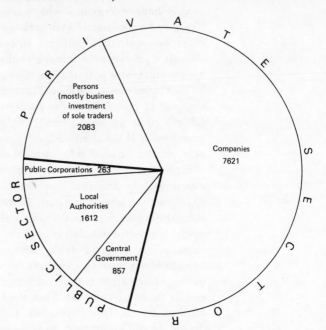

VI The control of cyclical unemployment

Analysis of the task

Employment depends upon the level of *AD* – the total amount of money spent on the goods produced. *AD* fluctuates according to the relationship between intended saving and investment:

(1) *AD* expands if: (a) investment increases but saving remains unchanged; (b) saving decreases but investment remains unchanged.

(2) *AD* contracts if: (a) investment decreases but saving remains unchanged; (b) saving increases but investment remains unchanged.

In practice investment is more liable to frequent change than is saving. Whereas firms' expectations are highly senstive to new conditions, people's spending habits are fairly stable.

To eliminate cyclical unemployment AD must be maintained at an adequate level. The responsibility for this must rest with the government. First, only the government can exercise the powers, particularly as regards collecting statistics and information, necessary for adequate planning. Second, the government's own spending forms such a large proportion (one-half) of AD that it can be used to balance changes in the private sector. Third, the knowledge that the government is committed to a full-employment policy will eliminate much of the uncertainty from which cyclical fluctuations begin. Fourth, any initial increase in spending generates further spending as people use their extra income. This 'multiplier' is estimated to be roughly 2.

The government's task, therefore, is to estimate the level of AD which willl produce full employment, and then, by increasing consumption, investment or its own spending, obtain the required level of AD.

The nature of government action

The role of the government in controlling the economy can be likened to that of the driver of a car. At no time can the car run on its own, and the man at the wheel has to make continuous steering adjustments. From time to time, too, he is concerned with more definite alterations, varying his pressure on the accelerator, changing gear, and even modifying his route to avoid traffic congestion.

But in all these manoeuvres different drivers act differently. Some use the gear lever rather than the accelerator in reducing speed. Others assess that traffic congestion will not be so bad as to warrant a detour. Nor does the same man do exactly the same things each day. He knows many different routes to work and, being flexible, he chooses that which is most appropriate to the particular traffic conditions.

So it is with the government. Like the driver guessing the traffic congestion along the route, the government has to work from incomplete information in estimating what change in AD is necessary to achieve the desired result and the extent to which the measures it adopts will produce that change. It has two main types of control – monetary and fiscal – but it usually has to combine them in different ways. Not only does one reinforce the other, but a different emphasis has to be placed on each according to the needs of the prevailing conditions. Where a quick change in the direction or tempo of the economy is required, more weight must be given to those measures which begin to work immediately, e.g. reducing taxes in order to increase consumption.

1 Monetary   Monetary measures are aimed at varying the cost and availability of credit.

The *cost of credit* is the rate of interest which has to be paid. Nevertheless, as we noted earlier, there are doubts regarding the effectiveness of interest policy in influencing investment. Moreover, apart from being ineffective, interest policy may be undesirable for the following reasons:

(a) It cannot be pursued independently of the general level of world interest rates. If, for instance, the UK retains interest rates which are low in relation to those of the rest of the world, there will be an outflow of sterling balances. On the other hand high interest rates mean a high cost of borrowing from abroad by the UK, increasing her 'invisible payments' (see p. 334).

(b) The Public Sector Borrowing Requirement may be so large that a high interest rate is necessary to attract loans (see Chapter 18). It must be remembered, however, that this adds to the burden of servicing the National Debt, necessitating higher taxation.

Even so, interest policy cannot be discarded completely as a weapon for regulating the economy. It can be applied quickly and to a fine degree and, if taken early, can provide an advance warning of the authorities' intentions. The psychological effects of changes may be more important than their direct effect on the cost of long-term investment.

In practice monetary policy, by varying the cost and availability of credit, is an anti-inflation weapon rather than one to promote full employment. Thus reducing the over-all level of liquidity, restricting credit and imposing selective controls, such as hire-purchase restrictions, may be useful in stopping people from spending, but relaxing restrictions may not stimulate them to increase spending.

2 Fiscal   Indirectly, fiscal policy, by changing the type of taxes levied, can influence private consumption and investment. Thus a switch from indirect taxation would tend to increase consumption, for it would mean greater spending power for poorer people (those having a high propensity to consume). Similarly a movement away from taxes on companies would tend to increase investment through improved profitability.

More directly, AD may be influenced by budgetary policy – adjusting the relationship between government taxation and expenditure. As we have seen, taxation represents an appropriation by the government of a part of private incomes, and will be retained in the circular flow of income only in so far as it is spent by the government (see Figure 16.7). Hence AD will be increased if taxation is less than government spending, and vice versa. If

Fig. 16.7
The circular flow of
income and
government spending
and taxation

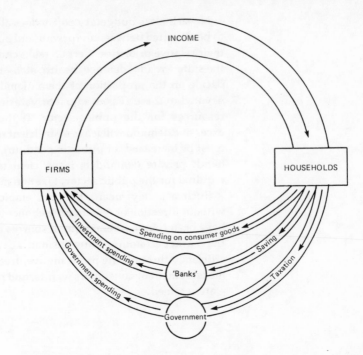

previously the budget were balanced, there would now be a
budget deficit, and vice versa.

Thus today the budget is regarded, not simply as the means of
raising revenue to meet the year's estimated expenditure, but as a
weapon to adjust private spending power to the output which
available resources can produce given the demands of the public
sector. Since the latter are largely determined by policy commitments, the ability to vary public expenditure is limited; it is
therefore taxation which takes the strain. Reducing taxation
increases disposable income and, provided this increase is not
entirely saved, spending will increase (expanding income according to the 'multiplier').

Such a policy is not without its difficulties. The convention of
annual budgets tends to dictate the timing of major adjustments
(see p. 56). Moreover, reducing taxes may, because of administrative difficulties, take time to be effective. With PAYE, for
instance, new tax tables have to be distributed. Thus fiscal policy
may often have to concentrate on putting extra purchasing power
quickly into the hands of consumers, e.g. by reducing national
insurance contributions and indirect taxes. Taxation, too, has
other objectives than adjusting AD, redistributing income for
instance. Thus policies can conflict. Finally, budgetary policy
does not direct demand into those districts and industries where
unemployment is highest. Again we see the necessity of having a
variety of measures.

Nevertheless budgetary policy does allow the national product to be allocated between the private and public sectors according to their relative priorities. Certain tasks can be undertaken better by the state – roads, defence, health, etc. – and the government must decide on the proportion of the national product which shall be devoted to these. Taxes adjust private demand in order to release resources for the public sector. If there is full employment, excessive demand will leave insufficient resources: either taxation must be increased, or public expenditure reduced. If, on the other hand, private demand is insufficient to employ resources not required for the public sector, taxation must be decreased.

Such a policy means that full employment can be pursued without direction of resources, for, once the public sector's claims have been covered, remaining resources can be allocated through the market economy. Thus the main advantages of that system – efficiency through the profit motive, freedom of choice, accurate measurement of consumers' wants, and provision for those wants – are retained.

17 Balanced Regional Development

I The nature of the problem

Regional unemployment

Even when there is no over-all deficiency of aggregate demand, unemployment may occur through changes in the conditions of demand and supply. Demand may be buoyant for some goods, e.g. electronic equipment and cars, and slack for others, e.g. ships, where workers become unemployed. On the supply side, too, technological change, e.g. automation, can lead to redundancies.

Because of the localisation of industry, the above changes result in some regions enjoying a high level of economic activity whereas others are depressed (see Table 17.1).

Table 17.1 *Percentage rate of unemployment by region, August 1979*

United Kingdom	6·0
Region	
South-East	3·8
East Anglia	4·3
South West	5·7
West Midlands	6·0
East Midlands	4·9
Yorks and Humber	6·1
North-west	7·6
North	9·0
Wales	8·3
Scotland	8·2
N. Ireland	12·6

Source: *Monthly Digest of Statistics* (Department of Employment), London, HMSO, 1979.

Frictions to the perfect operation of the price system

Theoretically the price system should move workers who become unemployed to other jobs. The fall in the demand for a good, and the consequent unemployment, should result in a relative wage fall. On the other hand where demand is buoyant wages should rise (assuming that AD is adequate throughout the economy as a whole). Such changes in relative wages should move workers from low-wage to high-wage industries, and industries from high-wage to low-wage areas.

In practice these movements take so long to accomplish that they cannot be left entirely to the free operation of the price system. Labour does not move easily from one industry to another because of occupational immobility, or out of depressed areas because of geographical immobility. Industry may not transfer to depressed areas because unemployed workers have not got the necessary skills, or because the saving in wage costs is insufficient to offset the loss of location advantages. Indeed, national wage agreements, by eliminating pay differentials, undermine the forces which set the price system in motion.

II Government policy

General considerations

In deciding upon specific measures to improve labour mobility the government must bear in mind that:

(1) Unemployment arising through immobility is far more difficult to cure when cyclical unemployment also exists for an unemployed man has little incentive to move if there is unemployment even in the relatively prosperous areas.

(2) Problems arise if only labour, and not industries, shifts. Where workers move out of an area, their spending power is lost. Here the 'multiplier' operates in reverse to make the area still further depressed. In contrast 'growth' areas could experience inflationary pressure which may eventually be transmitted throughout the economy.

(3) Other government interference in the economy may add to the problem of immobility. Thus high rates of income tax whittle away monetary inducements to move, unemployment benefit may reduce the incentive to seek a job elsewhere, while rent control leads to difficulties in finding accommodation. Similarly uniform national wage rates, insisted upon by many trade unions, eliminate the incentive of lower labour costs to attract firms to areas of high unemployment.

(4) Usually only a small fraction of the labour force may have to move out of a depressed area, since new industries can be attracted to provide work for the remainder. While it is easier for

younger workers to move, this should occur only if absolutely necessary, for their loss can further depress the area.

(5) Many changes of both occupation and area take place in a series of 'ripples'. Thus an agricultural labourer may move to road construction to take the place of the Irish labourer who transfers to the building industry.

(6) Since government measures take time to become effective, there should be a continuous policy of bringing greater diversity to those areas mainly dependent on one or two industries.

Specific measures to improve occupational mobility

The government's first task must be to improve occupational mobility. Entry into certain occupations should be made less difficult. Here the government can give information on opportunities in other industries and occupations and use its influence to persuade trade unions to relax their apprenticeship rules.

More important, people must be trained in the new skills required by expanding industries. The government's Training Services Agency is currently responsible for promoting industrial training. Over fifty government training centres have been set up, and trainees are given financial assistance. Lump-sum redundancy payments were introduced in 1966 to encourage workers to change jobs when their particular skills were no longer required. In the longer period the problem can be tackled by advising school-leavers on career prospects and further training. Today most industries have an industrial training board responsible for training facilities, paying grants for approved courses and imposing levies on employers to spread the cost.

Measures for dealing with geographical immobility

Obstacles to geographical mobility are more difficult to overcome. Where a whole area is 'depressed' the government can give first aid by placing its contracts there, e.g. for ships, and by awarding it priority for public works, e.g. schools, new roads, hospitals. In the long period, however, it must take measures which will on the one hand encourage the outward movement of workers, and on the other induce new firms to move in to employ those workers who find it difficult to move.

The first group of measures – 'taking workers to the work' – consists of granting financial aid for travelling to new work or towards the cost of moving, providing information on prospects in other parts of the country, and removing artificial barriers, such as the shortage of housing accommodation.

The second policy – 'taking work to the workers' – is now regarded as the real long-term solution. It avoids forcing workers to move out of areas to which they are attached, relieves the growing congestion in the Midlands and South-East England, and prevents depopulation in the North, with the loss of 'social capital' which this involves. Above all it recognises that the multiplier works in reverse so that moving workers out makes the region still further depressed.

On the other hand it can involve firms in higher costs: their desire to establish plant in the South-east is based on securing the advantages of localisation, such as a supply of skilled workers or close contact with customers on the Continent.

To move young expanding firms into the depressed areas the government may use either the carrot or the big stick. So far it has concentrated on the former, though there has been some oblique compulsion through planning requirements. A firm relocating in one of the assisted areas (Special Development Areas, where the need for jobs is most acute, Development Areas and Intermediate Areas – see Figure 17.1) is offered financial incentives, the most important of which are:

(1) *Regional development grants, depending on the type of area:*

	Buildings, works, plant and machinery (%)
Special Development Areas	22
Development Areas	15
Intermediate Areas	—

These grants are for specific activities in manufacturing, construction and mining. Since they are not limited to projects creating employment, they may be used to help with improvements and modernisation. In addition they do not reduce the capital expenditure which qualifies for capital allowances for tax purposes.

(2) *Removal grants* of up to 80 per cent for certain costs incurred in moving to a Special Development Area or Development Area.

(3) *Loans at favourable rates or interest relief* for projects which reduce unemployment.

(4) *Government factories* for sale or to rent on favourable terms.

(5) *Help for transferring key workers* essential to setting up a new plant.

All the above are in addition to the investment incentives through tax concessions available to manufacturing and service industries throughout the country.

Assistance is also obtained from the EEC's European Regional Development Fund, which was set up in 1975, and loans are available on favourable terms from the European Investment Bank and the European Coal and Steel Community.

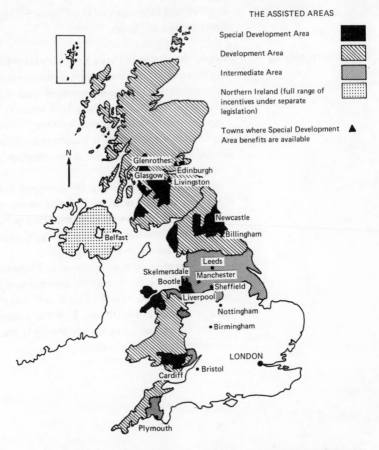

Fig. 17.1
The assisted areas in
1979

THE ASSISTED AREAS

Special Development Area

Development Area

Intermediate Area

Northern Ireland (full range of
incentives under separate
legislation)

Towns where Special Development ▲
Area benefits are available

N

Glenrothes
Edinburgh
Glasgow
Livingston

Newcastle
Billingham

Belfast

Leeds
Skelmersdale Manchester
Bootle Sheffield
Liverpool
Nottingham
Birmingham

LONDON
Cardiff Bristol

Plymouth

The Department of Industry controls the Industrial Estates
Corporation, which supervises government-sponsored industrial
estates in England. In Scotland and Wales the Industrial Estates
Corporations have become the responsibility of the Scottish and
Welsh Development Agencies, responsible to the Secretaries of
State for Scotland and Wales, respectively.

Northern Ireland also enjoys a full range of incentives under
separate legislation.

Through its planning powers the government can indirectly
use some compulsion. Consent of the local planning authority is
necessary for any new building or addition to an existing building. Moreover, if this would create industrial floor-space of more
than 50,000 square feet outside the assisted areas, an Industrial
Development Certificate is also required from the Department of
Industry which relates the request to the level of employment in
the region.

In the dispersal of industry the government has, wherever
possible, set an example. Thus the Department of Health and
Social Security is centred in Newcastle, the National Giro in

Bootle, and branches of the Department of Inland Revenue have been moved to Wales.

Regional planning

While development area policy deals with special districts needing extra help, planning now covers larger areas to ensure a sound infrastructure of public services and a broad-based industrial structure. To this end the whole country is now divided into ten regions (eight for England, one for Scotland and one for Wales), for each of which there is planning on a broad scale as regards the distribution of labour, the diversification of industry and the rate of growth.

Primary responsibility for regional development lies with the Department of Industry. In the seven regions requiring most assistance it has set up Regional Industrial Boards. These advise on applications for selective financial assistance for the development of industry in their regions.

Each region has an Economic Planning Board, consisting of civil servants from the main government departments concerned with regional planning. The Board's task is to formulate plans and to co-ordinate the work of the various government departments concerned. As far as possible the members are brought together in one building.

18 Currency Stability

I The effects of inflation

Today the control of inflation is given priority in government policy. To appreciate why this is so we have to look at the effects of rising prices, or – what is the same thing – a fall in the value of money.

Possible benefits

At one time a gently rising price level was not viewed with too much concern. It improved the climate for investment and so helped to maintain aggregate demand. Moreover, it tended to reduce the real burden of servicing the National Debt: while interest is fixed in money terms, receipts from taxation increase as money national income rises.

The snag, however, is that, once started, the rise in prices is difficult to contain. At first it becomes uncomfortable, producing undesirable results, both internal and external. Eventually the rate of inflation increases. The situation is then serious, for it is much more difficult to reverse the trend. Indeed it can develop into runaway inflation.

Internal disadvantages

(1) Income is redistributed arbitrarily. Not only does inflation reduce the standard of living of persons dependent on fixed incomes, e.g. pensioners, but it benefits debtors and penalises lenders. Thus the stability upon which all lending and borrowing depends is undermined.

(2) Interest rates rise, both because people require a higher reward for lending money which is falling in value and also because the government is forced to take disinflationary measures.

(3) Investment is discouraged by government anti-inflation policy. Controls imposed on prices are more effective than those on costs, particularly wages. The result is an erosion of profits and a disincentive to invest.

(4) Saving is discouraged because postponing consumption simply means that goods cost more later.

(5) Inefficiency is encouraged because a buoyant sellers'

market blunts competition as higher prices allow even inefficient firms to survive.

(6) Inflation generates social unrest since there is competition for higher incomes. Thus, because of rising prices, trade unions ask for annual wage rises. Often, demands exceed the rate of inflation, anticipating future rises or seeking a larger share of the national cake.

(7) The rate of inflation tends to increase, largely because high wage settlements in anticipation of higher future prices help to bring about what they fear.

External effects

Inflation can create serious difficulties for a country dependent on international trade, as Britain has discovered over the past thirty years. Where the level of domestic prices rises relative to those of foreign competitors, imports increase since they become more competitive with home goods. Moreover, exports are discouraged by being relatively dearer and because manufacturers find it easy to sell on the buoyant home market. This may lead to balance-of-payments difficulties (see later).

II Measuring changes in the general level of prices

Difficulties

The difficulty in measuring changes in the general level of prices is that different kinds of prices – wholesale prices, retail prices, security prices, import prices, etc. – change differently. If we tried to measure changes in all prices, therefore, our task would be stupendous. More than that it would lack practical significance, a measure which, for instance, included security prices having little interest to a working man owning no securities. It is usual, therefore, to concentrate on changes in the prices of those goods which are of most general significance – the goods bought by the majority of people.

The method of measuring changes in the price level

Since we are mainly interested in how much the price level has altered between one date and another, it can be measured as a relative change by means of an *index number*. The steps are as follows:

(a) A base year is selected.

(b) In order to ensure that the same goods are valued over the period under consideration a 'basket' of goods, based on the current spending habits of the 'typical' family (in 1979 where the head has a gross income of less than £160 a week), is chosen.

(c) The basket is valued at base-year prices, and expressed as 100.

(d) The same basket is revalued at current prices.

(e) The cost of the current basket is then expressed as a percentage of the base year. Thus if the cost of living had risen by 5 per cent, the index for the current year would be 105.

In practice the prices of the selected goods are compared, their percentage changes being 'weighted' according to the relative expenditure on the particular commodity in the base year. Suppose, for instance, that there are only two commodities, bread and meat, upon which income is spent. The index between two years is calculated as follows:

			Year 1			Year 2	
	Price	Units bought	Expend-iture	Weight	Price	Year 2 as % of year 1	Weighted price relative
Bread	20p	5	100	10	30p	150	1500
Meat	100p	11	1100	$\frac{110}{120}$	120p	120	$\frac{13200}{14700} \div 120$ $= \overline{122.5}$

	Index	
Year 1	(base)	100
Year 2		122·5

The price in year 2 is expressed as a percentage of the price in year 1. This is multiplied by the appropriate weight to give a 'weighted price relative'. These weighted price relatives are then totalled and divided by the total of the weights to give the new index number.

Defects of the Index of Retail Prices

The Index of Retail Prices is based on the method outlined above. But as a means of expressing changes in the value of money it has snags:

(1) The basket and the weighting are merely an arbitrary average. Different income groups have widely different baskets, and even within the same group the amount spent on each good varies. Thus a change in the Index of Retail Prices does not affect all people equally.

(2) The basket becomes more unreal the further we move from the base year. For instance, an increase in income changes patterns of expenditure. In an attempt to surmount this defect the weights are revised each January on the basis of the *Family Expenditure Survey* for the previous year. The index figure for the year is then calculated at current prices (January = 100) and then 'linked' to the main base date (15 January 1974) by multiplying the main index figure by the proportionate change in the year.

(3) Technical difficulties may arise both in choosing the base year and in collecting information. For instance, the base year may prove to be somewhat abnormal because of a particularly

high birth rate, while the development of discount stores may upset standardised methods of collecting prices.

Thus the Index of Retail Prices merely *indicates* changes in the cost of living. But if we remember its limitations, it provides a useful assessment of changes in the value of money.

III Money

Before we can examine government anti-inflation policy it is necessary to consider the nature of money and how its supply can be controlled. This will involve a brief look at the banking system.

What is money?

It is possible to exchange goods by direct exchange. But barter is rare in advanced economies. Where there is a high degree of specialisation, exchanges must take place quickly and smoothly. Hence we have a 'go-between' – money.

Anything which is generally acceptable in purchasing goods or settling debts can be said to be money. It need not consist of coins and notes. Oxen, salt, amber, woodpecker scalps and cotton cloth have at times all been used as money. In fact the precise substance, its size and shape, are largely a matter of convenience and custom. But whatever is used, it should be immediately and unquestionably accepted in exchange for goods and services. Thus the use of the particular good should be backed by custom, and people must feel that it will retain its value by remaining relatively scarce.

Sometimes an attempt is made to confer acceptability by law. In the UK notes have unlimited *legal tender*, in that a creditor *must* accept them in payment of a debt. But a commodity does not have to be legal tender for it to be money. Nor can legislation ensure that it will be acceptable. In West Germany after the Second World War cigarettes were preferred to the Reichsbank mark in payment for goods.

The functions of money

Money, it is usually stated, performs four functions:

(1) It is a *medium of exchange,* the oil, as it were, which allows the machinery of modern buying and selling to run smoothly.

(2) It is a *measure of value and a unit of account,* making possible the operation of a price system and automatically providing the basis for keeping accounts, calculating profit and loss, costing, etc.

(3) It is a *standard of deferred payments,* the unit in which, provided its value is stable, loans and future contracts are fixed. Without money there would be no common basis for dealing in

debts – the work for example, of such institutions as insurance companies, building societies, banks and discount houses. By providing a standard for repayment money makes borrowing and lending much easier.

(4) It is a *store of wealth*, the most convenient way of keeping any income which is surplus to immediate requirements. More than that, because money is also the medium of exchange, wealth stored in this form is completely liquid: it can be converted into other goods immediately and without cost. Indeed it is this 'liquidity' which is the most distinctive characteristic of money, and it results in money playing an active rather than a merely neutral part in the operation of the economy.

The supply of money

The supply of money consists of:

(1) *Coins and notes.* Since these are regarded as the small change of the monetary system, sufficient coins and notes are always provided for the everyday convenience of the community.

(2) *Bank deposits.* While purchases of everyday goods – bus-rides, cigarettes, petrol, etc. – are usually paid for in coins and notes, about 80 per cent (in value) of all transactions are effected by cheque. When a person writes a cheque he is instructing his bank to transfer deposits in his account to the person to whom he owes money. Bank deposits therefore act as money.

The two definitions of money in official use are: M_1, which consists of coins and notes and bank deposits held on current accounts, and M_3, which consists of M_1 plus bank deposits held in deposit accounts. M_3 is over twice as large as M_1.

A large part of bank deposits are 'created' by the banks. How this comes about will now be described.

IV   The creation of credit

The cheque system

There are various types of 'banks'. Here we are mainly concerned with the 'Clearing Banks', those whose cheques are cleared at the London Clearing House. These are dominated by the 'Big Four' (Lloyds, Barclays, National Westminster and the Midland), each having a network of branches throughout the country.

Banks are really companies which exist to make profits for their shareholders. They do this by borrowing money from 'depositors' and re-lending it at a higher rate of interest to other persons. Borrowers are private persons, companies, public corporations, the money market and the government. The more a bank can lend, the greater will be its profits.

Persons who hold a current account at a bank can settle their debts by cheque, a very convenient form of payment. But the use of cheques is also advantageous to banks. Thus, to advertise their business, induce customers to pay by cheque rather than by cash, and encourage people to keep sums of money with them, banks perform many services (often free of charge) outside their main business of borrowing and lending money – keeping accounts, making standing-order payments, providing night-safe facilities, paying bills by credit transfers, purchasing securities, transacting foreign work, storing valuables, acting as executors, etc.

The cheque as a substitute for cash

Cheques lead to a reduction in the use of cash. Suppose that I have paid £100 cash into my banking account. Imagine, too, that my builder banks at the same branch and I owe him £50. I simply write him a cheque for that amount, and he pays this into the bank. To complete the transaction, my account is debited by £50, and his account is credited by that amount. What it is important to observe, however, is that in the settlement of the debt no actual *cash* changes hands. A mere book entry in both accounts has completed the transaction.

Perhaps my builder will, towards the end of the week, withdraw some cash to pay his workers' wages. But it is likely that most of his payments, e.g. for building materials, petrol, and lorry servicing, will be by cheque. Similarly, while I may withdraw some cash from the £50 still standing to my account to cover everyday household expenses, the probability is that many of my bills, e.g. club subscription, half-yearly rates, mortgage repayments, will be settled by cheque or a credit transfer directly from my account. Furthermore, even where cash is withdrawn, this is often compensated for by cash being paid in.

With the development of the cheque system the proportion of cash required for transactions has decreased. Let us assume a simple model in which the banks operate free from government control but have discovered that in practice only 10 per cent of their total deposits need be retained in cash to cover all demands for cash withdrawals. In short only £10 of my original deposit of £100 is needed to form an adequate cash reserve.

The creation of credit

It is obvious, therefore, that £90 could be lent by the bank to a third party without my being the wiser. What is not quite so obvious is that the bank can go further than this – and does!

Let us assume that there is only one bank and that all lending is in the form of advances (see p. 304). When a person is granted a loan by his bank manager, all that happens is that the borrower's account is credited with the amount of the loan or, alternatively, he is authorised to overdraw his account up to the stipulated limit. In other words a deposit is created by the bank in the name of the borrower.

When he spends the loan the borrower will probably pay by cheque. If this happens, there is no immediate demand for cash. There is no reason, therefore, why the whole of my cash deposit of £100 should not act as the safe cash reserve for deposits of a much larger sum created by the bank's lending activities. But the bank must not overdo this credit creation. Our model has assumed that, to be safe, cash must always form one-tenth of total deposits. This means that the bank can grant a loan of up to £900. Because it is the only bank, there is no need to fear that cheques drawn on it will be paid into another bank and eventually presented for cash.

Fig. 18.1
How a bank creates credit

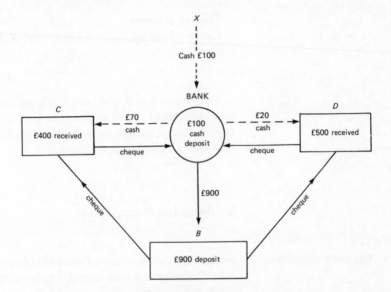

The process of credit creation is illustrated in Figure 18.1. *X* pays £100 in cash into the bank. This allows the bank to make a loan of £900 to *B*, who now settles his debts of £400 and £500 by sending cheques to *C* and *D*. These cheques are paid into the bank. C withdraws cash rather heavily, £70; but this is compensated for by *D*, who only withdraws £20 in cash. This leaves £10 cash – enough to cover the average withdrawal which *X* is likely to make. While these cash withdrawals are being made, other cash is being paid in, thereby maintaining the 10 per cent ratio.

In practice there are many banks, but for the purpose of credit creation they are virtually one bank, because they are able to eliminate a large demand for cash from each other by their clearing arrangements through the London Clearing House. While this consists of only six banks (the 'Big Four' dominating), other banks can do their clearing through one of these. Moreover, banks keep in line as regards their credit creation. Were one bank to adopt, say, a 6 per cent cash ratio, it would find that because its customers were making such a large volume of payments to persons who banked elsewhere, it would be continually called upon to settle a debit with other banks in cash at the end of the day's clearing so that its cash reserve would fall below the safe level.

The effect of lending on the bank's balance-sheet

Suppose that the receipt of the £100 in cash and the loan to B are so far the sole activities of the bank. Ignoring shareholders' capital, its balance-sheet will read:

Liabilities	(£)	Assets	(£)
Deposits			
Deposit account	100	Cash in till	100
Current account	900	Advances	900
	1000		1000

The advance to B is an asset; it is an outstanding debt. On the other hand his current account has been credited with a deposit of £900 – just as though he had paid it in. It can be seen, therefore, that *every loan creates a deposit*.

V Bank lending policy

The bank's objectives

In practice the structure of the bank's assets is more varied than this. Creating deposits in order to lend at a profit entails risks. First, the loan may not be repaid. Second, and more important, there may be a run on the bank for cash, the original depositor wishing to withdraw his £100, or B, C and D requiring between them an abnormally large amount of cash. Any suggestion that the bank could not meet these demands would undermine confidence.

Hence, although a permanent cash reserve is essential, a bank must have other lines of defence so that in an emergency it can raise cash easily and quickly. Instead of lending entirely by advances which a borrower usually requires for at least six months, some loans must be restricted to a shorter period, even to just a day. But the shorter the period of the loan, the lower will be the rate of interest the bank earns. On the other hand it wants profits for shareholders to be as high as possible. Thus it is limited in its lending policy both quantitatively and qualitatively. Not only must credit be restricted to a multiple of the liquid reserves but it must also afford adequate *security, liquidity and profitability*.

As regards security, the bank endeavours not to lend if there is any risk of inability to repay. Collateral, e.g. an insurance policy, the deeds of a house or share certificates, is regarded more as a weapon to strengthen its demand for repayment than as a safeguard against default.

Liquidity and profitability pull in opposite directions – the shorter the period of the loan, the greater the bank's liquidity but the less it will earn by way of interest. The difficulty is resolved by a compromise: (a) loans are divided among different types of borrower and for different periods of time; and (b) the different types of loan are kept fairly close to carefully chosen proportions. In short the bank maintains a 'portfolio' of assets.

The distribution of a bank's assets

We can see how in practice a bank reconciles conflicting aims by studying its sterling assets. These, apart from its cash, buildings and goodwill, are its debts outstanding – the loans it has made. The position is shown in Figures 18.2 and 18.3.

**Fig. 18.2
The nature and distribution of a bank's main assets**

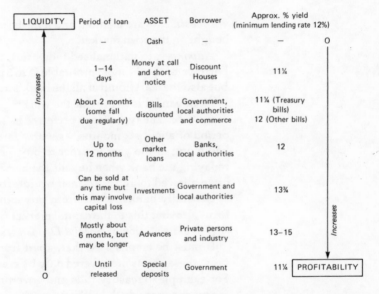

LIQUIDITY	Period of loan	ASSET	Borrower	Approx. % yield (minimum lending rate 12%)
	–	Cash	–	0
	1–14 days	Money at call and short notice	Discount Houses	11¼
	About 2 months (some fall due regularly)	Bills discounted	Government, local authorities and commerce	11¼ (Treasury bills) 12 (Other bills)
	Up to 12 months	Other market loans	Banks, local authorities	12
	Can be sold at any time but this may involve capital loss	Investments	Government and local authorities	13¾
	Mostly about 6 months, but may be longer	Advances	Private persons and industry	13–15
	Until released	Special deposits	Government	11¼ PROFITABILITY

Money at call and short notice are very short-term loans to discount houses which enable the latter to discount bills of exchange and hold them for a month or so before passing them on to the banks.

Bills, which are Treasury Bills, local authority bills and trade bills, are obtained chiefly from the discount houses (though some may be discounted directly for customers) and are held for the remainder of their currency, usually two months.

Other market loans are loans to banks, local authorities and trade bills above the 2 per cent limit, all of which are not 'eligible reserve assets' (see p. 306).

**Fig. 18.3
The pyramid of bank
credit**

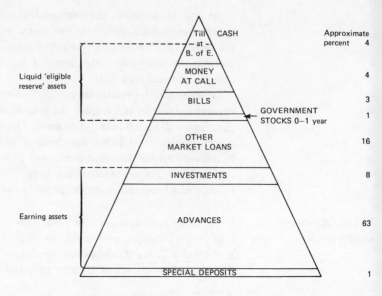

Investments are medium and long-term government securities
bought on the open market.

Advances, to nationalised industries, companies and personal
borrowers, are the most profitable (1 to 3 per cent above base rate)
but also the least liquid of all the bank's assets. The main object of
bank advances is to provide the working capital for industry and
commerce. The type of loan preferred is 'self-liquidating' within a
period of about six months, as with a farmer who borrows at the
beginning of the year in order to buy fertilisers and pay wages,
repaying the bank when he sells the harvest. Firms, however, are
often allowed to 'roll over' their overdrafts.

Generally banks refrain from providing long-term capital for
firms, leaving this to the capital market (see p. 213).

(For a discussion of *Special Deposits,* see p. 307.)

It must be emphasised that, apart from cash and bank buildings, these assets are covered only by credit created by the bank.
For example, Treasury Bills and government securities are paid
for by cheques which will increase the accounts of the sellers. If
they are new issues, there is an addition to the government
account at the Bank of England; if they are old issues, the bank is
virtually taking over from somebody else a loan already made to
the government. In writing these cheques the bank increases its
liabilities, for book-entry deposits have to be created to cover
them. This 'pyramid of credit', created to buy earning assets and
to make loans upon a minimum 12½ per cent liquid assets basis, is
shown in Figure 18.3.

**Modification of the
cash-ratio approach**

Our explanation of credit creation has followed traditional lines:
credit bears a fixed relationship to cash reserves. Today, how-

ever, the monetary authorities (i.e. the Bank of England acting as agent for the Treasury) now regard cash simply as the small change of the monetary system, to be varied according to the needs of trade. In any case banks are more concerned with their general liquidity position than with cash *per se*. This originally stemmed from the introduction of the Treasury Bill, which – through government support – became almost as good as cash. Improved markets for loans, e.g. the money markets described in Chapter 13, also increase liquidity to the extent that such loans can be regarded as 'near money'.

It follows, therefore, that if the authorities wish to control the money supply, they must operate on other assets which the banks hold so as to change total deposits.

VI Controlling the supply of money

The need to control the money supply

The government's economic advisers now consider that an increase in the supply of money which is proportionately greater than any increase in output will result in rising prices as the extra money is spent on goods and services – the doctrine of 'monetarism'.

In recent years the UK has experienced this sort of situation. An increase in the money supply in 1971–2 has been held to have been the cause of the 27 per cent inflation rate of 1973–4. Again, in 1975–6, the need to finance much of the large PSBR by increasing the money supply led to inflationary pressure and the run on sterling. Indeed one condition of the IMF loan to support sterling was that the money supply should be brought under control. Such a policy means restricting the ability of the banks to create credit, and is the responsibility of the Bank of England.

Functions of the Bank of England

The Bank of England, established in 1694, remained a joint-stock company until it was nationalised in 1946. However, nationalisation merely formalised its position as a 'central bank' – the institution which, on behalf of the government, exercises the ultimate control over the policies of banks and other financial institutions.

The Bank of England performs a number of functions. It issues notes, acts as banker to the government, holds the cash reserves of the commercial banks, manages the Exchange Equalisation Account in order to stabilise the sterling exchange rate or to protect the gold and foreign currency reserves, and co-operates in harmonising monetary policies with other central banks and international financial institutions, such as the International

Monetary Fund, the Bank of International Settlements, the International Bank for Reconstruction and Development (the World Bank) and the European Monetary Agreement. Above all it manages the monetary system of the UK in accordance with government policy.

The weapons which the Bank of England can employ

In broad terms monetary policy involves varying the cost and availability of credit. To achieve this the Bank of England has a number of weapons.

1 The minimum reserve-assets ratio   The policy by which credit is controlled is founded on the ability of the Bank of England to dictate to the banks and other lending institutions the minimum liquidity ratio which they shall maintain.

Each bank is required to observe a minimum reserve ratio (in 1979 $12\frac{1}{2}$ per cent) of 'eligible reserve assets' to 'eligible liabilities'.

Eligible reserve assets comprise: balances with the Bank of England other than Special Deposits; Treasury Bills; company tax-reserve certificates; money at call; local authority bills eligible for rediscount at the Bank of England (up to a maximum of 2 per cent of eligible liabilities); and British government securities with one year or less to maturity. Broadly speaking banks would regard these as their liquid assets.

Eligible liabilities refer broadly to net bank deposits (excluding foreign currency deposits and deposits having an original maturity of over two years).

It is important to note that this ratio applies to *all* banks, not merely to the clearing banks.

2 Open-market operations   With a liquidity ratio of $12\frac{1}{2}$ per cent a given change in eligible reserve assets held by the banks will change total deposits by eight times the amount. The Bank of England can therefore adjust the money supply by varying the eligible reserve assets held by the banks.

This it achieves by buying or selling government securities on the open market. Suppose, for instance, it sells long-term securities. The increase in the supply offered lowers their price (i.e. raises the rate of interest) until the total offering has been bought by the banks or by their customers. But cash will be necessary to pay for them, and so the banks' cash balances at the Bank of England fall. In other words the liquid reserve assets held by the banks are reduced and, if previously banks had made loans to the maximum possible, they now will be forced to squeeze their advances.

Alternatively the Bank of England may put the pressure on the 'short' end of the market by varying the weekly offer of Treasury Bills. Inasmuch as these bills are bought initially outside the banks the cash balances of the banks' customers can be made to fall, and hence the cash of the banks will likewise fall.

3 Funding   A deliberate policy of converting government short-term debt into long-term debt is known as 'funding'. It is achieved by open-market operations (as described above) over an extended period. What happens is that the Treasury Bill offer is reduced, the government raising the finance it requires by selling medium and long-dated securities instead.

4 Special Deposits   More fundamental changes in the supply of credit can be effected through calls for Special Deposits. Banks are required to deposit with the Bank of England a given percentage of their total eligible liabilities. These Special Deposits do not count as eligible reserve assets, and so the weapon really acts as a device to vary the liquidity ratio temporarily.

5 Supplementary deposits   When the money supply, chiefly bank credit, is rising too quickly, the Bank of England may apply the 'corset', requiring supplementary deposits from the banks. These are automatically payable if a bank's interest-bearing deposits (thus excluding current-account deposits) rise faster than a specified rate.

This target rate of growth is fixed by the Bank of England periodically while the 'corset' is operative. The proportion of the excess to be deposited with the Bank of England rises progressively according to the extent of the excess growth, and may be as high as 50 per cent.

Supplementary deposits, unlike Special Deposits, earn no interest. This means that when the target rate of growth is exceeded, it ceases to be profitable for a bank to compete for deposit money by paying high rates of interest. Thus the pace of monetary expansion is restrained without forcing short-term interest and bank lending rates to unacceptable heights.

6 Minimum Lending Rate   The Minimum Lending Rate (formerly Bank Rate) is the rate at which the Bank of England will help the discount houses as a lender of last resort. The rate is announced on a Thursday, and any change in it signals the direction in which the authorities require interest rates to move.

7 Requests   A policy of allocating credit by the market is not entirely satisfactory, especially when an attempt is being made to hold down the rate of interest. Thus from time to time the monetary authorities issue instructions to the banks, requiring them to discriminate against certain borrowers, e.g. property developers, but to favour others, e.g. exporters. Similarly, to enable building societies to compete with banks for deposits when interest rates are high, banks have been instructed not to pay more than $9\frac{1}{2}$ per cent on loans of less than £10,000.

8 Directives   The Bank of England, if authorised by the Treasury, can issue directives to any banker to ensure that its requests and recommendations are implemented. So far this power has not had to be used, the banks having observed the requests of the Bank of England.

Conclusion

Monetary policy is unlikely to rely on a single weapon since the use of one reinforces the others. While today the emphasis is on controlling the total money supply (see p. 305), the different weapons also enable the Bank of England to influence the structure of interest rates in order to induce shifts in the portfolios of both the public and the banks in the desired direction.

19 The Redistribution of Income

Redistribution of income takes place through:

(1) expenditure, e.g. welfare benefits, students' grants; and

(2) taxation.

However, both may promote other objectives, and so we have to consider the nature and the full economic effects of the government's fiscal measures.

I Government expenditure

Limits to government spending

In the 1970s taxation has taken about 40 per cent of the gross national product – a remarkable increase since 1910, when it was only about 10 per cent. The government is now spending on a much wider range of activities.

Many items of government spending, e.g. pensions, National Debt interest, grants to local authorities, are unavoidable since, by nature, they are basically contractual. It may therefore seem that the government has merely to estimate its expenditure and impose taxes to cover it. But this is not the case.

Since goods and services in the economy as a whole are limited, the government has to cut its coat according to its cloth, asking such questions as: What can be afforded for the Arts Council? How much can be given to local authorities? Can university education be expanded? Can National Insurance contributions be reduced? The economic problem, involving decisions at the margin, confronts private persons and the government alike. The government can only secure more of the goods and services by allowing the private sector less. In the last resort the division rests on a political decision.

The distribution of government expenditure

Government spending can be classified under the following headings:

(1) *Defence*, which has accounted for about one-sixth of all government spending.

(2) *Internal security* – the police, law enforcement and fire brigades.

(3) *Social responsibilities*, covering education, and protection against the hazards of sickness, unemployment and old age.

(4) *Economic policy*, covering subsidies to agriculture and industry, help to Development Areas, worker training and the provision of capital to the nationalised industries.

(5) *Miscellaneous*, including expenditure on diplomatic services, grants to local authorities and, the largest single item, interest on the National Debt.

How government expenditure is financed

In the same way that firms have to pay for both variable and fixed factors so the government has to spend not only on single-use goods and services but also on goods which render services over a long period. The first, which involves regular yearly spending, should be met out of regular yearly income. But capital spending, on such items as roads, loans to the nationalised industries and university building, is more fairly financed by borrowing, for the repayment of the capital then partly falls on future beneficiaries.

Current expenditure is met from two main sources:

(a) miscellaneous receipts, chiefly interest on loans, rents and charges on goods and services (such as on medical prescriptions); and

(b) taxation, described in more detail later.

Capital expenditure is mostly covered by government borrowing, which takes the form of:

(a) *Short-term loans* from the sale of Treasury Bills. Originally these were used to bridge the time gap between expenditure and receipts from taxation, but – because it is cheaper to borrow short than long – they eventually became a major means of government borrowing. Nevertheless the inflationary effects which followed have forced the government to adopt a 'funding' policy (see p. 307).

(b) Medium and long-term loans are obtained by selling stock having a minimum currency of five years. Some, such as $3\frac{1}{2}$% War Loan, are undated stock.

(c) *'Non-market' borrowing* through National Savings Certificates, Premium Savings Bonds, etc., and the deposits of the National Savings Bank and Trustee Savings Banks.

(See Figure 19.1 for a summary of government expenditure and revenue in 1978–9.)

II The modern approach to taxation

Taxation and government policy

Until the end of the nineteenth century the functions of the state were concerned mainly with defence and law and order, and

Fig. 19.1
Government revenue
and expenditure,
1978–9

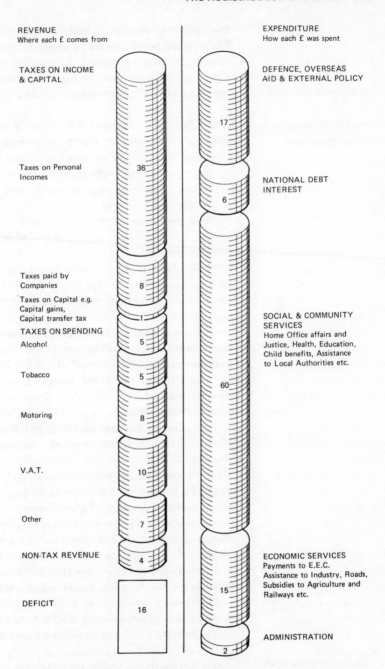

REVENUE
Where each £ comes from

TAXES ON INCOME
& CAPITAL

Taxes on Personal
Incomes — 36

Taxes paid by
Companies — 8

Taxes on Capital e.g.
Capital gains,
Capital transfer tax — 1

TAXES ON SPENDING
Alcohol — 5

Tobacco — 5

Motoring — 8

V.A.T. — 10

Other — 7

NON-TAX REVENUE — 4

DEFICIT — 16

EXPENDITURE
How each £ was spent

DEFENCE, OVERSEAS
AID & EXTERNAL POLICY — 17

NATIONAL DEBT
INTEREST — 6

SOCIAL & COMMUNITY
SERVICES
Home Office affairs and
Justice, Health, Education,
Child benefits, Assistance
to Local Authorities etc. — 60

ECONOMIC SERVICES
Payments to E.E.C.
Assistance to Industry, Roads,
Subsidies to Agriculture and
Railways etc. — 15

ADMINISTRATION — 2

taxation was levied primarily for revenue purposes.

To meet the vast increase in government spending over the last
fifty years higher rates of taxation have been imposed and new
taxes introduced. As we shall see, these additions have provided
new means for promoting economic and social policies. Briefly,
by its fiscal measures the government can: (a) *exercise an over-all*

control of the economy, mainly to achieve full employment or check inflation: (b) *promote economic growth,* e.g. through tax allowances for investment and subsidies to agriculture; (c) *redistribute income and wealth,* e.g. by welfare benefits, subsidised 'merit' goods and progressive taxation.

The attributes of a good tax system

In his *Wealth of Nations* Adam Smith was able to confine his principles of taxation to four simple canons: persons should pay according to their ability; the tax should be certain and clear to everybody concerned; the convenience of the contributor should be studied as regards payment; and the cost of collection should be small relative to yield.

While today the main purpose of any tax is usually to raise money, emphasis is now placed on other attributes. Indeed the ideal tax should be:

(1) *Productive of revenue.* All taxes cost money to collect and are unpopular. The yield of any tax should therefore at least cover the cost of collection, with something to spare to offset the vexation caused. In practice, too, a single tax with a high yield is better than a number of taxes each having a small yield, for these complicate the tax structure and make it difficult to understand and administer. The Chancellor should also be able to estimate the yield from a tax if the budget is to be used for adjusting over-all demand.

(2) *Certain to the taxpayer.* Not only should a taxpayer know exactly when and where he has to pay his tax but he should also find it difficult to evade payment. Indirect taxes score heavily here.

(3) *Convenient to the contributor.* Bad debts and evasion are reduced if the time and manner of tax payment are related to how people receive and spend their incomes.

(4) *Impartial between one person and another.* All persons similarly placed should pay the same tax. Thus while non-smokers do not pay the selective tax on tobacco, all smokers do. Yet, although there is impartiality in this sense, the concentration of indirect taxes on a few goods – chiefly tobacco, alcoholic drink, and motoring – penalises severely certain forms of spending. One of the objects of introducing VAT was to broaden the tax base.

(5) *Adjustable.* A tax should be capable of variation, both up and down, according to changes in policy.

(6) *Automatic in stabilising the economy.* As we have seen, varying the relationship between government expenditure and revenue is one of the major weapons for keeping the economy on an even keel – with full employment but a stable price level. Through tax changes the Chancellor of the Exchequer can vary the purchasing power of the community. Usually he has to make a deliberate adjustment in his budget, but it is helpful if taxes

operate automatically in the desired direction. Thus, when money income increases, so do income tax and VAT yields, thereby reducing inflationary pressure, and vice versa.

(7) *Unharmful to effort and initiative*. This becomes important as direct taxation increases. High rates of income tax, for instance, may induce the taxpayer to take his income in the form of leisure or reduce his willingness to undergo training or seek promotion. The extent to which this occurs, however, is ambiguous. If a person has fixed money commitments, e.g. hire-purchase instalments, mortgage repayments and insurance premiums, he may have to work harder to meet them when his income is reduced. Furthermore, if we assume that a high rate of income tax is a disincentive to effort, we infer that persons always look upon work as distasteful, while leisure is seen as a pleasurable alternative. This may be true for many, but among the high-income brackets there are some who find their work enjoyable. Last, most workers have to work a 'normal' week, and can only vary their hours as regards overtime.

The disincentive effect is more likely to occur when there is a sudden jump in the rate of tax between one income level and another. People reduce their effort at the higher marginal level.

High direct taxes can also affect enterprise and efficiency. By eroding the wage differentials between skilled and unskilled labour they reduce incentives. Similarly entrepreneurs are only prepared to accept risks if the rewards are commensurate.

Furthermore, high taxation of profits and income means that the penalty of inefficiency is not borne entirely by the taxpayer, for some falls on the government through loss of revenue.

(8) *Consistent with government policy*. While the tax structure should not change frequently, individual taxes must be constantly reviewed to see how they could be used to promote government policy. To encourage effort, should income from work be taxed at a lower rate than investment income? Will an indirect tax, by raising the cost of living, increase wage-push inflation? Indirect taxes can be adapted to specific objectives, e.g. cigarettes bear a high selective tax, while exports are zero-rated under VAT.

(9) *Minimal in its effect on the optimum allocation of resources*. An indirect tax on a particular good results in resources not being fully allocated according to the preferences of consumers. To maximise satisfaction consumers spend so that marginal utility relative to price is equal for all goods. This relationship is destroyed by a tax on one good, for its price rises, resulting in a redistribution of consumers' expenditure and thus of the factors of production. In addition taxing its products may dislocate the industry (see later).

Again, selective indirect taxes entail a greater loss to the consumer than an income tax yielding the same amount. Unlike the latter, selective indirect taxes change the relative prices of goods, so that consumers have to rearrange their pattern of expenditure. This substitution involves a loss of satisfaction in addition to that suffered through the reduction in income.

Finally, direct taxes can affect the supply of factors, particularly capital, to industry. High taxation may discourage saving; it certainly reduces the power to save. This is not serious for large companies, who can borrow on the open market. But the major sources of capital for small businesses are the owners' personal savings and profits ploughed back. Thus income tax and corporation tax deprive small, risky, but often progressive, companies of much-needed capital.

Not only that, but high direct taxes may repel foreign capital. Although the deduction of income tax on dividends may be refunded, the company still has to bear corporation tax on profits (at 52 per cent in 1979). The amount available to shareholders is therefore less, and the declared dividend correspondingly smaller. Consequently people may prefer to invest in companies operating in countries where there is a higher return to capital – a higher return which is the result not of superior efficiency but simply of lower taxes.

(10) *Equitable in its distribution of the tax burden.* Taxes can be classified according to the proportion of a person's income which is deducted:

(a) A *regressive* tax takes a higher proportion of the poorer person's income than of the richer. Indirect taxes which are a fixed sum irrespective of income, e.g. television licences, are regressive.

(b) A *proportional* tax takes a given proportion of one's income. In 1979 income tax was proportional for the first £10,000 of taxable income, 30 per cent of every £1 being taken in tax.

(c) A *progressive* tax takes a higher proportion of income as income increases (see Figure 19.2). Income tax is progressive above £10,000 taxable income. Capital transfer tax, which has gradated rates of tax, is also progressive.

Fig. 19.2
The difference
between regressive,
proportional and
progressive taxes

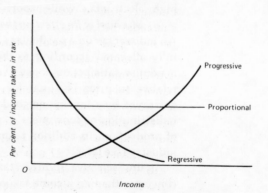

Justification for taxing the rich man higher than the poor man rests on the assumption that a law of diminishing utility applies to additional income – that an extra £50 affords less pleasure to the rich man than to the poor man. Thus taking from the rich involves less hardship than taking from the poor. Generally this can be accepted as true, but we can never be sure, simply because there is no absolute measure of personal satisfaction.

III The structure of taxation

Because there are so many effects of taxation no single tax is completely perfect. Consequently there must be a structure of taxation, combining a number of taxes which the government can vary from time to time according to changes in emphasis on different objectives.

The following classification of taxes is based on the method of payment – (1) direct taxes; and (2) indirect taxes:

(1)   Direct taxes

With these taxes the person makes payment direct to the revenue authorities – the Department of Inland Revenue or the local authority. Usually each individual's tax liability is assessed separately.

(a) *Income tax.* 'Taxable income', which is subject to a basic rate with increasing rates above £10,000, is arrived at after allowing deductions depending on marital status and other personal circumstances. Investment income above £5,000 per annum is subject to a surcharge of 15 per cent.

(b) *Corporation tax.* All profits, whether distributed or not, are taxed at the same rate (52 per cent in 1979). A part (3/7 at an income-tax rate of 30 per cent) is imputed to shareholders and deducted in advance when the divident is paid. This advance payment is allowed against the mainstream 52 per cent corporation tax payment (which is always paid in arrears), while for the shareholder it counts as a 'tax credit', and is refundable if income tax is not paid because of low income.

(c) *Capital gains tax.* A tax is now levied at 30 per cent of any capital gain when an asset is disposed of. Owner-occupied houses, cars, National Savings Certificates and goods and chattels worth less than £2,000 are excluded, and losses may be offset against gains. Depending on their circumstances individuals may achieve a lower rate and, where the disposal proceeds of assets do not exceed £1,000 in any year, no tax is payable.

(d) *Capital transfer tax.* Capital transfer tax replaced estate duty in 1974. it applies to lifetime gifts as well as to legacies, though the former generally bear only half the latter's rate of tax. The rates of duty are progressive, varying according to the size of the transfer – 10 per cent in the £15,000 to £20,000 band, increasing to 75 per cent above £2 million. Somewhat lower rates are payable by working farmers on the transfer of their farms.

(e) *Other taxes.* These consist of stamp duties (payable on financial contracts), motor-vehicle duties, Petroleum Revenue Tax and Development Land Tax.

Local rates, levied by district councils, can also be regarded as a direct tax.

Direct taxes yield nearly two-thirds of total revenue. Their great merit is that, being progressive and assessed according to the individual's circumstances, they ensure that the heaviest burdens are placed on the broadest backs. Their progressive character also gives additional weight to their role as a 'built-in stabiliser'.

Their main disadvantage is that, when the rate of tax is high, there may be disincentive effects. As a result indirect taxes also have to be levied.

(2) Indirect taxes

Indirect taxes on goods and services are so called because the revenue authority (the Department of Customs and Excise) collects them from the seller, who, as far as possible, passes the burden on to the consumer by including the duty in the final selling price of the good (see p. 318). They may be *specific* (i.e. a fixed sum irrespective of the value of the good) or *ad valorem* (i.e. a given percentage of the value of the good).

Indirect taxes may be divided into:

(a) Customs duties levied at EEC rates on goods imported from countries outside the EEC.

(b) Excise duties on home-produced goods and services, e.g. beer, whisky, petrol, cigarettes and gambling.

(c) Value-added tax (VAT): an *ad valorem* tax, levied on most goods and services at each stage of production at a given rate. Thus, using Figure 15.1 on page 262 as an example, VAT at 15 per cent paid by the consumer on the table in the shop would be £1·50, making a total purchase price of £11·50. The VAT, however, would have been paid at each stage of production: tree-grower 45p; saw-miller 30p; table manufacturer 45p; retailer 30p. In practice each producer would pay to the Customs and Excise the full 15 per cent tax on the goods as invoiced by him *less* the VAT paid by his suppliers of materials, etc., as shown on their invoices. Thus, for instance, the retailer pays the Customs and Excise 30p – £1·50 minus the VAT £1·20 charged to him. Some goods, e.g. food, coal, gas, electricity, new buildings, books, newspapers, public transport fares, medicines on prescription, are zero-rated. This means that the final seller charges no VAT *and* can reclaim any VAT invoiced by intermediary producers. Other goods, e.g. rents and medical services, are 'exempt'. Here no VAT is charged by the final seller, but any VAT paid by an intermediary, e.g. for building repairs, cannot be reclaimed. The main merit of VAT is that it is broad-based, the yield increasing almost proportionately to consumer spending. Moreover, since VAT covers most forms of spending, it does not distort consumer choice as much as a highly selective tax. On the other hand it can be argued that a general tax on spending is regressive, for its hits those on lower incomes hardest. This is tempered somewhat, however, by zero-rating goods regarded as necessities.

Indirect taxes give a certain and often an immediate yield and can be adjusted to specific objectives of government policy. On the other hand by being regressive they undo some of the redistributive effects of direct taxes.

The effect of an indirect tax on the size of an industry

The greater the elasticities of demand and supply, the greater will be the effect of a tax in reducing production. We can show this diagrammatically.

(1) *Elasticity of demand.* Before the tax is imposed total output is OM (Figure 19.3). The effect of the tax is to raise the supply curve from S to S_1. Two demand curves are shown, D_a being less elastic than D_b at price OP. The effect of the tax is to reduce output to OM_1, where demand is D_a, and to OM_2, where it is D_b. In the latter case consumers are more able to switch to buying substitutes.

Fig. 19.3
The relationship of elasticity of demand and production when a tax is imposed on a good

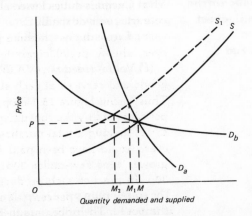

Quantity demanded and supplied

(2) *Elasticity of supply.* Before the tax is imposed total output is OM (Figure 19.4). The effect of the tax is to lower the demand curve from D to D_1. Two supply curves are shown, S_a being less elastic than S_b at price OP. The effect of the tax is to reduce output to OM_1, where supply is S_a, and to OM_2, where it is S_b. In the

latter case producers are more able to produce alternative goods. This proposition has important practical applications:

Fig. 19.4
The relationship of
elasticity of supply and
production when a tax
is imposed on a good

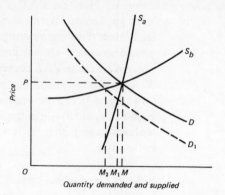

Quantity demanded and supplied

(*a*) The government may use a subsidy (which can be illustrated by moving the supply curve to the right) to increase the production, and thus employment, of an industry. The effect will be more pronounced where demand and supply are elastic.

(*b*) Because the effect of a tax is to reduce production, even a temporary tax may harm an industry. This is particularly so where home demand is elastic and production takes place under decreasing costs, for the smaller demand will raise export prices. Thus a selective tax on cars would not only reduce home demand but, by doing so, lose economies of scale, thereby putting up prices to both home and foreign markets. Even when the tax is subsequently withdrawn, foreign markets may not be regained.

The distribution of the burden of an indirect tax between consumers and producers

When a good is subject to a selective tax it does not mean that its price will rise by the full amount of the tax. Consider the following demand and supply schedules for commodity X:

Price of X (pence)	Demand (000 lb.)	Supply (000 lb.)
12	60	150
11	70	130
10	80	110
9	90	90
8	100	70

The equilibrium price is 9p. Now suppose a tax of 3p per unit of X is imposed. The price rises to 11p. (The quantity supplied to the market at 11p is only 70,000 lb., for the producer now really receives only 8p a unit. Alternatively the quantity demanded at each price is that for which the price is greater by 3p.) Thus we see that the buyer pays 2p more and the supplier receives 1p less per unit. This is shown diagrammatically in Figure 19.5.

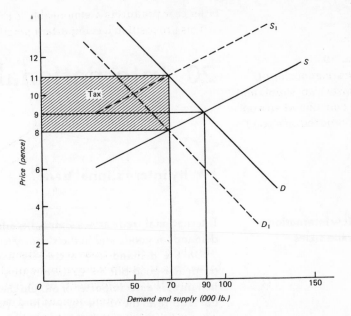

**Fig. 19.5
The distribution of a
tax between the buyer
and the seller**

The amount of the tax falling on consumers as compared with
that falling on producers is directly proportional to the elasticity
of supply to the elasticity of demand. That is:

$$\frac{\text{Consumers' share of tax}}{\text{Producers' share of tax}} = \frac{\text{Elasticity of supply}}{\text{Elasticity of demand}}$$

That this proposition is likely to be true can be seen from the
following argument. When a tax is imposed the reaction of the
producer is to try to push the burden of the tax on to the consumer,
while similarly the consumer tries to push it on to the producer.
Who wins? Simply the one whose bargaining position is
stronger. This will depend upon the ability to switch to producing
substitutes if the price falls as compared with the ability to switch
to buying substitutes if the price rises. Now the possibility of
substituting largely determines elasticities of supply and demand. Thus the relative burden of the tax paid by producers and
consumers depends upon relative elasticities of supply and
demand.

20 International Trade

I Why international trade?

How international trade arises

International trade arises simply because countries differ in their demand for goods and in their ability to produce them.

On the demand side a country may be able to produce a particular good but not in the quantity it requires. The USA, for instance, is a net importer of oil. On the other hand, Kuwait does not require all the oil she can produce. Without international trade most of her deposits would remain untapped.

On the supply side resources are not evenly distributed throughout the world. One country may have an abundance of land; another may have a skilled labour force. Capital, oil, mineral deposits, cheap unskilled labour and a tropical climate are other factors possessed by different countries in varying amounts.

Nor can these factors be transferred easily from one country to another. Climate, land and mineral deposits are obviously specific. Labour is far more immobile internationally than within its own national boundaries. Capital, too moves less easily: exchange controls, political risks or simply ignorance of possibilities may prevent investors from moving funds abroad.

Because factors are difficult to shift, the alternative – moving the goods made by those factors – is adopted. What happens, therefore, is that countries specialise in producing those goods in which they have the greatest comparative advantages, exchanging them for the goods of other countries.

The advantages of international trade

1 It enables countries to obtain the benefits of specialisation Specialisation by countries improves their standard of living:

(a) It is obvious that without international trade many countries would have to go without certain products. Britain, for instance, has no gold or aluminium, and Sweden no oil.

(b) More imortant, many goods can be enjoyed which if produced at home would be available only to the very wealthy, for instance bananas, spices, oranges and peaches in Britain. But this benefit can be applied generally to all imports. The 'law of comparative costs' shows that, provided countries differ in the relative costs of producing certain goods, they can probably gain by specialisation and trade.

Suppose that there are two countries, A and B, producing just two commodities, wheat and cars. Each has the same amount of capital and the same number of labourers, but A has a good climate and fertile soil compared with B. On the other hand B's workers are far more skilful. All factors are fully employed.

When both countries divide their factors equally between the production of wheat and cars, they can produce as follows:

Country	Wheat (units)	Cars (units)
A	500	100
B	100	500
Total production	600	600

But if A specialises in producing wheat and B concentrates on cars, total production would be 1000 wheat and 1000 cars. There is thus a net gain of 400 wheat and 400 cars to be shared between them.

Here the gains are obvious, because A is better at producing wheat and B at producing cars. But suppose A has skilled labour and capital and is better at producing *both* wheat *and* cars, as follows:

Country	Wheat (units)	Cars (units)
A	500	300
B	400	100
Total production (no specialisation)	900	400

Are there still gains to be achieved by specialisation?

Provided the rate at which cars can be exchanged for wheat lies within the range of 5/3 and 4, the answer is 'yes'. The reason for this is that A's superiority in producing cars is more pronounced than her superiority in producing wheat. In the production of the former she is three times as efficient but with the latter only $1\frac{1}{4}$ times. Relative, rather than absolute, advantages are what are really important. The result is that if A specialises in producing cars, leaving B to produce wheat, total production will be 600 cars and 800 wheat.

Suppose now that world conditions of demand and supply are such that two units wheat exchange for one car, i.e. the price of cars is exactly twice that of wheat. A now exchanges 200 cars for 400 wheat, giving her a total of 400 wheat and 400 cars, and B 400 wheat and 200 cars.

It can be seen, therefore, that through specialisation B is 100 cars better off. But has specialisation improved A's position? She now has 400 cars but only 400 wheat, a gain of 100 cars but a loss of 100 wheat. But by her own production she would have had to go without 166⅔ wheat in order to obtain the extra 100 cars. Thus we can conclude that she too is better off.

The above explanation must be refined to allow for:

(i) *Demand.* The law of comparative costs merely shows how two countries can specialise to advantage when their opportunity costs differ. But until we know the demand for goods we cannot say definitely whether specialisation will take place or, if it does, to what extent (see p. 321). Thus although a country may be favourably placed to produce certain goods, a large home demand and thus a relatively high price may mean that it is a net importer of that good (as the USA is of oil).

(ii) *Transport costs* reduce possible gains and therefore make for less specialisation. Indeed it is conceivable that transport costs could so offset A's superiority in making cars that B found it better to produce her own requirements.

(iii) *Changes in the conditions of supply.* Few production advantages are permanent. Climate and, to a large extent, mineral deposits persist, but new techniques can make factors more productive. Thus India now exports cotton goods to Britain!

(iv) *Interference by nations with the free movement of goods* by customs duties, quotas, exchange controls, physical controls, etc.

2 By expanding the market, international trade enables the benefits of large-scale production to be obtained Many products, e.g. computers, aircraft and cars, are produced under conditions of decreasing cost. Here the home market is too small to exploit fully the advantages of large-scale production. This applies particularly to small countries such as Switzerland. In such cases international trade lowers costs per unit of output.

3 International trade increases competition and thereby promotes efficiency in production As we have seen, any restriction of the market makes it easier for one seller to gain control. In contrast international trade increases competition. A government must always consider the risk of a monopoly developing when it gives protection to the home industry by tariffs, etc.

4 International trade promotes beneficial political links with other countries Examples of this are the EEC and the Commonwealth, where trade is still an important link.

II Pattern of UK overseas trade

Trade with other countries

From a study of the reasons for international trade we can deduce the likely pattern of UK trade. Since, in the first place, trade arises because resources are unequally disturbed, we have to ask: (a) What are the factors of production of which the UK can be said to have a relatively plentiful supply? (b) What are the factors of production in which she is deficient?

In answer to (a) we can point to her coal reserves, her skilled working population, and the stock of machinery and factories which has been built up in the past through the thrift of her people. In addition she has a high proportion of very skilled and highly educated administrators, engineers and technicians, and commercial and financial experts. All such persons can render services to other countries, particularly to the less developed. Thus administrators go abroad to start businesses, engineers plan and construct buildings and bridges, while commercial and financial experts and institutions perform services for countries other than the UK.

As regards (b), however, the UK lacks land (chiefly for agriculture because of the size of her population); plentiful supplies of very cheap, unskilled labour; certain minerals (such as nickel, zinc, aluminium and copper), certain chemicals (such as sulphur and nitrates); and the climate – which is necessary, both as regards warmth and rainfall, for the production of many foodstuffs (such as cane-sugar, vegetable oils and tropical fruit), beverages (such as tea, coffee and cocoa), and raw materials (such as cotton, rubber and tobacco).

Thus, analysing the problem simply from the aspect of the distribution of resources, we can say something in a general way, first about the nature of the goods in which the UK deals with the rest of the world, and second about the countries with which she trades.

1 The commodities of the UK's international trade The relative supply of the UK's resources suggests that she will export mostly manufactured goods and also render services to other countries. In return she will import raw materials and foodstuffs, together with minerals and chemicals not found in sufficient quantities within her own borders.

While the nature of the services rendered by the UK are considered later, the broad divisions of goods exported and imported support this surmise (see Table 20.1 and Figure 20.1): 40 per cent of the value of her total imports consist of food, drink, tobacco, basic materials and mineral fuels, while 81 per cent of the value of her total exports are manufactured goods.

Table 20.1 *The United Kingdom's imports and exports, 1977 (by value)*

	Imports (£m.)	(%)	Exports (£m.)	(%)
Food, beverages and tobacco	5937·0	16	2216·4	7
Basic materials	3604·7	10	894·9	3
Mineral fuels and lubricants	5254·8	14	2,092·0	6
Manufactured goods	21,677·0	59	27,171·6	81
Miscellaneous	504·8	1	956·0	3
Total	36,978·2	100	33,330·9	100

**Fig. 20.1
Percentage
distribution of the UK's
imports and exports,
1977**

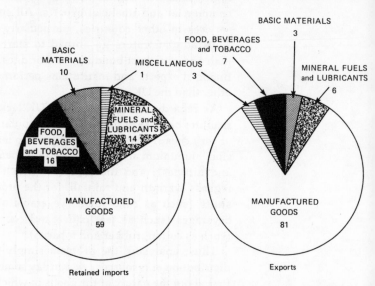

2 The countries with which the UK trades Again an analysis of the UK's resources as compared with those of other countries suggests that she will import goods from countries having relatively much agricultural land, from countries enjoying a tropical or semi-tropical climate, and from countries possessing the minerals and chemicals which she herself lacks (see Figure 20.2). Where these countries need the UK's manufactured goods, as in the case of Australia, imports from them can be paid for directly by the export of manufactured goods. But where the country, such as the USA, does not require these manufactured goods, then imports have to be paid for indirectly. This is achieved through triangular or multilateral trade. Thus Malaya and South Africa export tin and gold respectively to the USA, but the latter sends comparatively little to them directly in exchange. Instead she exports such goods as wheat, cotton, tobacco and

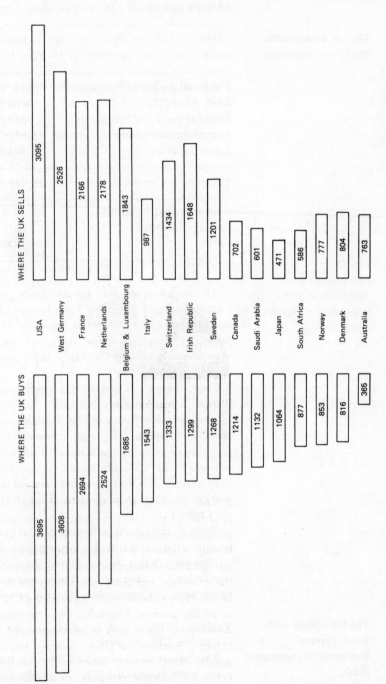

Fig. 20.2
The principal
exporters to and
importers from the UK,
1977 (£m.)

WHERE THE UK SELLS

USA	3095
West Germany	2526
France	2166
Netherlands	2178
Belgium & Luxembourg	1843
Italy	987
Switzerland	1434
Irish Republic	1648
Sweden	1201
Canada	702
Saudi Arabia	601
Japan	471
South Africa	586
Norway	777
Denmark	804
Australia	763

WHERE THE UK BUYS

USA	3695
West Germany	3608
France	2694
Netherlands	2524
Belgium & Luxembourg	1685
Italy	1543
Switzerland	1333
Irish Republic	1299
Sweden	1268
Canada	1214
Saudi Arabia	1132
Japan	1064
South Africa	877
Norway	853
Denmark	816
Australia	365

machinery to the UK, who in return settle the USA's bill from Malaya and South Africa by sending them manufactured goods.

The UK's trade with the Commonwealth

Table 20.2 shows that, in value, about one-eighth of the UK's trade is with the Commonwealth. Why is this?

Table 20.2 *Percentage distribution of the UK's foreign trade, 1938–73, between Commonwealth countries and the rest of the world*

	Imports (%)		Exports (%)	
	1938	1977	1938	1977
Commonwealth countries	38·9	10·8	44·6	13·6
Foreign countries	61·1	89·2	55·4	86·4
Total	100	100	100	100

The main reason has already been given – it arises because Commonwealth countries have factors of production which are complementary to those of the UK. However, this does not provide a complete picture, for as we suggested earlier there are special reasons why the UK's trade with the Commonwealth should predominate.

First, there exist certain ties which can be summed up in the phrase 'a feeling of brotherhood'. The development of the Commonwealth was pioneered by British emigrants, who took with them a common language, common trading methods and a common loyalty to the Crown. Today many people there still possess home ties with the UK. Because of such connections it is only natural that these countries should turn to the UK both for a market for their own goods and for their supplies of the goods they need.

Second, the return to British capital invested in the Commonwealth is earned mainly by exporting goods to the UK.

However, when Britain joined the EEC in 1973, preferential tariffs for Commonwealth goods was virtually ended and the importance of Commonwealth trade has decreased.

The UK's trade with the European Economic Community (EEC)

Table 20.3 shows that, in value, over one-third of the UK's trade is with the EEC countries.

Two points should be noted. Much of this increase in trade took place even before the UK joined the EEC, and it is likely to increase with the common external tariff (see later). Second, the trade is mostly in manufactured goods, particularly chemicals, machinery and cars.

Table 20.3 *Percentage distribution of the UK's trade between the EEC and the rest of the world*

	Imports (%)		Exports (%)	
---	1964	1977	1964	1977
EEC	23·0	38·3	27·6	36·45
Rest of the world	77·0	61·7	72·4	63·55
Total	100	100	100	100

The reason is that specialisation is now no longer confined to manufacturing as opposed to agriculture. Now, even within manufacturing, different countries concentrate on producing particular goods. Thus in cars, Japan's Toyota appeals to certain people in the UK, while British 'Minis' are wanted in Japan. Such specialisation can give rise to considerable trade between countries which have reached the same stage of industrial development.

III Free trade and protection

Controlling international trade

Our earlier analysis suggests that trade should be as free as possible, for only then can maximum specialisation according to the law of comparative advantage take place. In practice, however, all countries follow policies which, to varying degrees, prevent goods moving freely in response to differences in relative prices. Methods vary.

(1) *Customs duties.* Customs duties, e.g. the common external tariffs of the EEC, are both revenue-raising and protective. They become protective when the imported good bears a higher rate of tax than the similar home-produced good.

(2) *Subsidies.* While countries which subscribe to the General Agreement on Tariffs and Trade (GATT) cannot follow a policy of 'dumping' exports by giving direct subsidies, the volume and pattern of international trade may be influenced indirectly by other means, e.g. government assistance to the shipbuilding industry. Less obviously, welfare benefits, e.g. family allowances and income supplements which keep down labour costs, may give one country a price advantage over another.

(3) *Quotas.* If demand is inelastic, the increase in price resulting from a customs duty will have little effect on the quantity imported. Thus, to restrict imports of a good to a definite quantity, quotas must be imposed. For instance, foreign films can be exhibited only in a fixed proportion to British films. Compared with duties, quotas have two main disadvantages:

(a) As a result of the artificial shortage of supply, the price may be increased by the foreign supplier or by the importer. Hence, unless the government also introduces price control, it is these people who gain the advantage and not the public.

(b) Quotas are usually based on a firm's past imports, which penalises the efficient firm wishing to expand, and also makes the economy rigid.

(4) *Exchange control.* A tighter check on the amount spent on imported goods can be achieved if quotas are fixed in terms of foreign currency. This necessitates some form of exchange control. Until October, 1979 all earnings of foreign currency or claims to foreign currency had to be handed over to the Bank of England, which alone could authorise withdrawals to cover imports, foreign travel and capital movements.

(5) *Physical controls.* A complete ban – an embargo – may be placed on the import or export of certain goods. Thus narcotics cannot be imported, while the export of some strategic goods to Iron Curtain countries may be forbidden. Similarly strict regulations regarding the import of live animals (e.g. cattle, dogs and parrots) make trade more difficult.

Reasons for government control of international trade

In general trade is controlled because governments think nationally rather than internationally. Although people as a whole lose when trade is restricted, those of a particular country may gain.

Many reasons are put forward to justify control. Occasionally they have some logical justification; more usually they stem from a narrow self-interest. We can examine therefore the arguments, under three main headings: (1) those based on strategic, political, social and moral grounds; (2) those having some economic basis; and (3) those depending on shallow economic thinking.

1 Non-economic arguments   (a) *To encourage the production of a good of strategic importance.* Where a nation is dependent on another for a good of strategic importance, there is a danger of its supply being cut off in the event of war. Thus one argument for subsidising aircraft production in the UK is to ensure the survival of technical 'know-how', plant and skilled labour.

(b) *To foster closer political ties.* As a member of the EEC Britain must impose a common external tariff as part of a movement towards political as well as economic unity.

(c) *To prosecute political objectives.* Trade can be a weapon of foreign policy, e.g. sanctions against Rhodesia.

(d) *To promote social policies.* Although in the past Britain has subsidised her agriculture mainly for strategic reasons, today the purposes are basically social – to avoid depression in rural districts.

2 Economic arguments having some justification   (a) *To improve the terms of trade.* The incidence of a selective tax is shared between producer and consumer according to the relative elasticities of supply and demand (see p. 318). A government can, therefore, levy a tax on an imported good to improve the terms of trade if demand for the good is more elastic than the supply, for the increase in price is borne mainly by the producer, while the government has the proceeds of the tax. In practice this requires that: (i) the producing country has no alternative markets to which supplies can be easily diverted; (ii) her factors of production have few alternative uses; and (iii) the demand for the exports of the country imposing the tariff must be unaffected by the loss of income suffered by countries who now find their sales abroad reduced.

(b) *To protect an 'infant industry'.* It may be possible to establish an industry in a country if during its infancy it is given protection from well-established competitors already producing on a large scale. It is argued that the guaranteed home market will enable the 'infant' to get over its teething troubles and eventually be strong enough to compete with the rest of the world. Britain's car industry, for instance, benefited from such protection. The difficulty is that industries may come to rely on such protection, so that tariffs are never withdrawn, e.g. American duties on manufactured goods imposed in the eighteenth century are still in existence today. Moreover, industries are often encouraged which, without protection, would have no chance of survival. This leads to a maldistribution of the resources of a country.

(c) *To enable an industry to decline gradually.* Fundamental changes in demand for a good may severely hit industry. Such, for instance, was the fate of the British cotton industry in the 1970s. Restrictions on imports can cushion the shock, giving the industry more time to contract.

(d) *To prevent 'dumping'.* Goods may be sold abroad at a lower price than the home market. This may be possible because: (i) producers are given export subsidies; (ii) price discrimination by a monopoly is possible; or (iii) it enables the producer to obtain the advantages of decreasing costs. People in the importing country benefit directly from the lower prices. If, however, the exporter is trying to establish a monopoly which can be exploited once home producers have been driven out, there is a case for protecting the home market.

3 Economic arguments having little validity   (a) *To retaliate against tariffs of another country.* The threat of a retaliatory tariff may be used to influence another country to modify its restrictive policy. Thus in 1963 the USA threatened to impose higher import duties on a number of EEC goods to force a reduction of duties on imported American poultry. Here some concession was obtained, but such measures could induce counter-retaliation, with everybody losing.

(b) *To maintain home employment in a period of depression.* Countries may place restrictions on imports to promote employment on home-produced goods. The difficulty is that other countries retaliate, thereby leading to an all-round contraction in world trade. The General Agreement on Tariffs and Trade was set up to prevent this from happening (see p. 331).

(c) *To protect home industries from 'unfair' foreign competition.* The demand that British workers must be protected from competition by cheap, 'sweated' foreign labour usually comes from the industry facing competition and its workers. The argument, however, has little economic justification. First, it runs counter to the principle that a country should specialise where it has the greatest relative advantage. That advantage may be cheap labour. Carried to its logical conclusion the USA should refuse to import British cars because wages in Britain are much lower than in the USA. Second, low wages do not necessarily denote low labour costs. Wages may be low because labour is inefficient through low productivity. What is really significant is the *wage cost per unit of output.* Thus the USA can export manufactured goods to the UK even though her labour is the most highly paid in the world. The threatened industry can compete by improving productivity so as to bring about a lower wage cost per unit of output. Third, a tax on the goods of a poor country with cheap labour merely makes the country poorer and its labour cheaper. The way to raise wages (and the price of the good produced) is to increase demand in foreign markets. Indeed, if imports from poor countries are restricted, other help has to be given. Thus by importing cheap manufactured goods from Hong Kong, Britain reduces the amount of aid which is necessary. Fourth, protection, by reducing the income of the poorer countries, means that they have less to spend on Britain's exports. Last, the policy may lead to retaliation or aggressive competition elsewhere, thereby making it more difficult for the protecting country to sell abroad. One reason why Japan captured many of Britain's foreign markets for cotton goods was the restricted British market.

While restriction of trade tends to lower living standards, there may be benefits – economic, political and social. Thus protection to an industry may be given because home workers cannot adjust quickly to other occupations or industries. Usually, however, such economic gains are doubtful. Others cannot be measured, and it has to be left to the politicians to decide where the balance of advantages lies. But it must be remembered that protection creates vested interests opposed to subsequent removal.

**The General
Agreement on Tariffs
and Trade (GATT)**

The General Agreement on Tariffs and Trade, established in 1947, has three major objectives: (a) to reduce existing trade barriers; (b) to eliminate discrimination in international trade; and (c) to prevent the establishment of further trade barriers by getting nations to agree to consult one another rather than take unilateral action. It operates as follows.

Member nations meet periodically to 'agree' on a round of tariff reductions. Here the 'most-favoured-nation' principle applies – any tariff concession granted by one country to another must automatically apply to all other participating countries. Thus if the EEC agrees to reduce her tariff on American automatic vending machines by 5 per cent in exchange for a 5 per cent reduction in the American tariff on EEC man-made fibres, then both concessions must be extended to every other member of GATT.

Today over 100 nations subscribe to GATT. Through the organisation a progressive reduction in tariffs has been achieved, and the principle has been established that problems of international trade should be settled by co-operative discussion rather than by independent unilateral action. But difficulties have arisen:

(a) The principle of *reciprocity* means that low-tariff countries have to begin from an inferior bargaining position, and the concessions they can make are thus limited. Such countries may therefore prefer a low-tariff regional arrangement, such as the EEC.

(b) In certain circumstances the 'most-favoured-nation' principle may deter a country from making a tariff reduction to another country for the simple reason that it has to be applied to all.

(c) The Articles of the Agreement have had to be waived to allow for special circumstances – balance-of-payments difficulties, American protection of her agriculture, the UK's imports from the Commonwealth, the establishment of 'infant' industries in the underdeveloped countries, and the discriminatory character of the EEC.

IV The balance of payments

Paying for imports

Occasionally international trade takes the form of a barter arrangement, one country agreeing to take so much of another country's produce in exchange for so much of its own. Normally, however, exchanges are arranged by private traders who, according to relative prices, decide whether it is profitable to export and import goods.

But each country has its own currency – Spain (pesetas), France (francs), the USA (dollars), the UK (the pound sterling), and so on. This is important for two reasons: (a) sufficient foreign currency has to be obtained to pay for imports; and (b) a rate has to be established at which one currency will exchange for another.

We can approach the question of how imports are paid for by considering the purchases made by a housewife, Mrs Jones. Each week she buys a variety of goods. However, there are at least seven sources from which she could obtain the money to pay for them.

The most usual is the week's earnings. From her husband's allowance, say, Mrs. Jones pays the shopkeeper as she collects her goods. It must be noted, however, that what in fact Mrs Jones is really doing is exchanging the goods which Mr Jones has specialised in producing for the other goods needed. Thus if Mr Jones is a tailor, the money from the suits he sells buys Mrs Jones the goods she needs. Furthermore, money is often earned, not by making goods, but by performing a service. Thus Mrs Jones herself may earn wages by working for the shopkeeper. Also, interest on savings may provide some current income. Provided that all the weekly expenses are met out of this combined weekly income, we should say that the Jones family was 'paying its way'.

It might happen, however, that Mrs Jones's expenditure was not covered by the current weekly income. This might occur, for instance, because she bought a costly good, such as a washing-machine. In such circumstances Mrs Jones would have to raise the money from other sources. First, she could draw on her savings. Second, she could sell some goods from her household stock, such as the piano or the TV set, for which she had a less urgent need. Third, she might be able to borrow the money from a friend or, what amounts to the same thing, ask the shopkeeper to forgo payment for the time being. Finally, if she were extremely fortunate, she might be able to obtain a gift of money, say from a doting father. Such methods of payment would be fairly satisfactory provided that her savings were gradually replenished, or the assets sold were replaced by others of equal value, or the loan was repaid during the lifetime of the good. Otherwise Mrs Jones would not be 'paying her way'. If overspending continued, her savings would eventually run out, her home would be sold up, and more loans or credit from the shopkeeper would be unobtainable.

Broadly speaking a nation trading with other nations is in exactly the same position as Mrs Jones. The same alternatives are open to it in paying for imports. The main source is receipts from current exports. Figure 20.3 shows how exports earn foreign currency. Importing and exporting are undertaken by firms, and payments are arranged through banks, which exchange the currency of one country for the currency of another *provided that they have the necessary reserves of that currency.* Such reserves are earned by customers who export to foreign countries.

Fig. 20.3
How exports pay for imports

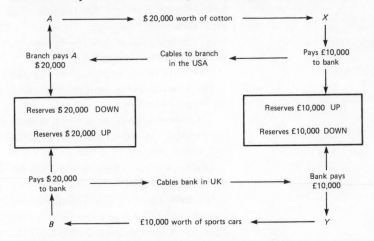

Let us assume that £1 sterling exchanges for $2 and that there are no currency restrictions. Suppose a British merchant *X* wishes to import cotton from *A* in the USA to the value of £10,000. The American exporter requires payment in dollars, for all his payments, e.g. his workers' wages, have to be made in dollars. Hence the importer goes to his bank, pays in £10,000 and arranges a 'documentary credit'. The bank cables its branch in New York, authorising it to make the equivalent dollar payment to *A* on production of the necessary documents, e.g. the bill of lading (see p. 209). (Most banks have branches in foreign capitals; if not, they engage local banks to act for them.) But how is it that the branch has dollars available to honour the draft?

We can see this if we imagine that another British firm *Y* has sold £10,000 worth of sports cars to an importer *B* in the USA. This firm wants payment in pounds sterling. Hence the American importer of the cars pays $20,000 into his bank in the USA, and the same procedure follows. It is obvious that the two transactions – buying cotton from the USA and selling sports cars to the USA – balance one another. The British bank's branch has had to pay out dollars, the American sterling. The British bank has received sterling, the American bank dollars. If the two get together, their requirements match. (In practice it is more likely that they would meet their needs through the foreign-exchange market.) The dollars to pay for the cotton are obtained by selling the sports cars, and vice versa. In short exports pay for imports.

'Exports' in its wider sense

In this connection the term 'exports' needs qualification. In the same way that Mrs Jones received payment for her services to the shopkeeper, so a nation may receive payment, not only for goods, but also for services rendered to other countries. Goods exported are termed 'visible' exports because they can be seen and recorded as they cross frontiers. On the other hand services cannot be seen and recorded; they are therefore called 'invisible' exports. Nevertheless, since services involve payments by persons from abroad, they are 'exports'.

The main sources of invisible earnings and payments are:

(a) *government expenditure abroad,* e.g. overseas garrisons, diplomatic services;

(b) *shipping services,* e.g. an American travelling in the *QE2* or shipping exports in a British merchantman;

(c) *civil aviation;*

(d) *travel,* e.g. sterling required by an American tourist for spending on a visit to London;

(e) *other services,* e.g. royalties earned on books and records, income from the transactions of overseas oil companies which ship direct from wells and refineries abroad to other countries;

(f) *interest, profits and dividends from overseas investments;* and

(g) *private transfers,* e.g. remittances to relatives abroad.

Payments for any of the above transactions involve changing into another country's currency. Thus they represent 'imports' to the paying country and 'exports' to the receiving country.

The balance-of-payments accounts

The accounts presented by countries of their monetary transactions with the rest of the world are known as the 'balance of payments' (see Table 20.4).

Current account

On the one hand the current account shows the foreign currency which has been *spent* on *imported goods* and *invisibles* in the course of the year, and on the other the foreign currency which has been *earned* by *exporting goods* and *invisibles*.

That part of the account showing payments for *goods* exported and imported is known as the *visible balance* (formerly the *balance of trade*). Where the value of goods exported exceeds the value of goods imported, we say that there is a favourable visible balance. If the opposite occurs, the visible balance is unfavourable. Too much, however, must not be read into the terms 'favourable' and 'unfavourable'. In the first place we have to know the reasons for the unfavourable balance. It may be brought about, for instance, by an increased demand for raw materials – which will later be exported in the form of manufactured goods. Second, a favourable or unfavourable visible balance can be reversed when invisibles are taken into account.

When we add payments and income on the invisible items to the visible balance we have the *current balance*.

Table 20.4 *The balance of payments of the UK, 1977 (£m.)*

CURRENT ACCOUNT

Visible trade

Exports (f.o.b.)	+ 32,182	
Imports (f.o.b.)	− 33,891	
Visible balance		− 1,709

Invisibles (net)

Government	− 2,600	
Shipping	+ 21	
Civil aviation	+ 244	
Travel	+ 1,077	
Other services	+ 2,247	
Interests, profits and dividends	+ 1,123	
Private transfers	− 114	
Invisible balance		+ 1,998
CURRENT BALANCE		+ 289

TOTAL CURRENCY FLOW

Current balance	+ 289
Investment and other capital flows (net)	+ 4,410
Balancing item	+ 2,662
Total currency flow	+ 7,361

OFFICIAL FINANCING—drawings on (+), repayments or additions to (−)

IMF	+ 1,113
Foreign currency borrowing	+ 871
Official reserves of gold and foreign currency	− 9,345
	− 7,361

Source: *Annual Abstract of Statistics*

There is no special reason why earnings from goods and invisibles exported between 1 January and 31 December in any one year should equal expenditure on the goods and invisibles imported during that period. How often, for instance, does what you earn during the week tally exactly with what you spend?

The current account is therefore likely to show a difference between earnings and expenditure. When the *value* of goods and invisibles exported exceeds the *value* of goods and invisibles imported, we say that there is a surplus current balance; when the reverse occurs, we say that there is a deficit. But again too much should not be made of the terms 'surplus' and 'deficit'. The current account is only part of the statement covering a nation's overseas financial transactions. Capital flows must also be scrutinised.

Investment and other capital flows   If current transactions were a country's only dealings with the world, the balance-of-payments accounts would be quite simple. A surplus of £100 million, for example, would add that amount to the reserves or allow the country to invest that amount overseas or to pay off short-term borrowings from abroad. A deficit would reduce the reserves or have to be financed by disinvestment or short-term borrowing abroad.

But capital flows also affect a country's ability to build up reserves or to pay off debts. Thus investment by private persons resident in the UK in factories or plant overseas (whether directly or by the purchase of shares), or a loan by the UK government to an underdeveloped country, leads to an outflow of capital and the spending of foreign currency. Similarly investment in the UK by persons overseas, by borrowing abroad by the UK government, local authorities, nationalised industries or companies, leads to an inflow of foreign capital and the receipt of foreign currency. Whereas the current account covers *income* earning and spending in the course of the year, 'investment and other capital flows' deals with the movement of *capital* in and out of the country. This capital may be short or long term.

Adding capital flows to the current balance gives the *total currency flow.*

Total currency flow   The total currency flow shows how much foreign currency is earned or is required to cover: (a) the current balance; (b) investment and other capital flows; and (c) the 'balancing item', the difference between the total value of transactions recorded and the actual amount of foreign currency gained or lost as shown by the Bank of England's accounts.

Official financing   Even a net currency *outflow* must have been covered by foreign currency. For instance, imports will have been paid for even though receipts may not have been currently earned. *Official financing* shows how this has been achieved. Similarly, if there is a net currency *inflow,* the financing account shows how the balance has been disposed of. It is in this sense that we can say that the balance of payments always balances (see Figure 20.4).

Suppose that there is a net currency outflow. This can be covered by the monetary authorities by:

(a) official borrowing from the IMF or from the monetary authorities of other countries; and

Fig. 20.4.
The balance of
payments, 1978 (£m.)

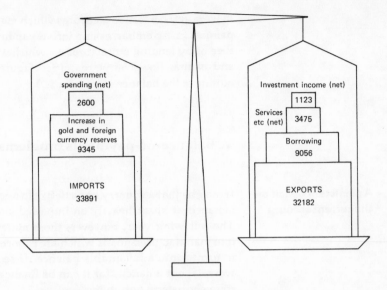

(b) drawing on the UK's reserves of gold and foreign currency.

As we shall see, a net currency outflow cannot go on indefinitely. Measures to correct the outflow, especially when the main cause is a persistent deficit on the current balance, will have to be taken.

Similarly a net current inflow enables the authorities to:

(a) repay official borrowing; and

(b) add to the UK's reserves of gold and foreign currency.

Fig. 20.5
The balance of
payments in outline

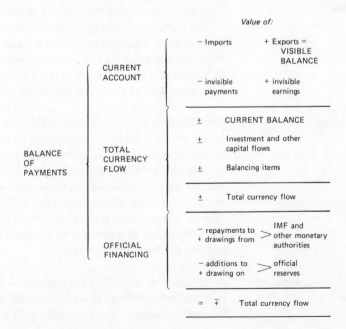

Here any corrective measures which may be necessary are less painful, for an embarrassing inflow can to a large extent be taken care of by lending more abroad – which will increase investment and capital flows outwards. (See Figure 20.5 for a summary outline of the balance of payments.)

V Balance-of-payments problems

A persistent deficit on the current account

It may be that a country has a deficit in a certain year because, for instance, it spent heavily on imported stocks of raw materials. The following year, however, those materials may be made up into manufactured goods which are exported, and thus the deficit is turned into a favourable balance. If so, there is little need to worry about a deficit, for it can be financed from the reserves or from short-term borrowing.

A different situation occurs where a deficit continues from year to year. Creditors will not lend indefinitely to finance a persistent deficit, and so action has to be taken to remedy the situation. A first-aid measure is to raise the Minimum Lending Rate and with it other short-term rates, in order to attract foreign loans. Eventually, however, exports must be increased in value, and imports decreased.

Export and import prices

To do this exports must be made cheaper and imports dearer. Because prices of internationally traded goods are composed of (a) the home price, and (b) the exchange rate, this can be achieved in two ways. Thus exports can be made more competitive by (a) lowering the price in the home currency, and (b) lowering the exchange rate so that fewer units of foreign currency are obtained for a given unit of the home currency.

Deflation

The first can be achieved by following deflationary policies at home to stop home prices rising (see Chapter 18). But the exchange rate remains fixed. This has the advantage that it encourages international trade by removing uncertainty as to exactly how much will actually be received when goods exported are paid for, something important to the UK which is so dependent on international trade to maintain her standard of living. On the other hand it has the grave disadvantage that deflationary policies produce unemployment.

Fluctuating exchange rates

An alternative method is to maintain incomes and prices at home but to allow exchange rates to fluctuate according to the demand for one's currency. Thus, if country A's exports to B are greater than her imports, the demand for A's currency will increase, for importers in B will be wanting it to pay for those imports. Consequently the exchange rate will move in favour of country A. Similarly, if A's imports are greater than her exports, the exchange rate will move against her. The effect of a fall in the value of the home currency in relation to that of other countries' currencies is to make imports relatively dearer and exports relatively cheaper, the very thing that is required to bring about equality in the values of total imports and total exports.

While this method avoids deflation of incomes at home, and thus further unemployment, it has disadvantages. Apart from inhibiting international trade it raises the prices of imported foodstuffs and raw materials, thereby adding to the cost of living. Furthermore, capital movements between countries will also influence the exchange rate, though this can be offset, as in the UK, by an Exchange Equalisation Fund.

The present position of the UK

After 1944 the UK, in common with other Western countries, followed a policy of 'managed flexibility' under the Bretton Woods Agreement (see later). But maintaining fixed exchange rates in the face of inflation prevented her taking measures to expand the economy. Hence in 1972 the 'pegged' pound was abandoned in favour of fluctuating exchange rates.

VI International institutions

Both the government and firms are influenced by decisions taken by international institutions, the most important of which are as follows:

(1) *The United Nations Organisation.* UNO is concerned with world political, economic and cultural activities. Although its own powers of action are limited by the need to obtain unanimous agreement of the Security Council, the consensus of opinion expressed exerts a strong influence on the actions of governments. Thus governments and multinational companies must respect world opinion in their policies.

(2) *The International Monetary Fund (IMF).* The Bretton Woods Agreement (1944) drew up an international code of monetary behaviour which operated through the IMF. Although much decided at Bretton Woods has been left high and dry, the IMF still monitors international affairs and acts as a 'lender of last resort' in order to tide member countries over temporary balance-of-payments difficulties. In return, however, it may require the recipient country to follow policies judged appropriate to correcting the imbalance.

(3) *The International Bank for Reconstruction and Development (The World Bank).* The World Bank, established under the Bretton Woods Agreement, provides long-term finance for reconstruction and development – roads, irrigation projects, power stations, etc., especially in the less developed countries. Funds are obtained by: (a) a 'quota' subscribed by member nations roughly in proportion to their national incomes; and (b) borrowing on the international market by the issue of bonds backed by the quotas of members. In addition, in order to encourage private lending, the World Bank will, in return for a small premium of $\frac{1}{2}$ to 1 per cent, guarantee repayment of the loan.

Countries which have economically sound projects but cannot obtain loans from private sources at a reasonably low rate of interest may borrow from the World Bank for a period of five to twenty-five years at about 4 per cent.

(4) *The General Agreement on Tariffs and Trade* (see earlier).

(5) *The Organisation for Economic Co-operation and Development (OECD).* The OECD, set up in 1961, has two main objectives: (a) to help member countries promote economic growth, employment and improved standards of living; and (b) to help promote the sound and harmonious development of the world economy and improve the lot of the developing countries. It consist of twenty-four member countries, mostly from Western Europe but includes Finland, Australia, Canada, Japan, New Zealand and the USA. It works through a number of agencies, monitoring economic problems, suggesting policies, and producing detailed statistics.

While the above organisations only have indirect influence on firms, the EEC has direct control in a number of spheres, and will therefore be considered in more detail.

VII The European Economic Community

Background to the EEC The First and Second World Wars convinced statesmen in Western European countries that some form of political unity was desirable, and in 1949 the Council of Europe was created, the basis, it was hoped, of a European Parliament. But organisations for definite functions – the Organisation for European Economic Co-operation (1948), the North Atlantic Treaty Organisation (1949) and the Western European Union (1954) – proved more fruitful than did the Council of Europe with its broad aims.

Although these organisations involved co-operation, they were merely voluntary associations, not federal bodies exercising supra-national powers in the interests of members as a whole. Federation was the ultimate aim of the European statesmen but they realised that it could only proceed piecemeal on a functional basis. The first supra-national organisation, the European Coal and Steel Community (ECSC), was formed in 1951 to control the whole of the iron, steel and coal resources of the six member countries – France, West Germany, Italy, Holland, Belgium and Luxembourg. The old divisions created by inward-looking national interests were thus broken down.

The success of the ECSC led to the setting up in 1957 of the Atomic Energy Community (EURATOM), a similar organisation for the peaceful use of atomic energy, and the European Economic Community (EEC), an organisation to develop a 'common market' between the six member countries. All three communities have now been brought within the EEC.

When first offered membership of these organisations Britain refused to join. Not only would joining the EEC have weakened Commonwealth ties but she was also unwilling to forgo the right to follow independent policies in economics and defence. Instead, with six other nations, Britain joined the looser European Free Trade Area (EFTA).

Contrary to Britain's expectation, the EEC grew in strength, for difficulties were resolved as they arose. Moreover, Britain's trade with EEC countries increased at a faster rate than that with EFTA since her goods were more complementary to their economies. Accordingly, after protracted negotiations, the UK joined the EEC in 1973.

The institutions of the EEC

The essential point to grasp is that the 1957 Treaty of Rome set up a 'Community' having a government and institutions developed from the old ECSC. Britain's position in the institutions is similar to that of France, West Germany and Italy, with the other members, Belgium, the Netherlands, Luxembourg and the Irish Republic, enjoying slightly less representation.

There are four main institutions:

(1) *The Commission.* This is the most important organ of the EEC. Its thirteen members (two from the UK) serve for four years. Once chosen, however, the members of the Commission act as an independent body in the interests of the Community as a whole, and not as representatives of the governments that have nominated them. The Commission is responsible for formulating policy proposals, promoting the Community interest, trying to reconcile national viewpoints, and implementing Community decisions.

(2) *The Council of Ministers.* Each member country sends a cabinet minister (usually the Foreign Secretary) to the Council of Ministers. This is the supreme decision-making body. Its task is

to harmonise the Commission's draft Community policies with the wishes of member governments. Proposals and compromise plans are exchanged between the Council and the Commission. If the Council becomes deadlocked, the Commission reconsiders the proposal in order to accommodate the views of the opposing countries. Originally it was intended that Council decisions should be on a weighted majority basis, but proposals affecting vital national interests now have to be unanimous.

(3) *The Court of Justice.* This consists of ten judges appointed by agreement of member governments for a six-year term. Its task is to interpret the Rome Treaty and adjudicate on complaints, whether from member states, private enterprises, or the institutions themselves. Its rulings are binding on member countries, Community institutions and individuals.

(4) *The Assembly, or European Parliament.* This is a body of 410 elected members (81 from the UK). Members sit according to party affiliation, not nationality. The Assembly debates Community policies and also examines the Community's budget. It can dismiss the Commission by a two-thirds majority.

(5) *Special institutions.* Apart from the four main institutions above, there are also special institutions to deal with particular policies, e.g. the Economic and Social Committee, the European Investment Bank, the European Social Fund, the European Monetary Co-operation Fund, etc.

Economic objectives of the EEC

The overriding aim of the EEC is to integrate the policies of the member countries. As regards economic policy this is based on two main principles; (1) a customs union; and (2) a common market.

1 A customs union We have to distinguish between a free-trade area and a customs union. The former simply removes tariff barriers between member countries but allows individual members to impose their own rates of duty against outsiders. A customs union goes further. While it has internal free trade, it also imposes common external tariffs.

The EEC has a customs union, since this is essential for an integrated common market. Otherwise goods would enter the market through low-duty countries and be resold in those imposing higher rates.

2 A common market In essence the common market of the EEC envisages goods and factors of production moving freely within the Community through the operation of the price system; only in this way can the full benefits of the larger market (see later) be realised.

However, this takes time to accomplish. Member countries had already developed their own individual taxes, welfare benefits, monopoly policies, methods of removing balance-of-payments imbalances, full-employment policies, and so on. Such differences could disrupt the working of the price system because they would give some members an advantage over others. For example, suppose, on joining the EEC, Britain had retained purchase tax on refrigerators but had removed it on binoculars. This would weight the possibilities of trade against Italy (which has a comparative advantage in producing refrigerators) in favour of West Germany (which has a comparative advantage in producing high-grade binoculars). Alternatively the comparative advantage of some countries may lie in the expertise of the professional services they can provide. Usually this means that such services have to be taken to where the customer is (e.g. know-how regarding property development). There must therefore be mobility of labour within the common market, e.g. for property developers.

Emphasis, therefore, has been placed on 'harmonisation' policies. Thus, when Britain joined, arrangements were made for her to adapt certain economic policies towards those of the original members.

The aims of EEC policy   The EEC is seeking to achieve:

(1) *Common external tariffs (CET).* All members will impose tariffs on imports from non-member countries at the same rates.

(2) *Free trade between member countries.* This involves the removal of all duties, quotas and other barriers to free trade between members.

(3) *A common agricultural policy (CAP).* Because the demand for agricultural products tends to be inelastic, changes in the conditions of supply can have far-reaching effects on the incomes of farmers (see p. 119). CAP seeks to support farmers' incomes by maintaining prices on the home market through import levies on imported foods. Three prices are fixed for each product:

(a) a *target price,* which, it is estimated, will give farmers an adequate return in a normal year;

(b) a *threshold price,* which is used as the basis for assessing levies on imports; and

(c) the *intervention price,* at which surplus supplies resulting from a good harvest or simply over-production through too high a threshold price are bought up by various agencies to be disposed of outside the EEC, e.g. butter sold to the USSR.

Obviously CAP confers greater benefits on countries in which agriculture is important (e.g. France) compared with countries which are more dependent on manufacturing (e.g. the UK).

(4) *Harmonisation of tax systems.* As already shown, some standardisation of taxation is necessary in order to remove any 'hidden' barriers to trade. This applies particularly to indirect taxes. In the EEC, VAT is to be the basic form of indirect tax, and

it is proposed that eventually it will be imposed by all member countries at the same rates. No proposals exist for harmonising income taxes, but most countries have adopted the 'imputation' system of corporation tax.

(5) *Free movements of persons and capital.* It is necessary that people and capital should be able to move as freely within the Community as within their own countries.

(6) *Complete monetary integration.* As we have seen, countries can adjust the prices of imports and exports by varying the exchange rate. If this were allowed within the EEC it could enable a member to obtain a competitive advantage over others by depreciating its currency. It is agreed, therefore, that eventually all currencies will have fixed exchange rates within narrow limits. However, world economic depression since 1973 has inhibited countries with relatively weak currencies (e.g. the UK) from committing themselves to a fixed exchange rate, as maintaining this could entail deflation (see above). Even so in 1979 all countries except the UK joined the European Monetary System, agreeing to keep their exchange-rate movements within a narrow band.

(7) *A common regional policy.* Just one nation cannot allow depressed areas to persist, so the EEC is expected to help regions of high unemployment. Northern Ireland and southern Italy are two such regions. Apart from the establishment of a Regional Development Fund, however, little has so far been done to integrate policies designed to encourage industries to go to problem areas.

(8) *A common transport policy.* By regulating such items as freight rates, licences, taxation and working conditions, the EEC can seek to ensure that transport undertakings compete on an equal footing. Any hidden advantages encouraged by one country would distort the free movement of goods within the Community.

(9) *Common rules on competition.* To prevent the distortion of competition in trade, uniform regulations have been introduced to cover price-fixing, sharing of markets and patent rights.

(10) *A Community budget.* A Community budget is necessary to meet the costs of administration and policies requiring expenditure, e.g. CAP and regional assistance. There are two main sources – import duties and a 1 per cent VAT.

Advantages of belonging to the EEC

Several advantages can accrue to countries by forming a common market.

First, it increases the possibility of specialisation. The EEC provides a market of 260 million people, larger than that of the USA. This allows economies of scale to be achieved, especially as regards sophisticated products requiring high initial research expenditure, e.g. computers, nuclear reactors, supersonic air-craft, and modern defence weapons. Member countries now combine to cover research costs, e.g. Concorde, the European Airbus.

Second, keener competition in the larger market can result in greater efficiency. Within the EEC there are no trade barriers – which do in fact protect inefficient firms. Free trade means that goods and services can compete freely in all parts of the market and that factors of production can move to their most efficient use, not merely within a country, but between countries also.

Third, a faster rate of growth may be achieved. In the first fifteen years the GNPs of the six original members grew twice as fast as that of the UK, giving them, Italy apart, a higher GNP per head than Britain's. To a large extent this faster rate of growth was the result of the increased economies of scale and competition enjoyed by the EEC countries. But it is also possible that the EEC generates growth by the mood it engenders.

Fourth, there could be significant political benefits. As already explained, the ultimate objective of the original advocates of European co-operation was some form of political union. A Western Europe which could speak with one voice would carry weight when dealing with other major powers, particularly the USA and the USSR. Moreover, the integration of defence forces and strategy would give them far greater security.

Problems facing the UK as a member of the EEC

While Britain's membership of the EEC can secure important benefits and allow her to influence its future development, it does pose special problems.

(1) *The CET could lead to the diversion of trade towards less efficient EEC suppliers.* The duties imposed by the customs union may allow firms within the EEC to compete in price with more efficient firms outside.

Suppose, for instance, that the same machine can be produced by both the USA and West Germany, but – because the American firm is more efficient – its machine is 10 per cent cheaper. In these circumstances Britain would, other things being equal, import from the USA. As a member of the EEC, however, Britain would have to discriminate against the American machine by the ap-propriate CET, say 20 per cent. This would make the German machine cheaper, and so trade would be diverted to the less efficient producer.

The main problem this poses for Britain concerns foodstuffs, for these have traditionally entered Britain duty free. As a result, for instance, dairy produce (particularly butter) from New Zea-land was able to compete with European producers. The imposition of a tariff against New Zealand thwarts this.

(2) *The CAP has particular disadvantages for the UK.* There are three main criticisms of the CAP

(a) The import duties levied on foodstuffs in order to maintain prices for farmers within the Community hits Britain particularly hard. Since she is dependent on imports for one-half of her food supplies, it is essential to obtain them from the most efficient producer. The CAP, on the other hand, requires Britain to switch her imports of foodstuffs to dearer producers within the EEC. In doing so she is subsidising, as it were, inefficient methods of farming, e.g. in West Germany.

(b) Over-production (as in the case of butter) occurs because high prices, *not* demand, encourage supply by EEC countries.

(c) The distortion of the normal pattern of international trade in foodstuffs widens the gap between the rich and poor countries since the latter are often food producers.

(3) *The UK's trade with the Commonwealth.* While Britain's former EFTA partners and the less developed nations of the Commonwealth enjoy a special association with the EEC, exporters of manufactured goods, among whom are Australia, Canada and Hong Kong, have lost their preferential treatment. In the past trade has been a strong link between the Commonwealth countries, though it must be recognised that the importance of Britain's trade with the Commonwealth has been diminishing over the past twenty years.

(4) *Certain producers, such as tomato and fruit growers, and fishermen, are particularly hit hard by EEC rules.*

(5) *Britain's contribution to the Community's budget is growing,* imposing an additional strain on her balance of payments.

(6) *Harmonisation of taxation and the adoption of a common monetary system involves some loss of economic sovereignty.* As regards taxation, two examples can be given. First, protection of agriculture by import duties rather than by deficiency payments means that consumers, not taxpayers, pay to maintain Community farmers' incomes. In effect, therefore, the change from subsidies to protective duties is regressive in nature. Second, a high rate of VAT also tends to be regressive since it does not impose progressively higher rates of tax on luxuries.

But it is through the adoption of the common monetary policy that Britain really stands to lose freedom of action over major economic policy, as this would mean the price of exports could only be reduced by a deflationary policy.

Against this, however, some economists might argue that this will present no problem for Britain provided she can hold her inflation in check – and adopting the European Monetary System's fixed exchange rate would impose the necessary discipline.

Conclusion   Britain's membership of the EEC provides the opportunity for an all-round improvement in her standard of living. But the benefits will only be secured if she braces herself to compete in the larger market. Two major problems must be faced: (a) increasing the rate of capital investment in industry; and (b) controlling the rate of inflation. Each is essential if Britain is to be cost-competitive within both the EEC and world markets.

21 The Community and Organisations

I A review

We started this book by looking at why organisations were formed. Basically their purposes are twofold: (a) to make and enforce rules so that people of the community can live in harmony together and promote their own and the common good; and (b) to provide the goods and services wanted by the community. The first is the task of government; the second is primarily the concern of business organisations, but also of clubs and societies.

We drew attention to the possible dangers of creating such organisations. Political institutions continually seek to exercise additional power over the people who have created them. Business organisations, too, by advertising and political influence may exercise a virtual monopoly position so that, as Professor Galbraith has pointed out, consumers tend to be puppets in their hands. Multinational companies in particular can arrange their operations so that certain communities suffer, e.g. by loss of tax revenue, in order to increase the profits of the organisation as a whole. We are reminded of Churchill's words: 'We shape our buildings and afterwards they shape us.' So it could be with organisations.

II Influencing organisations

Thus we come full circle: if organisations are to serve the community, then there must be means by which the community can influence the policies and activities of these organisations.

Most of the pressures and strategies which can be brought to bear by organisations and groups, and individuals within the community have been described in the main text. Here we bring them together in summary form.

Business firms

Firms are subject to internal and external pressures. The main internal pressure is exercised by the shareholders. But, as we have seen, with complex organisations this is a theoretical rather than a practical control.

In competitive conditions the main form of control is consumer reaction. Where the 'consumer is king' he simply takes his custom to a firm which gives him better service.

Unfortunately, if the good or service is produced by a monopoly, this is not possible. Moreover, certain firms may not consider the adverse 'spillover' effects of their actions on the community at large, e.g. as regards pollution. In such cases external pressures have to be exercised. Letters can be written to the company chairman or the press, and pressure groups, such as residents' associations, can be established to take concerted action and gain publicity for their ends. The Consumers' Association, which publishes *Which?*, also plays an important role. Television programmes, newspapers and magazines act as watchdogs to expose malpractices. And as regards the employment of labour, trade unions act on behalf of their members. When the above methods are deficient or the matters too important for them to be relied upon exclusively, control of firms has to be exercised by the government, through legislation backed up by administrative and judicial action.

Nationalised industries

The strength of the nationalised industries lies in the fact that many of them are virtual monopolies. While the above methods of control are appropriate, and indeed used, other forms of accountability have had to be devised. First, there are Consumer Consultative Councils which seek to work out acceptable solutions to problems and complaints by agreement. Second, the Minister exercises general control of policy. Above all, he is accountable to Parliament, the ultimate watchdog.

Government departments

In Chapter 1 we quoted Lord Acton: 'Power corrupts and absolute power tends to corrupt absolutely.' This is a factor which must always be borne in mind. With government departments control is exercised through political parties and political institutions, such as the Opposition, a press and TV which is free to comment and criticise, and individual pressure groups formed for specific purposes.

But the ultimate sanction is the watchfulness of the people in protecting their traditional liberties. Without this they are likely to become the servants of the organisations rather than the organisations fulfilling the objectives for which they were established – to serve the people.

Index